SAGE ANNUAL REVIEWS OF
STUDIES IN DEVIANCE
Volume 4

SAGE ANNUAL REVIEWS OF STUDIES IN DEVIANCE ⟶

Series Editors: **EDWARD SAGARIN**
CHARLES WINICK
The City College of the City University of New York

Deviance is one of the most important, exciting and stimulating areas in sociology. It covers the entire spectrum of activities and people who are disvalued, denigrated, punished, ostracized, and in other ways made to feel undesired and undesirable in society— whether this be for something that was done (as the commission of a crime), or for some peculiar stigmatic status. It extends into criminology, social problems, social pathology, and numerous other areas. Despite many texts, readers, and countless journal articles, there has never been a serial publication devoted exclusively to deviance. It is to fill this gap that this annual series is being launched.

Volumes in this series: ⟶

Volume 1. Deviance and Social Change (1977)
EDWARD SAGARIN, Editor

Volume 2. Deviance and Mass Media (1978)
CHARLES WINICK, Editor

Volume 3. Deviance and Decency: The Ethics of
Research with Human Subjects (1979)
CARL B. KLOCKARS and
FINBARR W. O'CONNOR, Editors

CRIME and DEVIANCE
A Comparative Perspective

Edited by
GRAEME R. NEWMAN

SAGE PUBLICATIONS   Beverly Hills   London

HV
6028
C72

For information address:

SAGE Publications, Inc.
275 South Beverly Drive
Beverly Hills, California 90212

SAGE Publications Ltd
28 Banner Street
London EC1Y 8QE, England

Printed in the United States of America

Library of Congress Cataloging in Publication Data
Main entry under title:

Crime and deviance.

    (Sage annual reviews of studies in deviance ; v. 4)
    Bibliography: p.
    1. Crime and criminals—Addresses, essays,
lectures. 2. Deviant behavior—Addresses,
essays, lectures. I. Newman, Graeme R.
HV6028.C72   364.3   80-11629
ISBN 0-8039-1076-2
ISBN 0-8039-1077-0 (pbk.)

FIRST PRINTING

CONTENTS

ACKNOWLEDGMENTS

Permission has been received to reproduce passages from the following works:

Law and Society Association for Kurczewski, J. and Frieske, K., "Some Problems in the Legal Regulation of the Activities of Economic Institutions," *Law and Society Review*, Vol. 11. Elsevier Scientific Publishing Company, Amsterdam for Elwin, G., "Swedish Anti-Terrorist Legislation," *Contemporary Crises,* Vol. 1. Canadian Association for the Prevention of Crime for Snider, D. L., "Corporate Crime in Canada," *Canadian Journal of Criminology,* Vol. 20. Pluto Press, Ltd. for Pearce, F., *Crimes of the Powerful,* Copyright © 1976, Pluto Press. Yves Brillon for "The Evolution of Crime in the Ivory Coast." Maurice Cusson for "Observations on the Problem of Juvenile Delinquency: The Case of Abidjan." Macmillan, London and Basingstoke for Ditton, J., *Part-Time Crime. Soviet Studies* for Treml, V. G., "Alcohol in the U.S.S.R.: A Fiscal Dilemma" (Vol. 27) and for Katsenelinboigen, A., "Coloured Markets in the Soviet Union" (Vol. 29). Prentice-Hall, Inc. for Conklin, J. E., *Illegal But Not Criminal.* Macmillan Publishing Co. for Jacoby, N.H. et al. *Bribery and Extortion in World Business,* Copyright © 1977, The Trustees of Columbia University in The City of New York. Charles C. Thomas, Publisher for Bassiouni, *International Terrorism and Political Crimes.* University of Illinois Press for Lewis, O., Lewis, R., and Rigdon, S., *Four Men: Living the Revolution.* Tavistock Publications, Inc. for Rock, P. and McIntosh, M. (eds.), *Deviance and Social Control,* Copyright © 1974, The British Sociological Association. Random House for Chalidze, V. (P. S. Falla, trans.), *Criminal Russia: Crime in the Soviet Union.* D. C. Heath, Ltd. for Hess, H., *Mafia and Mafiosi: The Structure of Power* (E. Osers, trans.), 1973. Routledge and Kegan Paul for Podgorecki, A. and Łoś, M., *Multidimensional Sociology.*

1

INTRODUCTION
The Limits and Possibilities of Comparative Criminology

GRAEME R. NEWMAN
FRANCO FERRACUTI

From the early beginning of criminology the great classic authors stressed the comparative approach. Works such as Tarde's ''La Criminalite Comparee'' (1890), and Lombroso's and Ferri's early writings were replete with comparative connotations, trying to verify across cultures and nations the scant facts that constituted, in those times, the crude body of knowledge of criminology. Mannheim (1965) has taken a similar posture in his widely known book, *Comparative Criminology*. Interestingly enough, Professor Mannheim did not even discuss the rationale for the use of the term ''comparative.'' He does make frequent use of facts and data across cultrues, but does not discuss why criminology must be comparative. Similar recent studies have been carried out by Cavan and Cavan (1968), Lopez-Rey (1970, 1976), and Radzinowicz and King (1977).

Within a sociological frame of reference, in the widely known monograph, *Crime in Developing Countries* Clinard and Abbott (1973), follow

Bendix's formulation about comparative sociology, define the goal of comparative criminology as that of developing "concepts and generalizations at a level that distinguishes between universals applicable to all societies and unique characteristics representative of one or a small set of societies." They also make reference to Durkheim's often-quoted statement:

> One cannot explain a social fact of any complexity except by following the complete development through all social species. Comparative sociology is not a particular branch of sociology, it is sociology itself, insofar as it ceases to be purely descriptive and aspires for facts [Durkheim, 1938].

Also, Friday (1973), discussing research problems, in comparative criminology, has quoted Cohen's (1959) blunt statement that "the plausibility of our own speculations about juvenile delinquency in the United States rests upon the findings of similarly oriented studies in the other societies."

It is a well-known fact that the concurrence of opinions on the need for comparative criminology has not been matched by a wealth of truly comparatied studies. All the efforts of the international bodies, both as scientific societies or as policy-oriented bodies such as the United Nations and the Council of Europe, have failed to produce major research findings. Of course, notable exceptions exist, many of which are described and reviewed in this volume.[1] Indeed, Professor Szabo has made it his life's goal to develop a sizable body of knowledge in the comparative field, with remarkably increasing success. Other concerted efforts, even when begun under auspicious circumstances, have failed for reasons which are difficult to assess. It could be remarked that so far the most international and cross-cultural production of the United Nations Social Defense Research Institute of Rome has been the recent rather incomplete and outdated *World Directory of Criminological Institutes*. The hundreds of institutes listed therein are testimony to the development and importance of criminology, but no evidence emerges of any crosscultural, comparative coordination of work, or even adequate exchange of information.[2]

Professor Szabo (1973) has repeatedly defined the meaning and goals of comparative criminology, tracing its history from its early European beginnings. In essence, moving from the original "crime as a universal phenomenon" formulation of early criminology, the interest has shifted toward, according to Glueck, "replication of researches designed to uncover etiological universals operative as causal agents, irrespective of cultural differences among the different countries" (Glueck and Glueck, 1964). Several such studies exist — for example, De Fleur (1967a, 1976b, 1969), Ferracuti et al. (1975), and others. Replication, however, is not really comparison unless a rationale is explicitly used for the selection of the countries or cultures. Too often, the selection of countries is determined by geographical opportunity or even availability of funds.

THE TASKS OF
COMPARATIVE CRIMINOLOGY

A very general formulation would define two posible main tasks for comparative criminology. One consists of confirmation — in different juridical, economical, and cultural systems — of universal data and constructs with the aim of achieving general validity from crosscultural verification. Much of this research is reviewed by Paul Friday in this volume. The second consists of using different cultures, arranged along various relevant socioeconomic, political, or developmental continua as "cells" or "units" in a natural experimental design, or as quasi-clinical cases, in order to test general theories against the varieties of facts and situations offered to the researcher by the existing variations in sociopolitical and ecnomic systems.[3] In this second approach, the comparative method becomes an integral part of the research effort; and existing differences among nations and cultures cease to be an impediment to research, becoming instead an essential methodological component of the research itself. The work reported by George DeVos in this volume represents essentially this approach. Relevant, of course, is the difference between comparative *methods* and comparative *content* of the research.

It might be advisable, at this point, to take a close look at what has happened to other social and behavioral disciplines in the comparative field. In this context, the comparative aspects of cultural anthropology are very important in view of the established comparative tradition of this discipline. According to Bock (1978), comparative methods can be used to achieve at least three different, albeit related, goals:

(1) *historical*, to follow developmental sequences and mutual relationships within cultural systems;
(2) *functional-causal*, to understand the general principles of development and of cultural integration; and
(3) *universals*, to discover and confirm content or process universals, detectable in all or a majority of the systems under consideration.

All three goals are relevant, although criminology has obviously failed to develop a universal model grounded either in the biology, sociology, or psychology of human beings, or in some combination. Perhaps universals do not exist in a "definitional metadiscipline" such as criminology. After all, not only natural crime has so far eluded us, but we are focusing our interests more and more on the interactional aspects of crime and deviance, reaffirming the cultural relativity of our object of study.[4]

On a more concrete level, the differences and vagaries of existing juridical systems and the objective difficulties (recently analyzed by Vetere and Newman, 1977) of comparing crime statistics internationally must not be underestimated. This is not to say that international factual and numberical comparison is impossible, but that its difficulties have to be faced and solved. Before international statistics can be usable, they must be made meaningful nationally, as Vetere and Newman remind us. This intranational analysis cannot be limited simply to criminal statistics, but must instead be extended to all other relevant social indicators which have a direct or indirect bearing on the crime phenomenon. This, however, is also a general problem for comaprative criminology, which cannot in any case be limited to national criminal statistics. It is also a question of comparative perceptions rather than statistics per se, which Scott and Al-Thakeb demonstrate in Chapter 3 of this volume,

"Perceptions of Deviance Cross-Culturally." The apparent relativity in the definition of crime, yet the possibility (or necessity?) of universal categories ("harms") is examined in this volume by Leslie Wilkins in his fascinating chapter on international crime statistics.

This point raises a problem that is rather special to comparative criminology: What can or should be the specific content of comparison? After World War II criminological theories developed to the point that they answered to the somewhat caustic connotation of "a dime a dozen" situations. Yet, most theories are still untested or only partially tested. A priority for comparative criminology is most certainly theory testing, particularly for those theories which are policy or action relevant.[5] Some "new" phenomena, such as transnational terrorism or large-scale multinational economic crimes, force us, by reason of the nature and content of the criminal behavior under study, to assume a comparative posture. These aspects of comparative criminology are reviewed in the chapters of this volume by Maria Loś, Daniel Georges-Abeyie, and Francis and Elizabeth Ianni.

HISTORICAL COMPARISON

C. Wright Mills (1959) has noted: "If we limit ourselves to one national unit of one contemporary (usually Western) society, we cannot possibly hope to catch many really fundamental differences among human types and social institutions."

It is perhaps a truism to say that what is historical is necessarily comparative. The reverse, however, is not true, and the overwhelming portion of research in all criminology has been ahistorical.[6] There are two ways in which comparative criminology must address this issue. First, it may draw on its many contributing disciplines and theories which derive from diverse cultures and try to assess the points of intersection of biography and history: the central problem of social science, according to Mills. S. Giora Shoham has attempted this near-impossible task in his books and in his chapter, "The Simple Standard Deviant," in this volume.

Second, historical comparison is crucial if one wishes to understand the evolutionary or change aspects of social phenomena (Bendix, 1968). In this regard, there is an important sense in which spatial comparative studies are also temporal, since a common assumption is that some kind of developmental dimension exists along which all societies can be arranged, so that particular societies may represent particular points in *time* in the evolution of societies. In their own ways, great social theorists from Marx to Sorokin and Parsons have amply developed this thesis. It is a very controversial issue, since it borders on making value judgments as to the comparative "immaturity" of societies, as Culbertson (1971) and McCord (1965) have indicated. It is, however, a central theme underlying the testing of any dynamic aspect of society, and few societies can be defined as static.

The importance of the temporal element to the comparative approach is accentuated when one compares subcollectives within the same culture. Here the argument against the arbitrary classification often used in "normal" social science methodology may apply, in that subcultures may be "contaminated" by each other or by the dominant culture. It is therefore difficult to make the *prima facie* claim that two such units of analysis are truly independent. The way in which one gets around this problem is to infuse into the research design a temporal analysis of the comparative histories of the two subcollectives, or the subcollective and the culture, depending upon one's theoretical interest. This approach is well demonstrated in this volume by George DeVos in his chapter on minority groups and crime, although the emphasis in his paper is more on spatial rather than historical comparison. In contrast, Cheryl Haft Picker's chapter takes the historical perspective as primary and uses the spatial comparisons as secondary in her wide-ranging review of the evolutionary aspects of subcultures. Together, these two chapters open the way to many new questions concerning the role of subcultures in criminology theory.

Haft Picker's chapter also gets to the core of criminological theory by identifying where "criminal law and criminal violence intersect." The implied thesis here is that there is "a little crime in justice and a little justice in crime," a position recently argued by Newman (1978). This view, in part, grows from the now well-established "social process" approach to the study of deviance in sociology, a tradition which is well demonstrated in Chapter 8 by Jerome Krase and Edward Sagarin on the informal social control of deviance. These authors show how important a comparative perspective is in shedding light on the emergence and maintenance of deviant behavior.

THE CURRENT
STATE OF THE "ART"

The papers assembled in this volume identify many serious shortcomings and failings of past comparative research on deviance and crime. Some of these shortcomings can be and have been overcome by improved research design and, more importantly, a better specification of theory. In fact, many of the methodological problems are simply those of orthodox methodology which, when they emerge in a comparative setting, appear far more accentuated.

Research knowledge has, nevertheless, accumulated. In general, some correlates of crime appear to be found throughout the world: for example, the significance of broken homes, unemployment, urbanization, and industrialization, cannot be overlooked. There are, of course, exceptional cases; and such variables, even where they represent identical patterns of behavior, may take on radically different meanings depending upon the culture in which they emerge. It would also appear that there are both similarities and differences across diverse cultures in the perception of crime and deviance. Right now, such findings are highly controversial and the subject of much ideological debate. For the moment, comparative criminologists would do well to try to withstand these ideological pressures which call for extreme philosophical solutions: After all, relativism is just as extreme as universalism. We see the challenge of comparative criminology to search out both unities and diversities. Given the current state of our knowledge and theory, to choose one or the other seems to us to prejudge the issue.

The chapters in this volume bring together for the first time a vast array of research findings and innovative theory from diverse settings, perspectives, and disciplines. We hope they add a few more pieces to the complex puzzle that is comparative criminology.

NOTES

1. For other reviews of comparative research in criminology see Clinard (1956, 1959), Clinard and Abbott (1973), Friday (1973), and Szabo (1973, 1978).

2. "Adequate exchange of information," although it is not exactly research, is probably the first much-needed step in comparative criminology. Some efforts have been made to develop crossfertilization through some journals and international societies. Yet, the knowledge and understanding of the vast amount of work in criminology in, for example, European countries, not to mention Marxist countries, is dismally low in the United States. The problem is not necessarily a question of the amount of comparative research that reaches the United States, but its quality and approach. Articles such as that by Maria Łoś and Luis Salas in this volume are needed to cut through the myths and stereotypes that U.S. researchers have of Marxist countries, and vice-versa.

3. The study of one culture with reference only to that culture ought to be impossible, since that culture is part of a universe or "world of cultures." Why do we not look to this world of cultures to give meaning to the analysis of one culture? Surely intensive "explanation" of a single culture, without reference to other cultures, must be a highly artificial explanation and must lack general meaning (Przeworski and Teune, 1970). Therefore, the significance of such research, its main variables of analysis, its findings, must remain in considerable question. This is not to say that within-culture studies are unimportant or meaningless. Of course, it is very useful to know that crime is distributed in the United States according to urban, poverty, or other dimensions. In order to explain these variations, we need to know whether or not such distributions are special to the United States, are similar in other countries, or are special to the United States today compared with yesterday. It is only through the spatial and temporal approach to research on crime that we can ever hope to explain it to the extent that explanations are achieved in our "meta-discipline."

4. This is true across cultures and across time. Yet, it is through comparative studies that interactional relativism must prove its tenets. Since the appearance of *Comparative Deviance* (Newman, 1976) more attention has been given to the question of relativism and universals in criminological theory (see Friday, 1979; Turk, 1978; and Toby, 1979 in relation to "radical" criminology). In fact, the question of relativism and universals is a central point of controversy throughout the whole of *Crimonology* in its February 1979 issue devoted to "radical criminology."

5. The failure of criminological theory to develop sound and effective policies should not stop us, since in most instances and in most countries theories have failed to attract the policy maker and policies have often been based on a limited, stop gap, crisis-solving perspective. Therefore, it is not a failure of theory per se that defines our discipline as ineffectual, but rather a failure of the policy makers to cross the bridges from theory to policy to action.

6. Recent trends suggest that this is changing. See, for example, Given (1977), Hay et ai. (1975), Newman (1978), Beattie (1974, 1975), and Gurr, et al. (1976), who combine both spatial and historical comparisons.

REFERENCES

BEATTIE, J. M. (1974) "The pattern of crime in England 1660-1800." Past and Present 62 (Fall): 47-95.
——— (1975) "The criminality of women in eighteenth-century England." Journal of Social History 8: 80-116.
BENDIX, R. (1968) "Concepts in comparative historical analysis," in S. Rokkan (ed.) Comparative Research Across Cultures and Nations. Paris: Mouton.
BOCK, P. K. (1978) Antropologia Culturale Moderna. Torino: Einaudi.
CAVAN, R. S. and J. T. CAVAN (1968) Delinquency and Crime: Cross-cultural Perspectives. Philadelphia: J. B. Lippincott.
CLINARD, M. B. (1956) "Research frontiers." Criminology, British Journal of Delinquency 7: 110-122.
——— (1959) "Crimninological research," pp. 509-536 in R. K. Merton (ed.) Sociology Today. New York: Basic Books.
——— and D. J. ABBOTT (1973) Crime in Developing Countries: A Comparative Perspective. New York: John Wiley.
COHEN, A. K. (1959) "Delinquent subcultures." Estudios de Sociologia 1: 96.
CULBERTSON, J. M. (1971) Economic Development: An Ecological Approach. New York: Alfred A. Knopf.
DEFLEUR, L. (1967a) "A cross-cultural comparison of juvenile offenders and offenses: Cordoba, Argentina and United States." Social Problems 14: 483.
——— (1967b) "Delinquent gangs in cross-cultural perspective: the case of Gordoba." Journal of Research in Crime and Delinquency 4: 132-141.
——— (1969) "Alternative strategies for the development of delinquency theories applicable to other cultures." Social Problems 17: 30.
DURKHEIM, E. (1938) [1895] "Les regles de la methode sociologique" (S. A. Solvay and J. H. Mueller, trans.), in G. E. C. Catlin (ed.) The Rules of Sociological Method. Chicago: University of Chicago Press.
EGAN, F. (1961) "Social anthropology and the method of controlled comparison," pp. 109-129 in F. W. Moore (ed.) Readings in Cross-Cultural Methodology. New Haven: HRAF Press.
FERRACUTI, F., E. ACOSTA and S. DINITZ (1975) Delinquents and Nondelinquents in Puerto Rican Slum Culture. Columbus: Ohio State University Press.
FERRI, E. (1895) L'omicidio. Torino: Fratelli Bocca.
——— (1929) Sociologia Criminale. Torino: Unione Tipografico, Editrice Torinese.
FRIDAY, P. C. (1973) "Problems in comparative criminology: comments on the feasibility and implications." International Journal of Criminology and Penology 1: 151-160.
——— (1979) "Developing a comparative approach to study deviance." Journal of Criminal Law and Criminology 10: 270-272.
GALWAY, E. (197) "United Nations technical assistance in crime prevention and control." International Review of Criminal Policy 34: 22-25.
GAROFALO, J. (1977) "Time: a neglected dimension in tests of criminological theories," pp. 93-116 in R. F. Meier (ed.) Theory in Criminology. Beverly Hills, CA: Sage.
GIVEN, J. B. (1977) Society and Homicide in Thirteenth-century England. Stanford, CA: Stanford University Press.
GLUECK, S. and E. GLUECK (1964) "Wanted: a comparative criminology," in Ventures in Criminology. Cambridge, MA: Harvard University Press.
GOODENOUGH, W. H. (1956) "Residence rules." Southwest Journal of Anthropology 12: 22-37.

GURR, T., P. GRABOSKY and R. C. HULA (1977) The Politics of Crime and Conflict. Beverly Hills, CA: Sage.

HAY, D., P. LINEBAUGH, J. G. RULE, E. P. THOMPSON and C. WINSLOW (1975) Albion's Fatal Tree. New York: Pantheon.

HOLT, R. T. and J. E. TURNER (1970) The Methodology of Comparative Research. New York: Free Press.

LOPEZ-REY, M. (1970) Crime: An Analytical Appraisal. New York: Praeger.

——— (1976) "manifiesto Criminologico." pp. 363-376 in Capitulo Criminologico. Maracaibo: Universidad del Zulia.

MANNHEIM, H. (1965) Comparative Criminology. Boston: Houghton Mifflin.

MARSH, R. M. (1967) Comparative Sociology. New York: Harcourt Brace Jovanovich.

MAYER, K. (1963) "The changing shape of the American class structure." Social Research 30 (Winter): 458-468.

McCORD, W. (1965) The Springtime of Freedom: The Evolution of Developing Societies. New York: Oxford University Press.

MILLS, C. W. (1959) The Sociological Imagination. New York: Oxford University Press.

MURDOCK. G. P. (1957a) "Anthropology as comparative science." Behavioral Science 2 (October): 229-254.

——— (1957b) "World ethnographic sample." American Anthropologist 59, 4: 664.

NEWMAN, G. R. (1976) Comparative Deviance. New York: Elsevier-North Holland.

——— (1978) The Punishment Response. Philadelphia: J. B. Lippincott.

PARSONS, T. (1971) "Comparative studies and evolutionary change," pp. 97-140 in I. Vallier, Comparative Methods in Sociology. Berkeley: University of California Press.

PRZEWORSKI, A. and H. TEUNE (1970) The Logic of Comparative Social Inquiry. New York: John Wiley.

RADZINOWICZ, L. and J. KING (1977) The Growth of Crime. New York: Basic Books.

REISSMAN, L. and M. HALSTEAD (1970) "The subject is class." Sociology and Social Research 54: 293-305.

SMELSER, N. J. (1973) "The methodology of comparative analysis," pp. 42-88 in D. P. Warwick and S. Osherson, Comparative Research Methods. Englewood Cliffs, NJ: Prentice-Hall.

SOROKIN, P. (1957) Social and Cultural Dynamics. Boston: Porter-Sargent.

SZABO, D. (1973) "Criminologie comparee — signification et taches." Annales Internationales des Criminologie 12: 1-2, 89-126.

——— (1978) Criminologie et Politique Criminelle. Montreal: Les Presses de l'Universite.

TARDE, G. (1890) La Criminalite Comparee. Paris: Felix Alcan.

TOBY, J. (1979) "The new criminology is the old sentimentality." Criminology 16, 4: 516-526.

TURK, A. (1978) "Comparative deviance." Sociology and Social Research 62, 1: 187-188.

UNSDRI [United Nations Social Defense Research Institute] (1978) A World Directory of Criminological Institutes. Publication 17. Rome: Author.

VETERE, E. and G. R. NEWMAN (1977) "International crime statistics: an overview from a comparative perspective." Abstracts on Criminology and Penology 17, 3: 251-267.

WOLFGANG, M. and F. FERRACUTI (1967) The Subculture of Violence. London: Tavistock.

2

WORLD CRIME
To Measure or Not to Measure?

LESLIE T. WILKINS

When you can measure what you are speaking about and express it in numbers, you know something about it, but when you cannot measure it, when you cannot express it in numbers, your knowledge is of a meagre, and unsatisfactory kind. [Attributed to Lord Kelvin, quoted in Pearson, 1945].

The above quotation appeared for several editions as a frontispiece to *Tables for Statisticians and Biometricians* — a classical reference work edited by Karl Pearson (1945). The attribution to Lord Kelvin has been challenged, and the quotation ceased to appear in editions published since 1950. Even in the eighteenth century, not all persons agreed with the view expressed in this phrase. Indeed, it is reported that academic statisticians were, at the time, extremely critical of the "political arithmeticians." Two quotations will provide the flavor of the dispute: "These stupid fellows disseminate the idea that one can understand the power of the state and the number of dumb beasts grazing around." "The machinations of these criminal politician statisticians in trying to tell everything by figures...[are] despicable and ridiculous beyond words" (quoted in Social Indicators, n.d.; without attribution).

Perhaps the zenith for belief in the power of statistical data and analysis to solve social problems was reached around the beginning of this century. The complexities of contemporary problems make the average social scientist today more modest in his claims to be able to attach meaningful numbers to all phenomena. This modesty is based upon ample evidence — the enthusiasms of the founders of statistical societies were not sufficient to resolve the problems, and many more problems are recognized today. Nevertheless, in the field of crime, there are those who seem still to be too ready to try to "say it in numbers" without adequate attention to precisely what may be said in these terms.

It is now beginning to seem possible that the failure to find "anwers" might be due, in some measure, to the inadequate or inappropriate statements of questions. This chapter will examine some current demands for statistical data on crime with particular reference to the expressed need for international comparisons of such data. The United Nations is among the various bodies calling for such developments with a view to improvements in international crime control. The chapter concludes with a suggestion of a different framework — a restructuring of the basic questions — but a restructuring that addresses the issues which it is claimed have previously been inappropriately specified.

EARLY CALLS FOR INTERNATIONAL CRIME DATA

It appears that Quetelet made the suggestion of an international statistical congress in 1851, and that this was realized in September of 1853. On the agenda for this meeting, together with ten other topics, was the problem of statistics of crime (Campion, 1949). This was almost 20 years before the first International Congress on the Prevention and Repression of

Crime, which was held in London in 1872. One of the declared purposes of this latter congress was stated to be the examination of "reliable criminal statistics...to gather information and compare experiences as to the working of different prison systems, and the effect of various forms of punishment and treatment" (Vetere and Newman, 1977: 251). In rather strange contrast, Beatie (1968) notes that in the most affulent country of the world, the United States of America,

> Before World War I the only information to be found, except for scattered state and local court or correctional reports, was the highly limited data collected by the Bureau of the Census describing persons incarcerated in correctional institutions. There simply was no public accountability of crime, let alone of the processes of criminal justice administration.

It is interesting to note that Beatie's comment relates to a period which dates some 60 years or more after the first internatoinal congress on statistics and over 40 years after the first international congress on the prevention of crime. Crime statistics have proved to be either too difficult or insufficiently attractive to show much progress over the decades, even up to the present time.

Sir Harry Campion, Director of the Central Statistical Office of England and Wales, in this presentation on the topic of "International Statistics" before the Royal Statistical Society in 1949 (one of the few occasions on which that society has considered the topic), named criminal statistics just once, and then only when noting that it was one of the topics dealt with at the 1835 International Congress. Thus, as Campion notes, although even at the first congress there were represented some 26 countries and the total attendance of 150 persons has increased rapidly and almost continuously since, the assigned task of "establishing comparability between statistics published by different countries" has made little progress in the field of crime.

It may, appropriately, be pointed out that the problem of establishing criminal statistics in the United States is a more difficult one than for some other countries. The problems are those of a multijurisdictional administration of criminal justice.

Comparability among the states within the country presents very similar problems to those involved in seeking comparability among countries. If the United States cannot succeed in obtaining statistical data on crime and criminal justice procedures which satisfy all necessary criteria, it seems most unlikely that the more intractable problems which would be faced by an international undertaking will be solved in the near future, if at all. Nonetheless, the idea (ideal)? of seeking national statistical data on crime which might be valid for international comparisons has not been challenged. Most countries now have considerable investments in their own particular forms of statistical data bases of crime, but it appears that this cannot be harnessed to any internationally comparable data base. Any attempt to provide a comparison must involve radical changes in or additions to the present systems. To demonstrate this and to suggest a possible approach requires an assessment which will take us through some historical and philosophical debates.

SOME HISTORICAL NOTES
ON CRIME STATISTICS

As we have noted, Quetelet is frequently credited with originating much of the work of social statisticians. There is no doubt that he was a great advocate of the value of statistical data and that he was a moving force in the setting up of organizations to review and communicate statistical issues at the international level. However, there is a much earlier history which, it is argued, still has significance in relation to current problems.

The chain of ideas which still has considerable impact upon social statistical thought may go as far back as the fourteenth century, although some may consider this claim tenuous at best. It is clear that in England, the Penitentiary Bill of 1778 "provided for regular statistical returns by the Governors of the intended new penal establishments" (Grunhut, 1951). Bentham, in 1778, stated that he had "begun sketching out a plan for a collection of Bills of Delinquency with analogy to the Bills of Mortality" (Grunhut, 1951). Note that the analogy between the proposed criminal statistics and the Bills of Mortality is that stated by Bentham himself. This statement provides a clear link with events two centuries before when the Bills of Mortality were first organized.

It was Thomas Cromwell who initiated the Bills of Mortality to which Bentham refers for this model. Thomas Cromwell is not given much credit for his important social invention, perhaps because, with this one exception, his activities are not seen as particularly commendable. During Tudor times, England suffered considerably from the plague, and various precautionary measures became to be regarded as necessary. Quarantine and isolation (an early form of preventive medicine!) seem to have been rather successful in obtaining some remission of the ravages of the plague (Wilkins, 1965).

In order to be able to put the necessary measures into effect, it was essential to have early warnings of the existence of the plague in specific areas; even to the extent of identification of particular houses. In order to obtain the required information, "searchers," usually women, were appointed under the supervision of the parish clerks. The searchers were required to report the causes of each death taking place within the parish. The parish clerk then sent these reports to the parish Clerks' Hall. The returns provided the basic data for the Bills of Mortality to which Bentham refers as his inspiration for his idea of Bills of Delinquency.

The Bills of Mortality were summaries of the data collected by the searchers, and from these it was possible to distinguish the areas in which the plague was currently present and those areas which were free from the plague. Accordingly, restrictions on movement and other precautionary measures could be taken. It is generally believed that the Bills of Mortality data from 1553, or perhaps slightly earlier. It is certain that the Bills of Mortality were systematically compiled in a standard form on a regular basis until 1841, when the Registrar General's Office began the implementation of the Births and Deaths Registration Act of 1836.

It is interesting to speculate what might have been the situation had Bentham pressed his analogy to the limit. We might have had something close to the latest idea in criminal statistical data — the victimization studies — some 200 years ago. Further stretching of the analogy would lead us to something close to that which we now know as epidemiological models and crime mapping!

Speculation aside, we may note one other important event: namely, the addition in 1728 of the age at death to the Bills of Mortality. This led, in turn, directly to the preparation of *Life Tables* on which life insurance was to be based. Before this, however John Graunt published a work entitled "Natural and-Political Observations," in which he made use of inductive methods based on the data relating to deaths in the period 1632-1661.

The link to the "epidemiological model" is not the only historical link which may be suggested to have had some influence upon the thinking of those concerned with the problems of crime. The idea of social accounting is considerably older, and indeed forms of "social accounts" were well established by the middle of the seventeenth century. It is interesting to note the work of Sir William Perry dealing with the concept of "national income" in the year 1665, and Berkeley's concept (1685-1753) of money as a "ticket of exchange." We may see this idea as an observation of the relationship between the flow of money and the flow of information.

Having digressed to the point of considering money (even if with emphasis upon its token features), it may not stretch the imagination too far to assume that the idea of "social accounting" was related to the idea of financial accounting. If this is not outrageous, we may observe that the first exposition of double-entry book-keeping was published in 1494 by Lau da Bargo Pacioli, while examples of the use of this method of recording may be traced as far back as 1340 (Davidson, 1968).

Perhaps it is surprising that "accounts" of crime were so late in appearing. It may be much more surprising that the utility of the data collected today, even in the "advanced" countries, is regarded as in considerable doubt. We may ask whether the failure to develop methods which could withstand examination and which could be useful for guidance for policy decisions about crime is due to a lack of effort or to inherent difficulties in the task. The lack of development of valid crime data does not seem to be due to any conscious rejection of the idea of quantification. Neither does there appear to be any lack of interest in the issues involved. Views may differ as to the adequacy of investment, but at various times this has been far from trivial. How can it be that a scheme of statistical data collection, based on a model which might compare well with many in vogue today, never reached maturity? Are there problems with the models? If so, these problems do not attract much attention; rather, we have two contrasting "camps," those who are calling for the development of the data bases and those who are claiming that the task is impossible.

It is probable that the uneven development of national crime data reflects the same problems as those which inhibit or prevent the development of internationally comparable data. We will concentrate on the latter issue, but in order to argue certain positions it will be necessary to return to both historical and national references.

ARE INTERNATIONAL COMPARISONS OF CRIME POSSIBLE?

No less an authority than that of the International Penal and Penitentiary Commission in joint session with the International Statistical Institute in 1946 declared that "a material comparison of national criminal statistics [has] been judged impossible from the beginning because of the diversity of penal law and of the statistical-technical methods of the various countries" (Vetere and Newman, 1977: 252). Notwithstanding, as Vetere and Newman (1977) note, "The United Nations, from the early days of its establishment... selected criminal statistics as one of its main areas of concern in social defense." Which of these two prestigious organizations is correct? Are international comparisons of crime impossible, or should the task of providing such materials be taken up with more vigor? Is it possible that both organizations are right, despite the apparent complete opposition of the views expressed in these quotations?

IS THERE CRIME EVERYWHERE?

It seems to be a simple matter to agree that all countries have problems with crime. Indeed, all or almost all of the countries now represented in the United Nations admit to having problems with crime and show concern about it. It might be thought that, given this basic agreement, there must be some methods whereby analyses of the experiences of one country could be of assistance to another. But clearly, as the International Statistical Institute points out, there are problems of definition. Why, then, have the experts not addressed this matter and produced a satisfactory definitional framework? This question clearly troubles many, including distinguished philosophers who have discussed crime and what is done about it. Hyman Gross (1979) affords one perspective: "[But] no one needs to consult the law to know that murder, rape and theft are criminal acts. One needs only consult common views in the community to find that out: and if somehow the penal code did not include these acts among its prohibitions, we should say... [it] was incomplete" (Gross, 1979:7). It has long been insisted by legal scholars that there are crimes which are wrong because they are declared to be so by law (*mala prohibita*), and other crimes which are wrong in themselves (*mala in se*). It may seem appropriate to conclude that the claim that there are crimes in the latter category is the same as a claim that universally accepted concepts (if not definitions) exist regarding "crime." The dichotomous category has been criticized. The Baroness Wootton (1963) for example, suggested that actions classified as *mala in se* are really only *mala antiqua*! However, it is often claimed that there are actions which are regarded as serious offenses everywhere, or almost everywhere, and that these actions (*mala in se*?) could form a basis for comparative statistical data on crime.

It might be inferred from the above perspective that it is "hair splitting" by the lawyers which prevents the development of social accounting of crime on a comparative basis. But let us look a little more closely at Hyman Gross's statement, "one need not consult the law." That is precisely what one *has* to do. There is absolutely no meaning to the word "murder" unless one refers to the law. Killing is not a crime, but once we decide to *call* a killing a "murder," we have by precisely the same token decided to call it a crime. So the most flattering thing we can say about Gross's comment is that it is tautologous. The classification of "murder" is like the idea of a "shopping basket" — it will have different contents in different parts of the world and at different times. To add together the number of murders is like adding together the number of shopping baskets found in different countries without reference to the contents! We may press the analogy of the shopping basket still further by noting that there is a good chance that some of the items in the basket at the start of the journey home will have disappeared along the way and found themselves in other kinds of shopping baksets! This is not a trivial matter of hair-splitting definitions. The same case may be made for all crimes in any catalogue, but let us take a more detailed look at the category of "murder" by way of example.

The definition of "murder" depends upon classifications of kinds of killings as presented in the law of any specific country. Many intentional killings may not be defined as murder and nations may object strongly to the inclusion of certain behaviors, maintaining that the elements of "murder" are quite different from those accepted as essential elements in other countries. Let us consider two or three examples to indicate that the problem is not as rare nor as simple as it might at first appear. In most countries following the English basis of law, the survivor of a suicide pact is regarded as having committed a murder and may be so charged. In other countries this definition would not be acceptable. Again, if two persons engage in a duel (as they do in some parts of the world) and one is killed, the survivor would often be charged with murder. Alternatively, it is argued, it is illegal to engage in a duel, but the risk of death is understood by the parties to be part of the contract — that is why it is illegal. Thus, the charge against the survivor would not be murder, but that he engaged in a duel. This would be precisely the same charge whether or not either party was injured or killed. The inclusion of the case of a death in a duel among "common murderers" would not be fitting for a gallant gentleman!

Perhaps one more example will be adequate to demonstrate that this is an issue of sufficient generality. In many countries (some in Europe), if a husband should find his wife in adultery, it is required by custom that he kill the offender. In those countries, such revenge for adultery is certainly not considered to be murder. Quite recently a migrant worker carried out his "duty" in such a case, and this involved his facing trial for murder in England — a situation which he found impossible to understand.

What is true of murder (should we now say, "murder"?) is, of course, generally to a greater degree also true of other "crimes." A charge of "attempted murder" in one country when described to lawyers in another would be seen as a mere misdemeanor. As though we require any further problems, we have not only spatial differences, but also time differences. By time differences we do not mean historical time which involves changes in the law, but changes in the way the act (or event) is described as it moves through the criminal justice machinery in any country. A case which originates as "murder" (the police initially so believe it to be) may later become accidental death, manslaughter, or may fit into any number of other categories, not all of which may even be regarded as "crimes." The problem then becomes, at what time in the processes of events is the label which will be used in the statistical data attached to the event? This is analogous to the basket having items removed and replaced or put into other baskets on the journey home, so that it is important to standardize the time at which the basket is intercepted and examined!

It seems that we must conclude that the declaration of the International Statistical Congress was correct — the task of producing "International Crime Statistics" is impossible. But...

IF THERE IS NOT CRIME EVERYWHERE...?

If we cannot say that there is "crime" everywhere, we may still argue that there are events everywhere which the societies of each country regard as crimes — to continue the shopping basket analogy, the contents of the baskets differ and there is no point in adding them up. However, by many individual and specific standards there are events which should be prevented or punished or both, and there are certainly victims who need protection. But is it only crime from which victims desire to be protected? Clearly not. We have here some clue as to how we might proceed. It seems that we cannot solve the problem of international criminal statistics because we have stated the questions in the wrong terms. It appears that the question has been posed in a language of answers. An answer-type language will not provide appropriate solutions. This is a broad generalization and a claim which needs some justification.

PROBLEMS SPECIFIED IN ANSWER-STYLE LANGUAGE?

Like the basic ideas of social statistics, the problem of stating appropriate questions has been recognized for centuries. Merton (1959) refers to the seventeenth century, when a certain John Aubrey noted: "Dr Pell was wont to say that in the Solution of Questions, the Main Matter was the well-stating of them: which requires Mother-wit and Logic. . . for let the Question be well-stated, it will work almost of itself." We may well agree with Dr Pell, but ask what he intends by a "well-stated" question. His invocation of "logic" and "mother-wit" is only an exhortation which provides no guidance as to how proper questions should be stated. It must be confessed that even today we have little scientific knowledge of how to state questions well. We have progressed considerably with regard to procedures for the testing of hypotheses, but we do not have as many techniques for their origin. There is no substitute for the scientific imagination. However, at great risk, perhaps some suggestions may be made in this area with particular reference as to how it affects our present problem.

To say that any question "stated in answer-style language" is a poor question provides no positive guidance, but it provides a test of appropriateness. Among the many questions which may be phrased in a particular problem area, we may use the test to reject those which are suspect. If we do not go that far, we may still find the test useful in raising our alertness to difficulties in our postulates. Perhaps the kind of language which is classified as being of the answer-type may best be indicated by two or three examples. The matter seems fairly clear in the field of occupational psychology — perhaps because this field has few emotional overtones.

A manufacturer might approach an industrial consultant and say that he "has a training problem with his staff," and request that the consultants work out a training program for his needs. A consultant who goes along with a package of training materials would be accepting a question posed in the language of answers. Consider another example and contrast it with the preceding. A manufacturer might approach an industrial consultant and say that he "has a selection problem." Accepting this as a statement of the problem, the consultant might go along with a battery of testing materials and guides for interviewing applicants. It will, perhaps, be quite obvious that the "selection problem" may well be a "training problem," or, conversely, the "training problem" may well be a "selection problem." The problem is not well specified when it suggests a form of answer or forecloses a thorough examination of the phenomena which are believed to be symptoms of the trouble.[1]

A more serious example, and one which is widespread, is an outcome of the belief of decision makers in almost every field that if only they had sufficient sound information they could make better decisions. The problems of decision-making are thus stated in answer-type language — the relevant information is more quickly accessible. The problems of the decision makers may have little or nothing to do with the quantity nor even the quality of the information. Certainly, the problems are unlikely to be related to the speed of access to information. It is known that the provision of more relevant information may make the decision maker less effective because of the problems generated by information overload (Hayes, 1962).[2]

In the field of criminal justice, it is easy to pose questions in the form of answers. It is easy to suggest that we might measure those things which can be measured and count those things which can be counted, such as dead bodies and money, or even the "crime baskets" noted above. The specification of questions in answer-type language is similar to the specification of operations in "closed systems" terms. Donald Schon (1971) has pointed out that when a firm of sandal manufacturers had sales difficulties, they received advice to the effect that they should not regard themselves as in the business of making and selling sandals, but as making and marketing leisure footwear. This may sound quite trivial. But consider an exactly similar linguistic transformation for a soap manufacturer. If he sees himself in the business of selling soap, then detergents will be the "enemy," but if he designates the purpose of his business as making and marketing "cleansing agents," then detergents may well be viewed differently and exploited by his comany. The change of language will at times seem trivial, but the consequences may be to advise opposing policies. The changes in these are from object language (sandals, soap) to the language of function (leisure footwear, cleansing agents). This kind of transformation of the statement of the criterion or purpose(s) is one of the ways of breaking the cognitive bind and of challenging the tendency for "more of the same" to be the only imagined remedy for a problem.

THE LANGUAGE OF CRIME

When we call an event a "crime" we do not describe the incident in any specific way. We are expressing our dislike of the act even if it is not, in fact, a crime. (It "ought to be a crime"!) Technically, we are stating that the act, as we see it at the time, fits into a category of acts which are prohibited by the criminal law in the location that the act took place. We are also saying that the act is "punishable," and certain other facts may be assumed if we are correct in using the term. Most precisely, however, we are saying what is to be done about the *actor* — he is to be dealt with through the machinery of government set up to deal with these cases: the criminal justice machinery. We are saying what will be *done about* the actor, but little about the act itself. Even a description in terms of a particular crime category tells us little. For example, robbery may mean one small boy threatening and taking the lunch money of another, up to and

including "The Great Train Robbery" (no train was stolen!).
Very similar procedures of criminal justice are employed to deal
with a wide variety of disapproved acts.

It seems that when we use the word "crime" in any question,
we are committed to stating the question in something like
answer-type language. Crime is, by definition, something
which we propose to deal with in (strict?) accordance with
specific procedures. If this can be accepted, a number of consequences follow, and these lead to a proposal for a system of obtaining what is required when we think of the potential utility of
international crime statistics.

A few consequences follow from the present specification and
are of some interest, although less central to the main concern.
The idea of "crime" is directly related to "acts" (rather than,
to states), and hence to the idea that these events can be
counted. It is often said that an offender was "found guilty on
both *counts*," although this may be coincidental. Not all crimes
can be counted, because many remain unreported by the public
or otherwise do not come to the attention of the police. The
standard term used to describe this unknown amount of crime
is "the dark figure," so the idea of number is used to describe
that which cannot be counted!

When we become committed to thinking about crime in terms
of summations of categorized items, we are taking a particular
approach which will condition our strategies of problem solving
in all kinds of ways. Problems of analysis and inference arise
mainly from the definitions which lead to the placing of items
into certain categories (baskets), rather than from counting the
categories or the items within them. The problems arise, in other
words, in the process of categorizing. As soon as we use
numbers in relation to categories, we cannot avoid the assumption that the data similarly categorized are strictly comparable
— comparisons are the essence of numbers. We have seen that
these assumptions of comparability are not satisfied, and hence
we may infer that any summations of data of these kinds will
not be satisfactory. We are, again, at the position stated by the
International Statistical Congress: International criminal
statistics are impossible. But we may have a clue as to how to

break out of this impasse. Can we restate the problem with a different question?

INTERNATIONAL — SUMMATION OF NATIONAL?

If we wish to enlighten international problems we must start our thinking and our questioning in terms of international models. We will have to abandon the idea that "international criminal statistics" should be some kind of summation of "national criminal statistics." We must start by thinking of "international criminal statistics" not merely as quantitatively different from national, but as qualitatively different. We should ask whether it is possible to find a set of constructs with which we might *perform the task* we initially had in mind when *we began* to look for international comaprisons of crime — that is, we must return to the question rather than consider varieties of answers. Note that we look for some means or process, not "a thing." What did the people who called for international comparative statistical data have in mind to *use* it for? Is there another way to assist them to do what they wanted to do without specifying the question in the language of answers?

AN INITIAL CONSTRAINT

It is useful to break the association between national and international, which merely defines the latter in terms of the former. While much of the work of the United Nations is carried out in terms of national units, it must be noted that there is extreme variety among countries in their abilities to undertake data collections, no matter how these may be organized. We must recognize also that some countries possess extreme varieties of sophistication. Nonetheless, throughout the world there are towns and cities with high levels of similarity — even in the developing countries there are urban areas which are quite similar to those in the most developed parts of the world. Many such cities even have their Hilton Hotels! It would seem that two factors lead us to suggest that international comparisons of "crime" (or whatever we substitute for this concept) should be limited to transurban data. In the first place, crime is usually regarded as mainly an urban phenomenon, and second, some reduction in the within-country variance might assist comparisons, since it is possible that the urban/rural variance would swamp any other variance.

REFERENCE DATA

Statistical data do not stand on their own. Countries have different forms of legal systems and procedures. The maintenance of law may not depend only upon "police," and indeed the definition of "police" will vary. A glossary of terms and the more important relevant background factors will be required. Of course, we may get into the same kind of problems as forced us to abandon the idea of international crime data from summations of national data. The key to this difficulty seems to be in separating the measures of "problems" from measures of what is done about them. Measures of "activity" by government agencies cannot act as very satisfactory proxy data for the problems addressed.[3] Arrests, for example, do not measure crimes — even if we wanted to measure crimes!

QUALITY OF LIFE

The concept of the "quality of life" has received considerable attention in recent times, but has yet to make any significant impact upon thinking in the field of "criminal justice." The United Nations (1978),[4] however, has suggested that the concept provides a central reference or "touchstone" by which to assess social policy. Thus, for the goals of the criminal justice system, we must look further afield than merely to actions defined as "crimes" and the official machinery set up to deal with these acts. It may be represented that it is not the task of criminologists to deal with such broad issues, and certainly the task is not theirs alone. Many disciplines must be involved in operationalizing the concept of quality of life as it may be assessed through the medium of "social indicators." No single discipline can arrogate to itself the right to pronouncements in this field, nor can many disciplines ignore an element of responsibility.

There are many thousands of persons who are interested in "crime" from the perspective of entertainment: playwrights, newsmen, some social scientists, and perhaps a large proportion of the public. The justification for collection of data is not that it be exploited for entertainment, nor merely for purposes of putting it "on record." The purpose of data collection is to inform decisions, and the decisions are related to the purpose of improving the quality of life. This may sound obvious and trivial, but it proves to be a very hard test of any proposed action in terms of the collection or analysis of data. To be able to say that it would be "interesting to know" does not justify expenditure on the collection of data. To be able to say that (X) is a fact is not sufficient justification — we must have some idea of how the knowledge or absence of knowledge of (X) will influence decisions (that is, its utility).

SOME PROBLEMS OF "QUALITY OF LIFE" IN RELATION TO CRIME

There may be fewer problems in relating the concept of the quality of life to economic issues than to those of crime and deviant behaviors, or it may be that more time and consideration has been given to the former. Perhaps one specific problem should be noted which may be central to the idea of "crime" but to few, if any, other areas. The quality of life cannot be defined only by positive factors or by things which exist. Negative factors are particularly important, as are also "absences" of factors. Philosophers have dealt at considerable length with the concept of freedom and noted that *freedom from* differs from *freedom to*. Freedom from (or the absence of) the fear of crime in a community may be a far more important indicator than any positive or "presence" factor. There are other "absences" which are relevant. It is, of course, difficult to count things which do not exist, but the absence of "ills" is not the same as the presence of "goods"; indeed, it is the former which is the more critical for the quality of life as seen from the perspective of criminal justice. We do not so much seek to do good as to prevent harm and damage. We may suggest that data on "harms" could be more useful than data on "crimes" as a basis for informed policy. This point will become the central aspect of the recommendations for action. But before we seek to see how this idea may be put into effect, there are a few more theoretical matters to be touched upon.

The concept of *freedom from* sits easily with the historical sphere of interest of criminal justice and criminal law. The concept of *freedom to* is more difficult and less specifically related to the idea of "social harm" and the traditions of law. Freedom to do something does not mean that a large proportion of the population actually does it or indeed would do it even if it could. I may value my freedom to go to the opera at a reasonable price, but the degree to which I value that freedom is not well measured by the frequency with which I attend. A measure of my appreciation of the freedom to is not obtained until the removal of that freedom is threatened.

Law is a social institution which for a particular society protects the individual from the capricious exercise of power by those in authority, as well as providing a list of prohibited acts for which penalties are prescribed. When we consier the problems of "crime" we are inclined to limit our thinking to the efficiency of the enforcement of the law rather than to extend it to the concept of the efficiency of law itself as a social invention. Focus upon the "touchstone" idea of the quality of life and the problems of reducing "social harms" increases the range of thinking and makes possible some new procedures. These procedures stand in relation to the idea of international crime statistics as the Bills of Mortality stand in relation to the procedures of contemporary Morbidity statistics.

BACK TO BENTHAM'S ANALOGY

It is fitting again, at this stage of the argument, to acknowledge the genius of Bentham for his suggested analogy of crime statistics to the system of compiling the old Bills of Mortality. Of course, no simple analogy may be pressed too far, but we know that for purposes of health planning the "surveys of complaints of sickness" provide a most useful tool (Slater, 1946).[5] (It should be noted that a "complaint of sickness" is not assumed to be the same as a "symptom," nor is it an "ailment.") The reference to which a "complaint" is assessed is the response to a question asking *how it affects* the complaint. A complaint of crime may have as little relationship to "actual" crimes as a complaint of sickness has to an actual diagnosis. Furthermore, in studies of complaints of sickness, it is not expected that the informant will provide a statement in any close degree similar to any ailment listed in the standard list of ailements.

The analogy has some interest, but it is obvious that in the case of sicknesses a diagnosis (professional assessment) is directly related to the indicated remedial action. The transformation from a "complaint of crime" (as in victim studies) has no such significance — the "treatment" is precisely the same no matter what the diagnosis of the harm suffered; namely, find the offender and punish him. But we know that this "treatment" has not reduced the social harms which we call crimes. Reduction of the problem of crime to the problem of the offender has not been successful. Perhaps if we were to examine the events in a wider framework in as much detail as we have examined the offender elements, we might be able to develop a more diversified strategy and perhaps be more successful. It seems essential, therefore, to examine carefully the link between the concept of a "social harm" and the concept of "crime" before any such enhanced strategy of action can be adequately thought about. This is, as we have noted, because the classification of the "harm" as a crime defines the activity to be taken to deal with one factor in the situation, namely the person who (if identified) can be accused of the act. It may be pointed out in passing that this approach limits our action in relation to these social harms almost entirely to a very small fraction of the events — that fraction of "crimes" which are detected and for which a finding of guilt is secured. The remainder of the social harms suffered provide little or no data and hence stimulate little or no remedial or preventive action.

A SUGGESTION FOR A NEW DATA BASE

If the previous argument can be accepted, even only partially,

a different form of data base is required. In order to begin this
process we need to think first of the kinds of issues which
should be addressed. We accept the national questions are relevant to national statistical data, and since law is statewide or
national, internal data bases will be generated and data of utility
within the countries or states may be expected to become
available. But international questions are appropriate for thinking about international data to inform international policy and
for purposes of comparisons between states. What are these
questions of international policy? Who has the right or duty to
ask them? Presumably, the international community of scholarship and the existing international bodies such as the United Nations and the other regional and international councils or
organizations of states.

The Organization for European Cooperation and Development (O.E.C.D., 1976) has begun work in this area, but it may
be that the thinking has not been sufficiently radical. (The term
"radical" is intended to be understood in its etymological
reference, not in its contemporary misuse as a political tag.)
There has been a tendency to try to press into service much of
the old styles of data without adequate challenge. It is necessary
to "get to the roots" of the matter and to give continuous and
vigilant attention to the focus on the concept of the quality of
life — the quality of life of people, rather than the qualities or
quantities associated with their institutions and administrations.
The cart must not get before the horse!

We are interested in the people's opinions as to what events,
persons, or organizations have prevented them from doing what
they need to do. We are interested not in complaints of
"crimes," but in "grievances." We limit our concern about
"grievances" to those which are regarded as causing harms. We
may further limit our concern to those events or acts which are
regarded as "serious" in terms of the ways in which they affect
individuals. If we wish to capture mainly those incidents which
fit closely into our time-honored concept of crime, we might
further restrict the listings of incidents causing harms to those
believed to be due to intentional acts, negligence, or to inappropriate exercise of power by other persons or organizations.

We might extend our concept of victims, as well as that of offenders, to organizations or collectives of persons. Thus, we might visualize a series of "filtering questions" which will take us toward those events which people believe to be crimes or which they would say ought to be crimes. It is possible that we might, by this means, produce a list of behaviors which may closely map on to the idea of *mala in se* which we rejected earlier in this chapter in terms of its present defintion. By conducting current research we would certainly avoid defining the idea of *mala in se* merely in terms of *mala antiqua*![6]

USING THE NEW LISTINGS OF "SOCIAL HARMS"

Given a listing of serious "social harms" meeting the requirements and constraints noted above, we may next move to consider how such material should be organized. We would, of course, now have direct information as to what degree the contemporary *mala in se* listings fit each other across the participating countries. We would know whether a meaningful "basket" might be made — a set of categories developed. It seems probable. As a tentative indication, the following cateogries may be examples of that which would materialize from this approach.

Area of Concern	How it Affects People
Personal liberty	Loss of liberty by reason of official action for whatever reason — legal or extra-legal Levels of constraint used
Individual suffering	External force injury Accident/crime Self-inflicted
Human dignity	Speed of trials Detention awaiting trials Confidence in legal processes
Fear of victimization	Fear of "crime Cheating or exploitation

TOWARD "SOCIAL INDICATORS"

Only when the grievances have been noted and the manner in which they affect people has been adequately described should there be a search for indicators of these "harms." It is not proposed to continue to survey the population with regard to their grievances and "harms" and the ways in which they are affected thereby. The listing of harms and grievance is intended only to provide a basic set of references of the "needs" of the community. A search would next be made to try to find indicators of the problems, needs, and harms as selected from the listing to be serious issues demanding the concern of public policy makers. It is not possible to say what precise form these indicators might take. Some of the kinds of items which may emerge from the study include the analogy of the use of the infant mortality rate as a proxy for "social class" and many other data. The "Dead-on-arrival" data from the emergency rooms of hospitals are an indicator of serious tragedies in the lives of people in a community; and so on. The aim would be to find indirect indicators which could substitute, either singly or by weighted equations, for the costly direct collection of data.

It is important at this point, to discriminate between measures of response and measures of the problem. At the risk of being repetitive, we again refer to crime as representing data about responses to a situation and *not* measures of the problem. Since the purpose of data collection and analysis is, among other things, intended to inform selection of responses, data which merely record these responses cannot be any guide!

The penultimate stage would be the identification of procedures which are assumed to be available to relieve the harms. And finally, we would seek indicators of the degrees of activity and effectiveness of such procedures. It is, of course, at this final stage that we seem to believe we have already arrived — most stastical data are in the category of measures of activity by agencies of government and other enterprises charged with the tasks of relieving ills. It is assumed that the intention to provide remedies and the amount of investment in that intention is adequate as a measure of the effects. Not only is this clearly unsound, but it may even be unsound in the inappropriate direction. The activities may not only fail to address the ills believed to be addressed, but these may be the wrong ills addressed in altogether the wrong ways.

IS A NEW APPROACH FEASIBLE?

The developed countries of the world have a very large investment in data-gathering bureaucracies, and a radical change will be difficult. However, there is no reason why these developed countries should assume that the procedures they have adopted are those which should be copied by the developing countries. One thing is clear: The foisting of the data-collecting procedures of the developed world upon the developing countries will not provide comparable data of any use to the developed nor to the developing. Any comparative data on deviance and crime must be independent of the legal structure of the countries concerned. The law enshrines both the culture and the history of the country where it exists. This is appropriate. But there is no culture-free statement of criminal law. There is not, and cannot be, an international code which sums the national codes. If we accept that there are commonalities among people (as people) everywhere, this seems somewhat more justified and provides a basis for comparisons. We should not *assume* that the concept of *mala in se* is valid, but it is just possible that we might empirically *find* something like it as a basis for our international data on the phenomena we now call "crime."

No large sums of money would be required to develop a data base, and the costs of maintenance would be less than the current investment in unusable data. If there is agreement as to those events which are common, serious grievances causing personal harm (*mala in se*?), a large sample is not required. Large samples are required where there is considerable variance. Thus, those who are most strongly attracted to the established ideas of consensus regarding serious crimes are those who should be among the first to support the proposed new approach. If there is considerable variance in the basic beliefs about the nature of crime, then we need to know that, and the task of obtaining cross-cultural comparable data is the more difficult.

It will be recalled that it was proposed to restrict the comparisons of the new data to data collected from a sample of cities, and not to atempt to include rural cultures. The argument was made then in terms of the values of such limited data bases, and the argument may now be extended to that of reduced costs.

In summary, the proposed exploration of a new data base may be seen as a series of simple stages. We begin, not by accepting the existing packaging of concepts (baskets) and adding these together, but we go back to identification of the contents of the "baskets." The items are to be identified by individuals within each society as those things which they find to be grievous harms or restrictions. The lists are then examined as to rational classifications (baskets) and provided with labels. Following the successful classification, social indicators are sought which will provide some measures of the "grievance baskets" or which serve adequately as proxy variables for these entities. The final stage attempts to provide measures of activity and effectiveness of agencies charged with finding remedies for or alleviation of these ills. It is hoped that the social ills will reveal a reasonable degree of comparability, while the measures taken to relieve the ills should show considerable variation. We might then learn how selected methods from the variety of remedies may serve to relieve the *similar* ills in countries which at present use *different* systems of social control.

Thus, we arrive at a possible scheme which uses as the major strength of our data base for international comparisons just those features which made cross-cultural comparisons impossible — the extremes of varieties of responses among countries. These data should serve to carry out the mission first envisioned as that of the first international congress on crime — namely, to provide data which might assist the making of policy decisions regarding the problem of "crime" and harmful deviant behaviors.

NOTES

1. This is not merely saying that we should avoid "begging the question."
2. See also articles by Burnham and Wilkins (1975).

3. Measures of activity have their place in statistical data which may inform policy decisions. Measures of the expenditure on medical services may be important in relation to measures of health, but not as substitutes for morbidity or mortality data.

4. See also monthly bulletins of the Ministry of Health for the year ended December 1945 for early examples of the use of sampling in morbidity (complainants of sickness data).

5. The author is indebted to those who took part in discussions at a meeting in Rome in 1977. A minority of those present raised issues along the lines noted in relation to "concerns" and "social indicators." 'No publication resulted from these discussions, which dealt with the minority views and proposals. Document U.N. E/AC 57/23:10 has some points of relevance to these concepts.

6. This is interesting rather than important.

REFERENCES

BEATIE, R. H. (1968) "A state bureau of criminal statistics," pp. 179-170 in M. E. Wolfgang (ed.) Crime and Culture. New York: John Wiley.

BURNHAM, R. W. and L. T. WILKINS (1975) Decisionmaking in the Criminal Justice System: Reviews and Essays. National Institute of Mental Health. Washington, DC: U.S. Government Printing Office.

CAMPION, H. (1949) "International statistics." Journal of the Royal Statistical Society Series A: 105-134.

DAVIDSON, S. (1968) "Accounting," in D. L. Sills (ed.) International Encyclopedia of the Social Sciences. New York: Macmillan.

GROSS, H. (1979) A Theory of Criminal Justice. Oxford University Press.

GRUNHUT, M. (1951) "Statistics in criminology." Journal of the Royal Statistical Society Series A: 271-297.

HAYES, J. R. (1962) Human Data Provessing Limits in Decision-making. Bedford, MA: Operational Applications Lab, Air Force Electronics, Systems Division.

MERTON, R. (1959) Sociology Today. New York: Basic Books.

OECD (1976) Measuring Social Well-Being: Progress Report on the Development of Social Indicators, MAS/WPI (76) 2. Paris.

PEARSON, K. [ed.] (1945) Tables for Statisticians and Biometricians. Cambridge: Cambridge University Press.

SCHON, D. (1971) The Reith Lectures. London: B.B.C. United Nations Document. E/AC. 57/23:10.

SLATER, P. (1946) Survey of Sickness. Government Social Survey Report. London: Her Majesty's Stationery Office.

Social Indicators (n.d.) Radical Statistics Pamphlet /4.

VETERE, E. and G. NEWMAN (1977) "International crime statistics: an overview from a comparative perspective." Abstracts in Criminology and Penology 17(3): 251-273.

WILKINS, L. T. (1965) Social Deviance. Englewood Cliffs. NJ: Prentice-Hall.

WOOTTON, B. (1963) Crime and the Criminal Law. London: Stevens.

United Nations (1978) Preparatory Papers for the 1980 Congress on the Causes of Crime and the Treatment of Offenders (prepublication draft).

PERCEPTIONS OF DEVIANCE CROSS-CULTURALLY

JOSEPH E. SCOTT
FAHAD AL-THAKEB

CRIME STATISTICS AND THE PERCEPTION OF CRIME

If asked, most Americans would undoubtedly express the belief that crime has increased dramatically during the last 10 or 20 years. Most would attribute this to the lenient manner in which the American criminal justice system deals with offenders. Most would undoubtedly feel that the American criminal justice system is more lenient with offenders than are comparable systems throughout the world. However, as most students of crime know, we have experienced more of a crime-reporting wave than a dramatic increase in crime, and our criminal justice system is possibly one of the more punitive in the free world. One should ask immediately: Why the divergence, then, between American beliefs and the reality of crime?

This chapter attempts to examine some of the research and writing concerning perceptions of crime not only in the United States but throughout the world, as well as to report on some resarch conducted by the authors in Western Europe, the Middle East, and the United States. Certainly, the perception of crime is a crucial issue given its impact on citizens' thoughts, fears, and actual behavior. Perceptions of crime also affect legislatures' movement to pass new laws, strengthen existing ones, or increase penalties for certain types of offenses. W. I. Thomas' oft-repeated proposition, "if men define situations as real, they are real in their consequences," may be taken to mean that a society's perception of its crime is more relevant than a society's actual crime rates or patterns as to consequences and policies.

There is a tradition in criminology to rely on official statistics concerning crime. This is understandable in terms of the reassurance which comes from quantification and thereby apparent objectivity. The conceptual inadequacy of much of our official statistics, however, is being recognized more and more. Much of the data for criminologists come from bureaucracies which produce this data for nonscientific purposes (Cicourel, 1964: 36-37), collected for wrong hierarchical levels (Biderman, 1970), and we know that the collection of crime data has been heavily influenced by the collecting agency's own ideology (Becker, 1973: 192-193; Cicourel, 1974: 93-94). The inadequacy of official statistics was well documented to the authors at the international Symposium on Selected Criminological Topics held in Stockholm during the summer of 1978. At this symposium, distinguished criminological scholars from approximately 50 countries were invited to present papers on crime trends in their respective countries since 1950. Many of these "scholarly' papers presented quantifiable data concerning crime not previously available. Certainly, the presentation of crime trends from the respective countries may have been more representative of someone's own perception of how crime should be perceived rather than their own perception or actual experience. A few examples are perhaps illustrative of this point.

Among a world heaving with social problems the first of which is loose family ties, ill upbringing, juvenile delinquency, use of

narcotics and strong drinks as means of escaping the unbearable
life situation, the Kingdom of Saudia Arabia has become the
land of peace where prosperity is and justice prevails.

The average crime occurrence in Saudi Arabia in the year 1966
was counted to be 0.32 per thousand of the population. This
year was selected as a starting point for criminal statistics
because statistical figures could only be available at that year.
From that time the average number of crimes started decreasing
till it reached a minimum of not more than 0.18 per each thousand of the population [Alganoubi, 1978: 2-3].

In Nigeria it is very difficult to obtain official criminal statistics
since law enforcement officers regard the data as secret. The
degree of confidentiality attached to criminal statistics is so high
that the Police Annual Report which usually contains such data
[is] normally prohibited from being circulated to the public. To
obtain the barest information on crime trends a researcher has to
go through a rigorous bureaucratic process which might take an
average of six months. Besides, the officers reserve the right to
provide the researcher with what information they believe he
should have and in what form they think proper.

According to the officials in charge of the criminal statistics,
such materials are believed to contain intrinsic security risk to
the society and there is a need to investigate thoroughly what information is given out, in what form it is given, to whom it is
given and for what specific purpose it is to be used [Olurun-
timehin, 1978: 1, 2]).

It is obvious that crime may only be understood by carefully
considering a country's social conditions. In Hungary, as we
have progressed with socialism and reduced the inequities of our
society, crime has consistently declined concomitantly. As social
injustices diminished, crime declined. This accounts for the
reduction of crime in Hungary during the last fifteen years
[Vign, 1978: 1, 3].

Why has Japan been enjoying low and decreasing crime rates
with all her remarkable industrialization and urbanization? This
is not an easy question to answer. Very often governmental
white papers enumerate plausible reasons; namely, homogeneity
of race and culture, traditional social values such as respect for
human relationships, strong ties of family, effective communal
control, the national character of highly law-abiding tendency,

widespread high educational level and low rate of illiteracy, low rate of unemployment, small income differentials, high social mobility, and so on [Iwai, 1978:2].

Crime has not yet become as serious a problem in India as in most of the industrialized countries of the world [Varma, 1978:].

It is clear that the collection and interpretation of criminal statistics may depend heavily on the agency's ideology as to crime. Kitsuse and Cicourel, in "A Note on the Uses of Official Statistics," emphasized that crime statistics are the result of decisions and action taken by persons in a social system which defines, classifies, and records certain behavior as criminal. The process is therefore crucially affected by the subjective attitudes of individuals and how they define and interpret behavior as criminal. Rates can be viewed as indices of organizational processes rather than as indices of the incidence of certain forms of behavior.

Most serious crimes known to the police are not discovered as a result of their direct initiative or detection, but are reported to the police by the public. Bottomley (1973:8-17), in a brilliant analysis of changing crime figures, identifies numerous factors affecting people's perception of crime and their willingness to call it to the attention of authorities. Perceptions of crime, national or international, are affected by broad sociocultural factors. Leslie Wilkins (1965) expressed the basic issue surrounding the definition of crime as "something that the police ought to do something about," and points out the likely changes in social attitudes toward criminal behavior that may occur from one generation to the next.

Cross-Cultural Studies of the Perception of Crime

There have been several creative efforts to assess perceptions of crime cross-culturally in several countries. Badr-El Din Ali (1978), using data from 34 countries, analyzes the perceived trend in each country's crime from 1965-1975 and the reason for these patterns. The countries utilized were Argentina, Australia,

Austria, Barbados, Belgium, Bolivia, Canada, Ceylon, Costa Rica, Cyprus, Denmark, Ecuador, Egypt, England, West Germany, Iceland, Israel, Italy, Jamaica, Japan, Kenya, Malaysia, Mexico, Nepal, Netherlands, New Zealand, Norway, Nigeria, Saudi Arabia, Scotland, Sierre Leone, Singapore, South Africa, Taiwan, and the United States.

Originally, questionnaires were mailed to investigators in 83 countries. These investigators were requested to report the trend in the rate of reported crime in general and for 11 specific types of crimes. Ali then ranked the 34 responding countries according to their level of developmnent (primarily a scale based on economics) to analyze the crime trend. Noteworthy is the fact that only two of the countries reported decreases in their overall crime trends for the period 1965-1975. The two were Barbados and Singapore (not Japan, Hungary, or Saudi Arabia, as reported at the International Crime Trends Seminar in 1978). Ali found that the highly developed nations as well as the less developed ones perceived greater increases in crime, while the intermediate nations had not perceived enormous increases.

A second major effort to assess the perception of crime in six different cultures was carried out by Graeme Newman (1976). This study, conducted under the auspices of the United Nations, relied on samples from India, Indonesia, Iran, Italy (Sardinia), the United States, and Yugoslavia to test a number of theories including the consistency theory of seriousness of crime cross-culturally. Newman's analysis is one of the most theoretically developed and thoroughly empirically tested that the authors are aware of in the literature. Nevertheless, one major limitation to Newman's study, in addition to the sample of countries where data were collected, is the number of "deviant acts" upon which responses were elicited. There were only nine acts on which data was gathered, and only three of these are definitely typical criminal acts (robbery, incest, and taking drugs); while the other six are crimes in some countries and more typical of moral guidelines in others (not helping, abortion, factory pollution, homosexuality, protest, and appropriation). Newman concludes that economically well-developed countries discriminate more clearly among classes of deviant behavior than do less-developed ones (1976:296). In addition, he found a definite pattern of disapprobation of traditional crimes across countries.

Is there a "consensus" in perceptions of crime? Social theorists have debated for years the "true" nature of society. Specifically, the debate has focused on the justification and purpose of a state and whether the mores and laws the state attempts to regulate and enforce reflect the views of the populace (consensus theory) or whether they reflect the ruling classes' desire to maintain the status quo for their own benefit (conflict theory). Criminology has not been immune from these diverse orientations with regard to its theories and research.

According to traditional criminology, the state exists to maintain order and stability, and laws are regarded as rules established by consensus by those who are governed. Acts are criminal, according to this perspective, because they offend the morality of the people (Chambliss, 1974:34). Radical criminology views the state as a creation by the elite to protect their material basis, and the legal system provides the mechanism for the forceful and violent control of the rest of the population (Quinney, 1974:18). According to radical criminologists, the ruling class uses the criminal law to secure its interests by preventing any challenge to its moral and economic structure. Acts are criminal according to this perspective because it is in the interests of the ruling class to so define them (Chambliss, 1974:37).

The crucial question appears to be the extent to which there is a consensus concerning traditional crimes and deviances, not only within the United States but across different national samples. There has been considerable research on whether consensus concerning the seriousness of crimes exists across different substrata within the United States. Conflict or radical criminologists reject these efforts inasmuch as the elite in a capitalist society control the mass media and thereby manage the peoples' thinking as to right and wrong. However, by examining this question across national samples composed of both capitalist and social welfare type countries one may better test whether traditional perceptions of right and wrong exist concerning crime and deviance. Anglo-Saxon criminal law has traditionally drawn the distinction between criminals acts as being *mala in se* and *mala prohibita*. Acts of *mala in se* are considered "real criminal acts" while *mala prohibita* are acts of "quasi-criminal" conduct (Devlin, 1968). The assumption is that *mala in se* crimes are natural wrongs, while *mala prohibita* crimes are man-made wrongs. Social scientists have been critical of this division inasmuch as it assumes some division of absolute or natural wrongs. Assuming there may be some consensus concerning right and wrong not only within the United States but across national samples, it would lend some credence not only to the traditional criminologist's orientation to the consensus of law, but also perhaps to the claim of legal jurisprudence concerning the existence of *mala in se* crimes.

There have been numerous studies of the American public's perception of the seriousness of various criminal acts over time comparing various substrata's views concerning seriousness. One of the best known of such attempts was Sellin and Wolfgang's (1964) study, which attempted to develop an index of the seriousness of criminal acts. A wide range of offense descriptions was presented to various groups who were presumed to represent the morality of the community. These authors found the intensity of reaction to various acts similar across all groups. Akman and Normandeau (1968) replicated the Sellin and Wolfgang study in Canada and found similar consensus to reactions to criminal acts between groups participating. This study has been replicated in at least five other countries, with the conclusion that reactions to crime appear to be similar between various substrata within a country. Makela (1966) assessed various sanctions preferred by judges to other community groups and found that the differences in the severity of punishments demanded were minimal.

Hogarth (1971) studied Canadian judges' behavior in comparison with the community values as reflected by suggested punishments by various groups from outside criminal justice and found little difference in their perception of wrongful conduct. Boydell and Grindstaff (1971), using mailed questionnaires, found little difference on the choice of sanctions between respondents as to education, although older people and those more active religiously were found to be somewhat more punitive.

There have been numerous other studies concerning appropriate sanctions by different groups in a community (too many to review for this short chapter), but it appears that the majority of the research within a country favors the consensus model with regard to a sharing of seriousness by various subclasses of the society. Where a lack of consensus has been found, it appears to be related to religious rather than social class differences.

None of the research that the authors are aware of has attempted to take a wide variety of crimes (traditional, economic, and victimless crimes) and determine whether consensus exists among citizens of various countries as to the ordered seriousness of a variety of crimes between more capitalistic countries and more socialistic countries. This research attempts to test the consensus theory of seriousness of crime between such countries. The central thesis of this study is whether there is an ordering among countries as to the seriousness of offensive behavior and whether the ordering, if it does exist, reflects similar appropriate sanctions for those convicted of committing such offenses.

METHODOLOGY

The data for this study were gathered on a criminology-penology study tour of six European countries during the spring and summer of 1974. In all, 12 upper-class criminology students from Ohio State University were involved in all phases of the research. The study tour involved observations and research in Finland, Sweden, Norway, Denmark, the Netherlands, and Great Britain. In each of these countries, students studied the criminal justice system and the respective correctional programs.

Before embarking on this research, students spent five weeks at Ohio State University delving into some of the pertinent specifics of each nation's history, values, culture, and social problems, with special emphasis on criminal law and criminology. Prior to and during this orientation phase, a questionnaire was developed to measure public attitudes and feelings about the proper punishment for 22 criminal offenses including all seven U.S. major index crimes, eight white collar offenses, three public order victimless violations, and four drug-related offenses. Each offense was presented in vignette style:

> The offender is a 30-year-old man who rapes a 19-year-old woman.

> The offender is a man who breaks into a neighbor's home to steal money.

> The offender is a person who uses marijuana.

> The offender is an executive of a drug company who allows his company to manufacture and sell a drug knowing that it may produce harmful side-effects for most individuals.

Following each of these 22 vignettes, the same penalty alternatives were listed in rank order from no penalty to execution, with appropriate gradations, and the respondent was requested to select the appropriate reaction to be taken:

   (1) No penalty
   (2) A fine
   (3) Probation
   (4) 30 days or less in jail
   (5) 31 days to 6 months in jail
   (6) 6 months to 2 years in jail
   (7) 2 years to 5 years in jail
   (8) 5 years to 15 years in jail
   (9) 15 years or more in jail
 (10) Life imprisonment
 (11) Execution

The choice of penalty in each instance reflected respondent punitiveness and the wrongfulness of the act. Thus, the stiffer the penalty, the more serious the perceived crime.

    The questionnaire was pretested in Columbus, the capital of Ohio, using 60 nonrandomly selected respondents. The reliability and validity (using Cronbach's alpha) as well as the comprehensibility of the questionnaire items were measured and necessary modifications were made. The vignettes combined with standard sociodemographic items and several criminal justice policy action questions comprised the final questionnaire.

The questionnaire was then translated into five languages: Finnish, Swedish, Norwegian, Danish, and Dutch. The translator in every case was a native of the country involved, and all but one was visiting in the United States at the time. After the initial translation, another native was hired to render the foreign questionnaire back into English. This second translation was done independently of the first translation. Differences in translation were resolved in a conference of the two translators and the project coordinator. As testimony to the effectiveness of this procedure, respondents in the various countries were most laudatory of the specificity and comprehensibility of the questionnaire.

In order to obtain comparable respondents from the several countries, a system was devised to administer the questionnaires in the capital city of each nation and in Columbus, Ohio. Each of the 12 students was responsible for the selection of 20 persons willing to cooperate in filling out the questionnaire. Of those approached, almost 95 percent were wholly cooperative.

Respondents were selected according to the following general guidelines; 10 of the respondents were to be male: all had to be over 18; not more than 10 percent were to be drawn from the local university campus, and the remainder from local hotels, trains, parks, and streets. In every country the same guidelines were used and every student was instructed to draw his or her sample in the identical fashion as before. In addition, this same questionnaire was administered in a similar manner by university students during the spring of 1975 in Kuwait; the one difference being that the students were this time native Kuwaitis. Otherwise, every effort was made to make this eighth sample comparable to the earlier seven groups of respondents.

Obviously, these procedures do not ensure a representative sample in the countries involved. However, whatever biases occurred were similar in each nation, lending comparability to the study. No claim can or should be made for the similarity of the sample to the national population, a failing of which we are only too aware. In view of the inordinate difficulties and costs in securing cross-cultural samples, and the limited resources available, the data obtained are adequate for testing the perceived seriousness consensus hypothesis.

In addition to questionnaire administration, considerable data were gathered from the courts, the police, correctional personnel, and official criminal statistics, as well as on the general operation of the various criminal justice systems. Much additional understanding and insight was obtained in seminars and discussions at the various criminological institutes in the respective countries.

The final composition of the sample (N = 1909), including the socioeconomic characteristics of the respondents by country, is given in Table 3.1. Overall, the sample is fairly comparative from country to country with minor exceptions. The samples from the Netherlands and Kuwait both have more male than female respondents compared with other countries. The Kuwaiti sample also has a much lower percentage of respondents who are divorced, separated, or widowed, undoubtedly because of the strong Moslem influence. In addition, the Kuwaiti sample is composed only of residents from a metropolitan area because of the demographic characteristics unique to that country. Finally, income data are not available for the Kuwaiti sample.

One of the major objects of the research project was to determine the level of seriousness concerning certain types of behavior generally considered to be illegal. Respondents in each country were therefore asked to read 22 vignettes describing both the individual and the behavior considered to be offensive. They were then requested to select the appropriate sanction the state should impose from the 11 types listed earlier. For simplicity's sake in this analysis, the average sanction selected by country will be given as the time such offenders should be incarcerated. These levels were calculated by taking the median punishment for each category, multiplying that by the number of respondents advocating that level for each offense, and

TABLE 3.1   Sociodemographic Characteristics of Sample by Country

		Total	(N)	United States	(N)	England	(N)	Finland	(N)	Sweden	(N)	Norway	(N)	Denmark	(N)	Netherlands	(N)	Kuwait	(N)
SEX	Male	56.1	(1070)	50.2	(119)	53.8	(120)	50.2	(120)	54.8	(126)	55.2	(127)	52.1	(122)	61.4	(140)	68.1	(196)
Percentage	Female	43.9	(839)	49.8	(118)	46.2	(103)	49.8	(119)	45.2	(104)	44.8	(103)	47.9	(112)	38.6	(88)	31.9	(92)
AGE	Median	26.57		28.75		27.21		27.15		26.30		25.75		25.00		27.42		27.9	
	Mean	32.35		36.15		32.26		30.04		31.79		31.55		29.25		35.44		29.2	
MARITAL	Married	40.9	(775)	47.0	(111)	44.8	(99)	42.4	(101)	31.2	(72)	38.8	(88)	32.2	(73)	41.2	(93)	48.1	(138)
STATUS	Single	51.1	(967)	40.7	(96)	48.4	(107)	51.3	(122)	59.3	(137)	54.6	(124)	55.5	(126)	50.4	(114)	49.1	(141)
Percentage	Divorced, Separated, Widowed	8.0	(151)	12.3	(29)	6.8	(15)	6.3	(15)	9.5	(22)	6.6	(15)	12.3	(28)	8.4	(19)	2.8	(8)
NUMBER OF	Having None	59.3	(1073)	54.0	(127)	60.9	(131)	60.3	(135)	63.0	(138)	59.2	(126)	59.3	(134)	59.3	(115)	59.2	(167)
CHILDREN	Having 1	12.9	(233)	15.3	(36)	12.6	(27)	17.4	(39)	11.0	(24)	9.9	(21)	15.0	(34)	10.3	(20)	11.3	(32)
Percentage	Having 2	14.2	(1256)	13.2	(31)	14.9	(32)	16.1	(36)	14.2	(31)	18.3	(39)	17.7	(40)	11.9	(23)	8.5	(24)
	Having More Than 2	13.6	(1246)	17.4	(41)	11.6	(25)	6.2	(14)	11.8	(26)	12.6	(27)	8.0	(18)	18.5	(36)	21.0	(54)
	Mean Number of Children	.89		1.12		.87		.70		.80		.91		.78					
SCHOOL	Median Years Completed	12.31		13.90		12.74		12.63		12.02		13.01		10.19		11.71		11.8	

TABLE 3.1 Continued

	Total	(N)	United States	(N)	England	(N)	Finland	(N)	Sweden	(N)	Norway	(N)	Denmark	(N)	Nether-lands	(N)	Kuwait	(N)
INCOME																		
Earning Percentage																		
Under $5,000	18.6	(260)	12.6	(27)	30.0	(60)	18.4	(39)	21.1	(41)	14.9	(30)	14.9	(30)	19.1	(33)		
$5,000-$7,999	19.8	(276)	15.0	(32)	19.0	(38)	31.1	(66)	18.6	(36)	17.4	(35)	13.9	(28)	23.7	(41)		
$8,000-$9,999	19.7	(275)	15.0	(32)	19.5	(39)	18.9	(40)	18.6	(36)	19.4	(39)	20.4	(41)	27.7	(48)		
$10,000-$14,999	21.1	(294)	23.8	(51)	16.0	(32)	21.7	(46)	22.7	(44)	21.4	(43)	27.4	(55)	13.3	(23)		
Over $15,000	20.8	(290)	33.7	(82)	15.5	(31)	9.9	(21)	19.1	(37)	26.9	(54)	23.4	(47)	16.2	(26)		
Median Income	$8,173.91		$9,627.19		$6,652.45		$6,574.48		$8,111.94		$8,819.59		$9,053.47		$7,279.24			
RESIDENCE: Percentage																		
Living in a Large City*	66.3	(1248)	71.7	(167)	56.1	(125)	67.2	(160)	55.1	(124)	64.6	(144)	61.8	(144)	43.6	(96)	100.0	(288)
Living in a Medium City**	13.1	(246)	12.4	(29)	16.1	(36)	15.1	(36)	18.2	(41)	4.0	(9)	16.7	(39)	25.5	(96)		
Living in a Small City***	10.0	(188)	8.2	(19)	4.9	(11)	12.6	(30)	14.7	(33)	13.0	(29)	11.2	(26)	18.2	(40)		
Living in a Small Town or Rural Area	10.6	(201)	7.7	(18)	22.9	(51)	5.0	(12)	12.0	(27)	18.4	(41)	10.3	(24)	12.7	(28)		

* = 100,000 or more; ** = 25,000-100,000; *** = 5,000-25,000

54

dividing by the total number responding. For example, those indicating no penalty, fine, or probation in this report are all treated as advocating zero days incarceration. Those selecting 30 days or less are assumed to be advocating 15 days on the average or .04 years (the median between 0 and 30 days). Similarly, those advocating 5 to 15 years are calculated as advocating 10 years (the median between 5 and 15 years). Those selecting 15 years or more were calculated as advocating 15 years; life imprisonment was assigned 20 years, and execution was calculated as 25 years in a rather arbitrary manner. The numbers under each country in Figures 3.1-3.4 and 3.6 represent the average number of years (as calculated in the manner explained above) suggested by respondents in each respective country for the particular offense. The numbers under each country in Figure 3.5 represent the average number of months suggested by respondents. Months are reported in Figure 3.5 because of the extremely mild punishments suggested in comparison with the other categories of crimes.

FINDINGS

Figure 3.1 presents the average recommended punishment by country for what in the United States are referred to as the four violent index crimes. A great deal of similarity exists among countries as to the rank-ordered seriousness of these violent offenses, although considerable differences exist as to the relative seriousness of these offenses or the appropriate sanction. Each country's respondents agree that murder is the most serious or repulsive of the four violent offenses. However, appropriate sanctions differ significantly among countries as to how an offender should be dealt with. Kuwaitis appear to advocate the most harsh sanctions, averaging the equivalent of 15 years of incarceration. Swedes, on the other hand, recommend on the average only 4.4 years.

Rape, armed robbery, and aggravated assault were evaluated as being approximately equal in seriousness and deserving of similar state sanctions. There is some variation among countries in the rank-ordered seriousness of these crimes, but the recom-

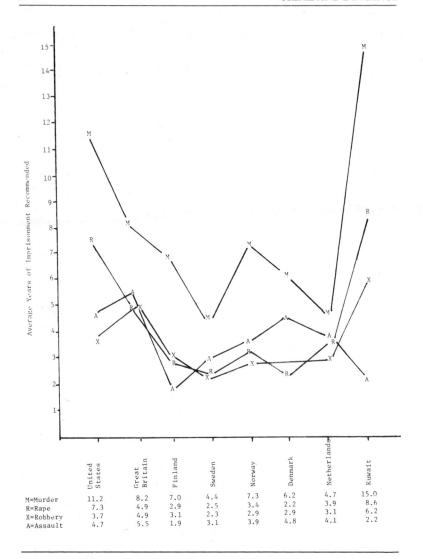

	United States	Great Britain	Finland	Sweden	Norway	Denmark	Netherlands	Kuwait
M=Murder	11.2	8.2	7.0	4.4	7.3	6.2	4.7	15.0
R=Rape	7.3	4.9	2.9	2.5	3.4	2.2	3.9	8.6
X=Robbery	3.7	4.9	3.1	2.3	2.9	2.9	3.1	6.2
A=Assault	4.7	5.5	1.9	3.1	3.9	4.8	4.1	2.2

FIGURE 3.1   Perceived Seriousness of Various Violent Offenses by Country

mended sanctions are similar for the most part. Rape is viewed as the second most serious violent crime by respondents from the United States and Kuwait and as the third most serious violent offense by respondents in five other countries. The suggested sanctions for rape, armed robbery, and aggravated assault are very similar for most countries, however. Differences in the recommended sanctions for rape vary from a high for the Kuwaiti sample of 8.6 years to a low for the Danish sample of only 2.2 years.

The other two violent offenses, armed robbery and aggravated assault, are both rated as deserving of more severe sanctions in seven of the eight countries than any of the property offenses shown in Figure 3.2. The one exception was the Kuwaitis, who ranked burglary as deserving more harsh sanctions than aggravated assault. This may be due to the vignette selected to portray aggravated assault: "The offender is a man who deliberately stabs his wife during a fight; she does not die." This type of violence is so uncommon in Kuwait that the respondents may have had a difficult time conceptualizing its seriousness in comparison with other offenses with which they could identify somewhat more readily.

Figure 3.2 presents the average recommended punishment by country for what in the United States are referred to as the three property index crimes (burglary, larceny, and auto theft). The rank-ordered seriousness of the various property offenses across countries is strikingly similar. In fact, there is only one exception to a perfect ordering; that being the Danish respondents, who ranked larceny as slightly more serious than burglary. Otherwise, respondents in each country ranked burglary as most serious, followed by larceny and auto theft as the least serious of the property crimes.

The variation among countries in the average recommended period of incarceration for offenders convicted of these offenses shows the United States and Kuwaiti respondents most punitive with burglars (2.5 years and 2.3 years, respectively), while the Danish are least punitively inclined to punish burglars, recommending only nine months on the average. United States respondents also recommended the most severe sentences for those convicted of larceny, averaging 1.5 years compared with only 4.5 months on the average for the Swedish respondents. Kuwaitis recommended the most severe sentences for those convicted of auto theft (1.3 years followed by the Dutch, who

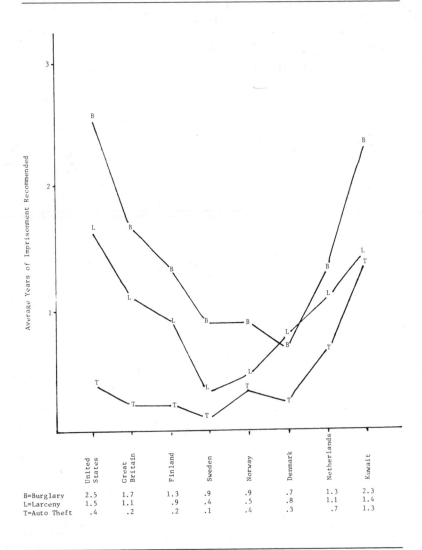

FIGURE 3.2   Perceived Seriousness of Various Property Offenses by Country

recommended nine months), while Swedish respondents were most lenient, recommending only 1.5 months on the average.

Figure 3.3 reports the perceived seriousness by country for eight types of white-collar or economic offenses. No data are available for the Kuwaitis on the seriousness of income tax eva-

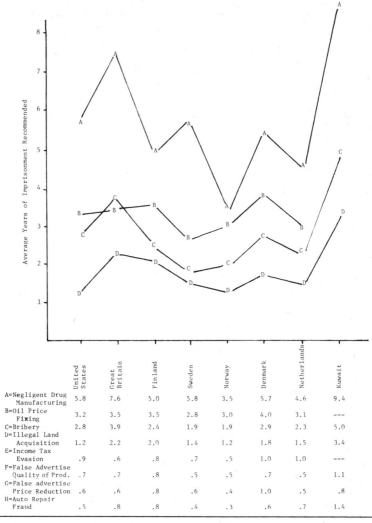

	United States	Great Britain	Finland	Sweden	Norway	Denmark	Netherlands	Kuwait
A=Negligent Drug Manufacturing	5.8	7.6	5.0	5.8	3.5	5.7	4.6	9.4
B=Oil Price Fixing	3.2	3.5	3.5	2.8	3.0	4.0	3.1	---
C=Bribery	2.8	3.9	2.4	1.9	1.9	2.9	2.3	5.0
D=Illegal Land Acquisition	1.2	2.2	2.0	1.4	1.2	1.8	1.5	3.4
E=Income Tax Evasion	.9	.6	.8	.7	.5	1.0	1.0	---
F=False Advertise Quality of Prod.	.7	.7	.8	.5	.5	.7	.5	1.1
G=False advertise Price Reduction	.6	.6	.8	.6	.4	1.0	.5	.8
H=Auto Repair Fraud	.5	.8	.8	.4	.3	.6	.7	1.4

FIGURE 3.3   Perceived Seriousness of Several Economic Offenses by Country

sion (since they, fortunately enough, have no income tax) nor on oil price fixing (an impossible act in Kuwait). Only the four acts perceived as most serious are charted in Figure 3.3 inasmuch as the remaining four received such low scores of perceived seriousness either within countries or among countries that it would have been difficult to interpret in the figure. However, their respective seriousness scores are reported at the bottom of the figure along with the four acts represented in the figure.

One overall observation is apparent in Figure 3.3; namely, the consistency in ranking the economic offenses among countries as to their seriousness. The four economic offenses considered to be most serious were negligent drug manufacturing and distribution, oil price fixing, bribery, and illegal land acquisition and disposition. As stated above, the other four economic offenses were all rated inconsequential and were considered by all eight samples as very minor transgressions.

The perceived seriousness of the four economic offenses with one exception (Great Britain ranking bribery as slightly more serious than oil price fixing) are consistent across eight countries. Kuwaitis were again most punitive overall but otherwise there appears to be no consistent pattern as to one nation's respondents evaluating the various crimes as more serious than another's. This was somewhat surprising inasmuch as we expected the more socialistic (or social welfare) countries' respondents to evaluate the seriousness of economic crimes greater than respondents from the more capitalistic countries.

The perceived seriousness of four drug offenses by country is reported in Figure 3.4. Again, there is almost universal consensus as to the seriousness of these four offenses, the only exception being the Kuwaiti respondents, who ranked the scale of marijuana as more serious than the sale of heroin. Also, the Kuwaitis were least tolerant and most punitive for anyone engaging in these four types of behavior. In fact, Kuwaitis ranked selling heroin or marijuana to be a more serious offense than rape, robbery, or any offense listed except murder. United States respondents were next most punitive concerning the sale or use of heroin. Conversely, respondents in the United States were most tolerant and advocated the most lenient punishment for those apprehended selling marijuana. Somewhat surprising was the perceived similarity in seriousness across all nations for marijuana and heroin use: Little variation exists as to the perceived seriousness of these two acts.

Responses by country for three sex crimes are reported in Figure 3.5. The suggested sanctions are reported in months in-

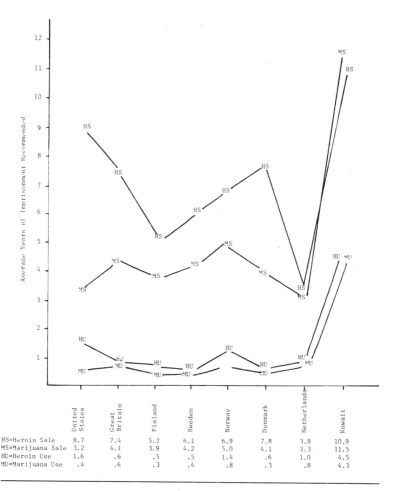

	United States	Great Britain	Finland	Sweden	Norway	Denmark	Netherlands	Kuwait
HS=Heroin Sale	8.7	7.4	5.2	6.1	6.9	7.8	3.8	10.9
MS=Marijuana Sale	3.2	4.1	3.9	4.2	5.0	4.1	3.3	11.5
HU=Heroin Use	1.6	.6	.5	.5	1.4	.6	1.0	4.5
MU=Marijuana Use	.4	.6	.3	.4	.8	.3	.8	4.3

FIGURE 3.4   Perceived Seriousness of Various Drug Offenses by Country

stead of years for this figure due to the minor sanctions suggested. Prostitution was perceived as most serious in five of the eight countries and as the second most serious offense in the remaining three countries. Kuwaitis ranked this offense as considerably more serious than did respondents in other countries — they suggested on the average that the appropriate penalty would be 7.7 years incarceration. Homosexuality was viewed as the most serious of the sex offenses in three countries and as the second most serious in three additional countries. Women who

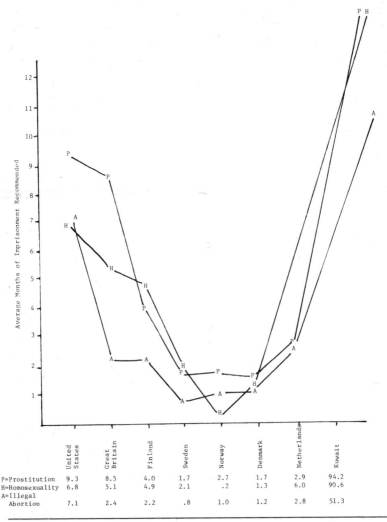

	United States	Great Britain	Finland	Sweden	Norway	Denmark	Netherlands	Kuwait
P=Prostitution	9.3	8.5	4.0	1.7	2.7	1.7	2.9	94.2
H=Homosexuality	6.8	5.1	4.9	2.1	.2	1.3	6.0	90.6
A=Illegal Abortion	7.1	2.4	2.2	.8	1.0	1.2	2.8	51.3

FIGURE 3.5   Perceived Seriousness of Three Sex Offenses by Country

have illegal abortions were not considered by any of the countries to be committing as serious an offense as were homosexuals and prostitutes. Securing an illegal abortion was considered the least serious offense in six of the eight samples. Overall, prostitution was perceived somewhat more serious than homosexuality, while obtaining an illegal abortion was considered least serious. While there was less consensus overall among

respondents from various countries on the seriousness of these
sex offenses, there was still considerably more consensus than
there were differences. Moreover, one apparent reason for the
variation may be the minimal sanctions being suggested.

In order to assess potential consensus better across countries
for various categories of crimes, the average suggested punishment was calculated for each category and plotted in Figure 3.6.
The five categories were *violent offenses* (murder, rape, armed
robbery, and aggravated assault); *property offenses* (burglary,
larceny, and auto theft); *economic offenses* (auto repair fraud,
bribery, oil price fixing, negligent drug manufacturing, illegal
land acquisition, false advertising concerning costs, and false
advertising concerning quality and income tax evasion); *drug
offenses* (marijuana sale, heroin sale, marijuana use, and heroin
use); and *sex offenses* (prostitution, homosexuality, and illegal
abortion). The average penalty by category of offense was then
calculated for each country. This was done by adding the
average number of days for each offense in each category by
country, dividing by the number of offenses, and then dividing
by 365 (the number of days in a year). This figure represents the
perceived seriousness of these types of offenses by country, and
the exact number represents the average punishment suggested
by respondents from each country as to the proper punishment
for individuals convicted of these types of offenses in years.

Figure 3.6 presents the recommended punishment by category
of offense by country. In all eight countries violent offenses
were considered the most serious. There is, in fact, only one exception in the entire graph which prevents total consensus as to
the seriousness of these five categories of crime: sex offenses,
which were considered to be the third most serious category of
offenses by Kuwaitis and least serious by respondents from the
other seven countries. With this one exception, violent offenses
were considered most serious, followed by drug offenses,
economic offenses, and property offenses, with sex offenses
considered least serious.

Similarities in perceived seriousness are common not only
with regard to the ordering of categories of offenses but to the
suggested average sanction. In comparing the United States,

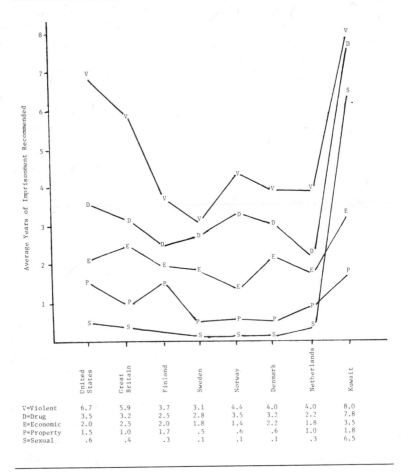

FIGURE 3.6   Perceived Seriousness of Violent, Drug, Economic, Property, and Sex Crimes by Country

for example, with other Western European countries, the only striking difference with regard to appropriate sanctions for offenders is with violent crimes. In that regard, the U.S. respondents favored considerably harsher penalties than the Scandinavian countries. In examining drug and economic offenses, little difference in perceived seriousness is apparent. One might have hypothesized that economic offenses would be perceived as considerably more serious in the more social welfare type countries such as Finland, Sweden, Norway, Denmark, and the Netherlands than in the United States, given the critical or radical criminologists' arguments. This does not appear to be the case. The economic offenses are considered more serious than the property offenses in all countries, but the difference in their perceived seriousness as reflected by the recommended sanctions is similar across countries for both categories of offenses.

The research is supportive of cross-cultural similarities in perceived seriousness of criminal acts. Certainly there are gross differences in the suggested sanctions that various criminal acts arouse in respondents from different cultures. Nevertheless, there is a great deal of similarity in the perceived seriousness of various offensive behavior across nations.

CONCLUSIONS

Now that considerable interest and research is being conducted on crime cross-culturally, a number of rather micro-level theories may be better tested. The previous research conducted by Scott and Al-Thakeb (1971) appeared to indicate a definite trend in the perceived wrongness of various offensive behaviors across nations. Undoubtedly, the reader may have noted with interest the different responses of the Kuwaiti sample as to the seriousness of various criminal acts. Research conducted in the spring of 1979 in Kuwait by Al-Thakeb and Scott and only preliminarily analyzed at this time introduced new questions as to the "perceived wrongness theory."

This most recent study asked 600 respondents living in Kuwait to select the proper sanction of some 40 acts presented in vignette style. The penalties included those utilized in the previous research of Scott and Al-Thakeb (1977) plus traditional Islamic penalties including those spelled out in the Koran such as whipping, severing a limb, and stoning to death. Significant differences are apparent in the seriousness of various acts between Kuwaiti citizens' responses and the non-Kuwaitis' responses who live in Kuwait. The major difference ascertained between these two groups was their religiosity. Kuwaitis' religiosity scores, as measured by an Islamic fundamentalism scale, were considerably higher and directly related to choosing traditionally Islamic penalties. This finding is consistent with those of two previous studies (Newman, 1976; Newman and Articolo, 1974) where religiosity was found to be significantly related to punitiveness.

One of the major problems in conducting cross-cultural research was discovered through this research concerning the severity of punishment as measured by choice of different sanctions and its relationship to religiosity. Here respondents chose traditional and nontraditional Islamic penalties. These were not perceived in the same way by different groups or by subsequent western students as to their harshness.

As more and more of these nuances are taken into cosideration, it is hoped that cross-cultural crime research can progress from its relatively embryonic stage to answering with confidence many of the questions we have for some time simply taken for granted.

REFERENCES

AKMAN, D. D. and A. NORMANDEAU (1968) "Towards the measurement of criminality in Canada." Acta Criminologica 1: 135-154.

ALGANUUBI, A. I. (1978) "Comparative field research on the effect of application of Islamic Criminal law on the security of Saudi Arabia" (unpublished).

ALI, Badr-el-din (1978) "Factors responsible for crime trends: a crosscultural analysis." Ohio State University. (unpublished)

ALI, B. (1978) "Factors responsible for crime trends: a cross-cultural analysis." Ohio State University. unpublished.

BASSIOUNI, M. C. (1974) "A survey of the major criminal justice systems in the world," in D. Glaser (ed.) Handbook of Criminology. Chicago: Rand McNally.

BECKER, H. (1973) "Labeling theory reconsidered," chapter 10 in H. Becker (ed.) Outsiders. New York: Free Press.

BIANCHI, H., M. SIMONDI and I. TAYLOR (1975) Deviance and Control in Europe. London: John Wiley.

BIDERMAN, A. (1970) "Information, intelligence, enlightened public policy: functions and organization of societal feedback." Policy Sciences 1: 217-230.

BOTTOMLEY, A. K. (1973) Decisions in the Penal Process. South Hackensack, NJ: Fred B. Rothman.

BOYDELL, C. L. and C. F. GRINDSTAFF (1971) "Public attitudes toward legal sanction for drug and abortion offences." Canadian Journal of Criminology and Corrections, 13: 209-232.

CHAMBLISS, W. J. (1974) "The state, the law, and the definition of behavior as criminal or delinquent," in D. Glaser (ed.) Handbook of Criminology. Chicago: Rand McNally.

CHANG, D. H. (1976) Criminology: A Crosscultural Perspective, vols I and II. New Delhi: Vikas Publishing.

CICOUREL, A. V. (1974) "Police practices and official records," pp. 86-95 in R. Turner (ed.) Ethnomethodology. Harmondsworth, England: Penguin.

——— (1964) Method and Measurement in Sociology. New York: Free Press.

CLINARD, M. B. (1978) Cities with Little Crime: The Case of Switzerland. Cambridge, England: Cambridge University Pres.

——— and D. J. ABBOTT (1973) Crime in Developing Countries. New York: John Wiley.

CONNER, W. D. (1972) Deviance in Soviet Society. New York: Columbia University Press.

DEVLIN, P. (1959) The Enforcement of Morals. Oxford, England: Oxford University Press.

EDGERTON, R. B. (1976) Deviance: A Crosscultural Perspective. Menlo Park, CA: Cummings Publishing.

HENSHEL, R. L. and R. A. SILVERMAN (1975) Perception in Criminology. New York: Columbia University Press.

IWAI, H. (1978) "Crime trends in Japan" (unpublished).

HOGARTH, J. (1971) Sentencing as a Human Process. Toronto: University of Toronto Press.

KITSUSE, J. I. and A. V. CICOUREL (1963) "A note on the uses of official statistics." Social Problems 11: 131-137.

MAKELA R. (1966) "Public sense of justice and judicial practice." Acta Sociologica 10: 42-67.

NEWMAN, G. (1976) Comparative Deviance: Perception and Law in Six Cultures. New York: Elsevier.

NEWMAN, G. and D. ARTICOLO (1974) "Authoritarianism, religiosity, and reactions to deviance." Journal of Criminal Justice 2: 249-259.

OLURUNTIMEHIN, O. (1978) "Crime trends in Nigeria — a preliminary analysis" (unpublished).

QUINNEY, R. (1979) Criminology. Boston: Little, Brown.

——— (1974) Critique of Legal Order. Boston: Little, Brown.

SCOTT, J. E. and F. AL-THAKEB (1977) "The public's perceptions of crime: Scandinavia, Western Europe, the Middle East, and the United States," in C. Ronald Huff (ed.) Contemporary Corrections. Beverly Hills, CA: Sage.

SELLIN, T. and M. E. WOLFGANG (1964) The Measurement of Delinquency. New York: John Wiley.

VARMA, P. (1978) "Crime trends in India" (unpublished).

VIGN, J. (1978) Criminality and the means against criminality in Hungary" (unpublished).

WILKINS, L. T. (1965) "New thinking in criminal statistics." Journal of Criminal Law, Criminology and Police Science 56: 277.

——— (1963) "The measurement of crime." British Journal of Criminology 3: 321.

WILSON, A. A., S. L. GREENBLATT and R. W. WILSON (1977) Deviance and Social Control in Chinese Society. New York: Praeger.

4

THE STUDY OF CRIME IN MARXIST COUNTRIES
Notes on Method for Outsiders, With Special Reference to Cuba

LUIS P. SALAS

This chapter is an outgrowth of this author's experiences and frustrations in conducting research on deviance and social control in Cuban society. Recent years have seen a rapid expansion of criminological research, both intra- and cross-culturally. Not intending to lag behind other disciplines, criminologists have expanded the scope of interest beyond their own borders. During this same period there has been a corresponding increase in the body of literature devoted to communist systems as well as a rebirth of Marxist approaches to the study of crime. Even though these trends have coexisted, there has been little effort devoted to the study of crime in socialist countries.[1] This largesse on the part of western scholars is due to a variety of factors, not the least of which is a reluctance to engage in research which is alien to traditional methodological approaches. The purpose of this Chapter shall be to examine Cuba as a case study and present to the reader some of the problems encountered by the writer in dealing with the study of crime in that socialist system.

A number of factors complicate the task of the investigator examining Cuban society. The first discovery to be made is that, except under very unusual circumstances, the researcher must rely upon secondary sources, since only a few social scientists have been allowed access to Cuban projects. Although travel restrictions to the island have been relaxed, the scientist will find it very difficult to obtain permission from Cuban authorities to conduct on-site experiments or surveys. Even when barriers are overcome and permission obtained, free movement and inquiry are not always possible. "The government's screening of visitors to Cuba introduces another problem, i.e., the ideological bias of the outsider has often been a distorting factor in the search for truth" (Mesa-Lago, 1969:53). In a great many instances works devoted to Cuban society have been very misleading; either the visitor has based his/her conclusions on inaccurate data or is biased in favor of or against the socialist regime and has allowed this to cloud the conclusions reached.

Doing Field Research in Cuba

Although a number of foreigners, specifically Americans, have been allowed to conduct field research on the island, most of them have found the experience frustrating and difficult. Perhaps the best-known case is that of Oscar Lewis. In 1968 he was invited by Fidel Castro to come to Cuba and replicate the study which he had performed in Mexico. In 1969 he and his colleagues undertook a three-year research project on the island. The following comments are illustrative of their experience:

> I can say flatly that there was not a single important aspect of the field work that was not affected in some degree by the great societal changes in Cuba, above all the ubiquitous presence of the state. In non-socialist countries, anthropologists doing research are normally on their own and, whether in an urban or rural or jungle setting, must spend a great deal of their time, energy and funds establishing themselves in the field. In Cuba such self-reliance was impossible. Although we made the basic

decisions concerning whom and what to study, there were many things we could not do or get on our own. With the government as the source of all goods and services, we were unavoidably dependent on them for material things such as food and housing. Almost everything had to be done through the proper channels, a process involving a good deal of bureaucratic red tape [Lewis, et al., 1977:xiii].

Even though these are restrictions which are common to all socialist countries and to some extent many nonsocialist developing countries, the Lewis saga was complicated by the fact that he was ordered to terminate the research and his notes were confiscated. In addition, one of his informants, who had been openly antagonistic during the interviews, was arrested. The closing of this project was not solely the result of the interviews but was part and parcel of a general crackdown on foreign intellectuals during the summer of 1970. The government in 1971 openly declared its policy to be the establishment of a "strict system for inviting foreign writers and intellectuals, to avoid the presence of persons whose works and ideology are opposed to the interests of the Revolution, especially in formation of the new generation, and who have participated in ideological diversionist activities encouraging their local flunkeys" (*Granma Weekly Review*, 1971:5).

The Lewis case presents some problems which must be considered by every researcher. Although the distrust of these years is now subdued, the investigator must consider political issues not commonly taken into account. The seizure of Lewis' notes is of some concern, but even more disturbing is the arrest of one of his informants. This is not an isolated occurrence. In 1971 an assistant of Rene Dumont helped him prepare a list of black market prices in the course of research on the Cuban economy. After publication of a book critical of Cuba's economic policies, the assistant was arrested and charged with being a CIA agent (García, 1971). Concern over the safety of informants should and must remain a primary preoccupation of researchers conducting field research in Cuba.

While Lewis was given ample opportunity to interview anyone he wished, others have found themselves severely limited in their scope of inquiry. Persons to be interviewed are selected by the government or the researcher is compelled to rely on native personnel whose loyalty may be questioned.

In addition to these practical problems, the investigator is faced with the most difficult task prior to even receiving permission to conduct research in Cuba. Making contact with the Cuban government is somewhat akin to dealing with a roll of jelly: Once you think you finally have a handle on it, it slides away. For example, the author asked the Cuban government for permission to have some notes on the Cuban legal system reviewed by a member of the University of Havana or the Ministry of Justice. Contact was made with the Cuban Mission to the United Nations in New York and after several months the reply came back affirmative. Upon my arrival in Cuba I would be met by an official of the Ministry of Foreign Relations who would process my request. Only the first name of the official was furnished, a factor not uncommon in dealing with Cuban officialdom. Upon arrival the official was nowhere to be found. After explaining the dilemma to an employee of the Institute for Friendship with Other Peoples (ICAP) I was told that she would accept the papers and get back to me prior to my departure. Needless to say, I never received a reply. After speaking with others engaged in Cuban research I found that this was not unusual. First, it is very rare for the Cuban government to deny any request outright; rather it relies on postponing decisions. Second, the seeming bureaucratic inefficiency is a product of a variety of factors including overbureaucratization, newness in these matters, and suspicion. The end result is an extremely frustrating experience for the researcher, since encouragements are constantly made and a sense of eventual resolution remains present.

The foregoing are merely words of warning to the inexperienced researcher and are not meant to discourage those who may wish to try on-site investigations. Suspicion is one of the primary barriers to be overcome by the researcher engaged in Cuba, or indeed research conducted in any other underdeveloped country. The image of U.S.-sponsored social science has deteriorated throughout Latin America and its legitimacy seriously questioned. More and more — especially after the scandal of Project Camelot (Horowitz, 1967) — there has arisen a perception that U.S. economic and political interests have been closely linked to social science endeavors in this continent. As a result, the situation has drastically changed in many of these countries. Whereas the U.S. scholar was previously welcomed, only under unusual circumstances are foreign studies presently being conducted (Portes, 1972). These problems have compelled the investigator to rely more and more on secondary data, something which many social scientists are reluctant to accept.

Availability of Secondary Data

In addition to the difficulties in obtaining permission for onsite visits which result in reliance on secondary sources, the researcher is also faced with the problem of locating these sources in the United States, not as easy a task as it might seem. The primary reason for the unavailability of sources is directly linked to an American blockade which for many years prevented access to Cuban materials.[2] The result has been the development of an intricate and secretive collection network. In order to bypass American regulations, librarians resorted to a variety of schemes whereby payments could be made through Canadian banks or imaginary exchanges set up with Cuban institutions. In order to safeguard their holdings, American institutions initiated special security systems so that many materials could be locked behind cages or could remain uncatalogued. Discovery of these major sources is one of the primary barriers presented to the researcher. Often the job is reminiscent of a detective searching for his/her prey. Location of materials in the most unusual place is not uncommon. Direct contact with Cuban institutions is almost impossible, unless the investigator visits the island, due to the difficulty in telephoning and the inefficiency of the postal system. In many instances one finds that the source material may not be found in Cuba at all and that the institution issuing the documents asks you to send them a copy since theirs is lost or misplaced.

The difficulties of the researcher are intensified by other factors operating inside Cuba. This is, after all, a developing country in which statistics on social problems are fairly unsophisticated, if collected at all. Since American social scientists place a great deal of reliance on satistical data, this is the subject which shall be considered first.

Unlike the United States, social science data do not appear in specialized journals or reports. Rather, this information may be found in a myriad of sources ranging from reports of the Ministry of the Interior to speeches by major political figures. The most thorough statistical report of crime in Cuba, for example, appeared in a Cuban newspaper article published in 1969 as a result of a forum of internal order (*Granma Weekly Review*, 1969), while the most complete overview of criminological theory was recently published as a speech by the chief of the Supreme Court appearing in the *Journal of the Havana Psychiatric Hospital* (Hernández de Armas, 1977). Some of the principal statements affecting regimental concerns, sometimes including valuable statistical data, have often appeared in major political speeches reported in the Cuban press. After a while the investigator discovers that such speeches are consistently made on the same days every year, for example the founding of the Ministry of the Interior or the Committees for the Defense of the Revolution. Referral to these speeches simplifies the task of the social scientist.

Specialized journals published by the Ministry of the Interior are not generally available to the public. Until recently the ministerial organ, *Moncada*, was not publicly distributed. Recently the policy has changed, but the astute investigator will discover that there are now two publications, one which is only distributed to members of the ministry and another which is openly circulated. The latter concentrates on popular stories and seldom carries any hard data.

As in many other Latin American countries, sociology is a recent addition to social sciences, and criminological studies are traditionally pursued by lawyers and psychologists. Articles on crime-related subjects often appear in these types of journals, rather than in publications such as the *Journal of Social Sciences*.

As the Revolution has become more institutionalized, it has begun to increase its reliance on statistical surveys and appears to be publishing more and more information on all subjects. Examples are reports of the Ministry of the Interior, the Supreme Court, and the Procuracy. A short article appeared in the Cuban press about these reports. An American scholar conducting research in Cuba managed to obtain a copy of the reports, which were published in a form similar to the U.S. Congressional Record. This presents to the reader the most thorough statistical information furnished by the Cuban government to date. The fact that it was discovered by the author by accident, in a conversation with the owner, highlights the haphazard manner in which sources of data are obtained.

RELIABILITY AND QUALITY
OF STATISTICAL DATA

In examining Cuban statistical sources the reader is impressed by its primitive nature and the absence of traditionally crucial variables. Unlike Soviet sources, which are frequently expressed as percentage distributions of unknown integers (Connor, 1973), Cuban data are "hard." The problems of a primitive statistical system are compounded by the political ideology of the reporting state. The reliability of communist statistics is a topic which has concerned many students of Marxist societies. The dominant argument maintains that most socialist data are fairly reliable due to the fact that inconsistencies would be revealed by cross-checks. A dual accounting system that is, one for internal consumption and another for propaganda purposes — is an unlikely proposition. The opposite view is maintained by those who argue that all data emanating from socialist countries must be reviewed with the utmost caution. They argue that statistical reports are clothed in the ideological biases of the reporting state (Nove, 1961; Schwartz, 1963; Orleans, 1965). But as socialist countries become more industrialized and the needs for accurate reporting mechanisms develop, the danger of statistical alteration recedes. Although Cuba has not yet reached this stage of development, it is highly unlikely that statistical figures concerning crime have been consciously and continuously altered. The rates and statements of concern are too serious for this conclusion. It is more likely that some figures have been withheld, however, due to their embarrassing nature.

In addition to data published by the Cuban government, some international organizations also publish statistics furnished by the regime. This is the case with health statistics published by the World Health Organization. This information is especially helpful in examining criminal homicides, abortions, suicides, and all accidents resulting in death. Cuban homicide statistics are illustrative of the problems enountered by the researcher attempting to determine the reliability of Cuban statistical data.

Cuban homicide rates may be obtained from two sources, (1) medical authorities, and (2) police agencies. The first type is based upon "cause of death" information appearing on death certificates and is derived from local medical authorities or coroners. These figures are then processed by the Ministry of Health, which reports them to the World Health Organization, which therafter releases them. The classification system utilized in listing cause of death is one developed under the auspices of the United Nations, and thus all nations utilizing this system publish homicide victimization rates that are intended to be comparable. Figures utilizing the standardized format are published in editions of two U.N. publications, the *World Health Statistics Annual* and the *Demographic Yearbook*.

The second type of homicide statistics are derived from figures released by police officials. These have appeared at

TABLE 4.1   Cuban Homicide Rates per 100,000 Population as Reported to the United Nations and the Police

Year	UN Rate	Police Rate
1959	15.5	38.2
1960	5.7	36.7
1961	15.3	37.2
1962	10.4	35.0
1963	10.3	13.7
1964	6.2	8.0
1965	5.1	8.4
1966	—	7.6
1967	—	6.8
1968	6.2	6.1
1969	7.3	—
1970	7.8	—
1971	7.2	—
1972	3.7*(6.0)	—
1973	3.8*(6.0)	—
1974	3.8*(6.1)	—

*The rates reported by the U.N. for the 1972-1974 period include only homicide and injury purposely inflicted by other persons and legal intervention (such as justifiable homicide, executions, etc.). The rates reported by the U.N. for 1959-1971 include death by "all other external causes," thus encompassing homicides and injury purposely inflicted by other persons and injuries resulting from operations of war. If the categories included in the U.N. rates for 1959-1971 are added to the 1972-1974 period, there appears to be less of a decline in the homicide rate. The figures in parentheses indicate the rate if the same categories are used in 1972-1974 as were used in 1959-1971.

SOURCES: *United Nations Demographic Yearbooks* from 1959 to 1974; *World Health Statistics Annuals* (Geneva: WHO), for the years 1970 to 1976; *Cuba, 1968 Supplement to the Statistical Abstract of Latin America* (Calif.: University of California Press, 1970); Jorge Domínguez, *Cuba: Order and Revolution* (Cambridge, Mass.: Belknap, 1978), p. 507. The Domínguez figures are taken from the *Anuario Estadístico de Cuba-1972* (Havana: Inst. del lib., 1973).

different times in popular Cuban periodicals and reports to the National Assembly of Popular Power. Comparison of the two sets of figures — medical and police — for Cuba, or indeed any other nation, is problematic in view of the differences in the type of homicide classifications included in the two types of rates and the changes over time in the reporting format of the U.N. figures. Table 4.1 contains a comparison of both of these rates for those years in which figures are available. The U.N. rates include all types of homicide, criminal as well as justifiable, and undertermined deaths and injuries resulting from operations of war; the police statistics supposedly reflect only criminal homicides. Thus, one would expect the broader U.N. category to result in larger rates than the police figures, since the latter involve a more restrictive category. However, a quick perusal of Table 4.1 reveals that the reverse is true: Police rates are much larger than the U.N. rates in the earlier years but approach U.N. rates by the mid-1960s. There appears to be no readily apparent explanation for this contradiction. It would seem that either the U.N. rates are too low or the police rates are too high. It could be assumed that the U.N. figures are more reliable, since 95.9 percent of all cases certified by medical authorities as being homicides are based upon a determination by a physician rather than a lay person. However, some doubt is cast on this thesis when one finds that in countries such as Jamaica a similar situation exists and yet the police figures were found to be more reliable than those reported to the United Nations (Wilbanks, 1979).[3] It is conceivable that some countries might choose to report a lower rate for international publications while maintaining a true rate for police figures which are aimed at a select audience. Another possible explanation for the divergence between police and health statistics is suggested by a set of figures recently released by the Cuban government that give the frequency of occurrence of different types of homicide for 1976 and 1977. The types of homicide along with the reported number for these years are, respectively, "simple homicide," 202, 96; "aggravated homicide," 84, 74; "attempted aggravated homicide," 0, 22; quasi-parricide, 6,

6; assistance in a suicide, 934, 602; culpable homicide (undefined others), 423, 221; and vehicular homicide, 620, 737 (Asamblea Nacional, 1979). Since the latest U.N. homicide rates for Cuba, reported for 1974, are based on an absolute number of 343 homicides, it may be that only simple and aggravated homicides are reported to the United Nations (the total for these two offenses for 1976 would approximate the U.N. figure). The police may be counting the larger number of culpable homicides (no definition is given for this category) and even those charged with assistance in a suicide.

Cuban statistics have been known in the past to be substantially incorrect. In some cases of erroneous data, the fault lies with the flaws in the system, including the limitations of underdevelopment. In other cases figures have been deliberate misrepresentations (Mesa-lago, 1969:47). While such statistics as demographic and social indicators are often flawed, others — primarily those dealing with foreign trade and economic matters — are extremely accurate and consistent over time. Especially susceptible to manipulation are those types of crimes which might bring some embarrassment to the regime. Prostitution is one of those examples in which the figures have constantly shifted. Some estimates gave as many as 270 bordellos operating in Havana in 1959, not counting the number of prostitutes working the streets and bars (Moreno, 1973). The official in charge of rehabilitation programs for prostitutes gave figures of 10,000 prostitutes working in Havana and 30,000-40,000 employed in the island as a whole (Lewis, 1977:279). Others, including Fidel Castro, have placed the figure at 100,000 (Castro, 1977), while others have reported figures of as many as 25,000 whorehouses in operation in Havana (Cardenal, 1976:279).

Legal Classifications

One of the most difficult problems in reviewing foreign crime statistics is the variety of legal definitions for crimes which we sometimes accept as being universal. Researchers, especially those not trained in the law, frequently assume that

TABLE 4.2   Crimes Against Property in Cuba

Year	Crimes Per 100,000 Population	Percentage of Total Amount of Reported Crime
1959	543.1	18.70
1960	482.7	18.17
1961	461.6	20.37
1962	489.4	20.00
1963	232.6	9.59
1964	133.2	6.55
1965	272.2	17.80
1966	317.0	19.35
1967	335.2	26.40
1968	341.4	28.96
1969	203.8	33.0
1977	608.3	36.64

SOURCES: Jorge I. Domínguez, *Cuba: Order and Revolution* (Cambridge, Mass.: Belknap, 1978); "As Servants of the People We Have Been Able to Achieve an Even Greater Understanding," *Granma,* May 11, 1969, pp. 7-9; "Dictamen sobre el informe de Rendición de Cuentas del Tribunal Supremo, leído por Julia Meceda," *Granma,* July 1, 1978, p. 2; Appendix A, herein.

these definitions are universal, yet there are vast differences in statutory codes. The problem is compounded by the fact that even after determining a correct classification it cannot be assumed that it remains in force over a long period of time. The case of property crimes in Cuba is particularly illustrative.

Table 4.2 presents a breakdown of all property crimes which took place from 1959 to 1977 (some years were excluded due to lack of information). A cursory review of these figures would indicate that there was a drastic reduction in these offenses in 1963-1964. This reduction has been attributed by Cuban officials to a draconian law which reclassified robberies of inhabited dwellings as political rather than common crimes. The modification also included robberies in which the perpetrator impersonated a police or military official or participated with a minor (Law 1098). The fact that the death penalty could be imposed in these cases was seen by Cuban officials as a deterrent resulting in a decrease (*Granma Weekly Review*, 1969). One factor, however, that must be considered is that during this period these crimes would be reported as political rather than common crimes and would not appear in property crime reports. By 1965 the courts began to treat these offenses as common crimes once again and the rates began to climb back to their original levels.

Another danger in examining statistics which are based on unknown crime categories is presented by reports of overall crime rather than specific offenses, something which is quite popular in Cuban literature. For example, the Cuban government released a graph that purported to show the "General Total of Crimes During the Period 1959-1968" (*Granma Weekly Review*, 1969:7). The graph shows a steady reduction in the overall crime rate, but there is no information anywhere that indicates which crimes are included and which are excluded. For example, if one includes traffic offenses in the 1968 figures, the rate would be several times larger than the 1959 rate. There is no telling what would happen if political crimes such as burglary and others were included, or even whether they are or not. Ignorance of these factors makes this type of data useless. It is perplexing that these figures are some of the most popular among American writers. The fact that this error has been repeated by socialist and nonsocialist scholars is even more confusing, since often these figures have a tendency to snowball and reappear in publication after publication (Domínguez, 1978:507; Wald, 1978:289; Liazos, forthcoming).

The same danger faced by American criminologists, of placing undue reliance on criminal statistics is repeated in the Cuban case. Arrest rates, for example, may merely represent shifts in the level of enforcement or definitional modifications rather than increased criminality. A concrete example of the former appeared last year when, after criticism by Fidel Castro and other prominent figures, the police arrest rates increased by seven percent (*Granma Weekly Review*, 1978). In reporting the increases, the Minister of the Interior warned officials to be careful in assuming rises in the levels of criminality, since the figures most likely represented improvements in police efficiency and greater efforts devoted to the suppression of crime. The largest rise was reported in cases of child abuse and negligence, with an increase of 41 percent in reported incidents. The police explained that rather than being a substantial rise the increases merely reflected the efforts of police, educational personnel (*Granma Weekly Review*, 1978) and political figures in exhorting greater reporting of this offense.

The Political Nature of Criminal Statistics

The political nature of crime would rarely be disputed by most criminologists, but this phrase is most often used in discussing the process of defining behavior rather than the manner in which criminal data is utilized. The political uses of criminal statistics become evident from any cursory reading of articles in the communist or capitalist press (Brohkin, 1975; Chalidze, 1977; Connor, 1970). Cuban writings on crime often use American data in order to reinforce negative impressions of the capitalist system and to downgrade the problems of rising crime in their own country.

The political uses to which crime figures are put are illustrated by the fact that most information presented to the Cuban public on the Cuban crime picture is usually compared with similar offenses in the United States. The rationale for using this comparative method is to demonstrate that even though crime may be on the rise it is not as pervasive a problem as found under capitalism. Comparison of rates is not limited to Cuba versus the United States, but is also made in relation to crimes in Cuba prior to the Revolution. These figures have been presented by Cuban and foreign observers to praise revolutionary improvements (American University, 1976; Wald, 1978; Thomas, 1971). While some observers have used crime statistics to buttress arguments of revolutionary success, others have employed them as standards in weighing the progress of complex social issues. For example, Domínguez, one of the foremost academicians studying Cuba in the United States, has often referred to crime statistics in analyzing the Cuban political culture and measuring the development of the "New Man" (Domínguez, 1978:507). While the former are easily dismissed due to their impressionistic and politicized arguments, the latter are often taken seriously by researchers and analysts. Yet, both conclusions are equally dangerous. Not only are the statistics on which these conclusions are reached suspect, but using crime statistics as a measure of social instability or regime failure is a dangerous and foolhardy effort.

The purpose of this review of Cuban statistics on crime has not been to claim that they should be ignored, but merely to indicate some of the pitfalls to readers interpreting this information. Many American criminologists have been reluctant to undertake research in communist forms of deviancy and crime because of the lack of adequate data, while others have placed an inordinate amount of importance on them without questioning their validity or reliability. This deficiency should not bar investigators; rather, it should spur the search for alternative or complementary sources.

OTHER STATISTICAL SOURCES

The foregoing discussion has been limited to Cuban statistical sources which deal specifically with crime, but it is becoming more and more accepted that crime cannot be understood in isolation from the total social system.

> For this reason we need to broaden the scope of traditional crime statistics, so as to extend them to all sectors of the system of crime control on one hand (endogenous variables), and, on the other hand, to include some exogenous variables of the whole social system such as population, social class, education, mental health and political climate [Newman and Vetere, 1977:260].

While it is concededly difficult to obtain and analyze demographic and political information on Cuba, the task is worthwhile. There are numerous publications which contain a great deal of valuable statistical information on Cuban demographic variables. Some of these are reported in Cuban editions such as the *Anuario Estadistico de Cuba*, published annually, and longer studies such as the 1970 census. Luckily, most of this information can be reviewed in U.N. publications as well as those of specialized institutions, such as the *Statistical Abstract of Latin America* published by the University of California. While many of the same cautions voiced in discussing crime statistics are also relevant in examining other statistical sources, their value cannot be underestimated (Mesa-Lago, 1969).

Of special interest to the criminologist are sociological studies and surveys conducted by both the Cuban government and outsiders. Maurice Zeitlin, for example, was given permission in 1962 to measure the relationship of variables such as economic insecurity, political ideas by generations, and race upon political radicalism and revolutionary support (Zeitlin, 1962). While studies as thorough as Zeitlin's are hard to find, they are invaluable in making determinations as to deviance and crime.

Many American scholars automatically dismiss surveys taken in socialist countries as being unreliable or sometimes even assume that such surveys are not done. Criticism is essential to any self-governing system. Since there is relatively little open criticism in closed political societies, there is a greater reliance on surveys to determine a broad variety of public attitudes. Only a small sample will be discussed here so that the reader can gain an impression as to its significance.

Gustavo Torroella conducted a survey among Cuban students for the United Nations (UNESCO) which measured a variety of attitudes and values among the respondents. Among the several values which he measured were attitudes toward civil liberties. He found that 59 percent of his 1070 respondents thought it unjust to punish an individual for an act committed in good faith; 54.1 percent thought evil intentions should be punished even if they resulted in no harmful actions, and 48.3 percent thought an individual should be punished for actions of a group to which he belonged even if the individual was personally blameless (Torroella, 1963).

The value of this type of survey is that it could be easily compared with identical responses from other surveyed countries.

Paired surveys have also been conducted across time allowing the reader to compare changes among similar populations over time. One such study allows the reader to see changes in familial patterns and clashes between different generations, a factor considered by Cuban and American criminologists crucial to the generation of delinquency (Jones et al., 1965).

Surveys have also been conducted among rural and urban populations to measure their concerns. One such survey involved 202 persons in the small town of Santa Fe in the Isle of Pines. When asked to identify local problems; 36 percent mentioned lack of recreational facilities; 35 percent referred to inadequate housing; 32 percent the need for increased production; while others spoke of more facilities to free women from housework, improved transportation, and poor water supply (DuMoulin, 1968). In none of the reported cases has crime or fear been an issue.

Attempts can also be made to measure the public's perception of the criminal justice system. Marifeli Pérez-Stable, for example, conducted a survey of 57 workers in 1975. When asked where they would go if a problem arose at the work site, very few indicated that they would seek protection from the Worker's Council, a legal institution set up for the protection of workers and empowered with judicial powers (Pérez-Stable, 1978). Other figures released by the Cuban government can also be used in conjunction with survey data in order to determine societal attitudes toward authority. For example, during one six-month period in 1977-1978 more than 300,000 traffic tickets were issued to drivers, but only 27.7 percent of these fines were voluntarily paid (Asamblea Nacional, 1978).

One of the most complete surveys conducted in Cuba involved a study of 26 divorced men and 43 divorced women in metropolitan Havana. Though the sample is small, the sampling procedures were extremely thorough (Hernández et al., 1973). This survey suggests that basic patterns about the family and traditional sexual roles had not been substantially affected by the revolutionary changes, though practical considerations had given rise to a cultural clash resulting in one of the highest divorce rates in the world. For a student of delinquency and, indeed, crime in general, knowledge as to familial relationships is essential in reaching any conclusions.

While sources of secondary data in Cuba certainly are not as abundant as in the United States, they are far less scarce than one generally assumes. From these studies only univariate distributions are generally reported, and statistical conclusions must be double-checked, since they are sometimes erroneous. While it may be argued that even if data availability does not constitute a major obstacle to secondary analyses, the quality of most of the Cuban data leaves much to be desired. This might suggest to many that the data should be ignored, but it should be remembered that (1) there are means for assessing the quality of secondary data; and (2) close examination reveals that the quality of the information is often no worse than that collected and analyzed in the United States. The value of much data, traditionally ignored by American criminologists in making comparative studies relevant to an understanding of the political, economic, and social climate of a nation, cannot be underestimated in reaching valid conclusions.

SEARCHING OUT VARIABLES

Essential to the examination of the data presented is a review of the variables which are considered by the researcher. Unfortunately, much of the Cuban data ignores or masks traditionally important variables. While age, sex, and marital status are usually furnished, the researcher encounters problems when attempting to review others such as race and socioeconomic status. In addition, the investigator encounters new variables which are not examined in the United States. A brief discussion of three of these variables will give the reader a better understanding of the difficulties.

Race is one of the most significant variables to be examined by any student of Cuban politics whether a criminologist or not. The author, however, has been unable to find a single Cuban study which considers this factor. This is due to a variety of reasons, the primary one being a conscious effort to erradicate race as a consideration for decision-making. Thus, while this information is collected, it is never reported. The 1970 census, for example, contained a question on the race of the respondent, yet the published results do not give any information on this subject (Dirección Central, 1971). The researcher does not even have a good idea of the racial composition of the Cuban population, not to mention the group being examined.

This difficulty has prompted students of Cuban politics to produce innovative measurement mechanisms to overcome this difficulty. Domínguez, for example, performed content analyses of pictures appearing in the Cuban military publications in order to arrive at a percentage figure of the racial composition of the Cuban Armed Forces (Domíguez, 1978). He also compared changes in height and illness reports in order to measure the impact of the Revolution's improvements on the health and living standards of Black Cubans. Casal, on the other hand, reached population conclusions based on the growth of Oriente province, which had the largest concentrations of Blacks on the island prior to the revolutionary takeover (Casal, forthcoming). Based on the growth rate of this province she approximated the racial composition of the nation as of the latest census.

It should be pointed out, however, that there are some pitfalls which hamper this type of study. For example, government statements have often linked adherents of Afro-Cuban religions, primarily the Abakúa and Náñigo, to a large percentage of the homicides which have taken place in urban areas (del Valle, 1969). In one of these statements the figure was placed as 75 percent of all homicides. Since these religious sects are primarily composed of Black Cubans, it would appear that this racial group experiences a disproportionate share of homicides. This conclusion is risky, however, since in the past it has been governmental policy to condemn many "subcultural religions," as in the cases of the Abaká and Jehova's Witnesses, by ascribing to them a large share of the nation's social problems. Thus, it was not unusual to see a majority of criminals being portrayed as "santeros" in government stories. Whether these statements merely reflect a propaganda effort or are realistic is not known.

In sum, while many of these methods have severe limitations for the researchers and their conclusions should be reviewed with some caution (for example, Domínguez utilized reviewers who were aware of the purpose of the study, which thereby severely biased the conclusions), they do present some innovative techniques in overcoming serious limitations in the quality of the data.

Another variable which often presents problems to the researcher is socioeconomic status. Even though the government does not recognize the existence of privileged and underprivileged classes in Cuba, it does report some information which is often useful to the investigator. Thus, the educational status, often described as "educational achievement," of the respondents is regularly included in studies (*Granma Weekly Review*, 1969). Income is rarely released, but it sometimes finds its way into the reports. For example, one study, of 523 children found that there was a direct relationship between errors in child rearing and family income and parental educational achievement (G. García et al., 1976). Specific mention of family income is usually omitted from the study, although this can be derived from those in which the occupations of the respondents are included. An example can be derived from a study of all suicides which took place in Matanzas province during a one-year period. The Matanzas study considered occupation as one of the variables in its research. Its conclusions were based on categorizations which included the following: persons with no classifiable occupation; new workers entering the job market for the first time; retired persons; recipients of government assistance; the handicapped; nonfarm labor; farm labor; housewives; directive personnel; and professionals and service personnel (Fierro and Bajos, 1977).

One of the variables most perplexing to the foreign researcher is that of political integration. This is a factor which is routinely considered in governmental studies. Some can be totally disregarded: For example, during a period in 1968 in which most small businesses were being nationalized, Castro went to great extremes pointing out to the population that as a result of a comprehensive survey the government had determined that the majority of the owners were not politically integrated or were outright opponents of the regime (Domínguez, 1978). In other cases, however, the data can be extremely helpful. The García study (1976) focused on errors in child rearing and placed primary emphasis on "revolutionary integration." As defined, this included such factors as membership in the Party and mass organizations as well as attendance therein (G. García et al., 1976). The most unusual characteristic of this variable is that it can be quantified and may be useful in determining other unknown factors such as socioeconomic status. In any case, only in exceptional instances, such as those presented in the nationalization survey, should this information be ignored, since it obviously represented to the Cuban researcher a very important variable. While some of these factors may not be considered useful by the American criminologist, the fact that they are essential to an understanding of Cuban political culture should make their ignorance a result of careful examination.

ANTHROPOLOGICAL STUDIES

Social sciences vary in importance from nation to nation and the criminologist is foolhardy in giving up his/her search solely because there are not sufficient sources in the discipline for which he/she has been trained. In Cuba, sociology is a relatively new science. Indeed, during the first years of revolutionary rule sociology was abolished from the curriculum of the University of Havana. Anthropology, on the other hand, has flourished under revolutionary rule.

A few fairly complete studies have appeared in Cuban publications which can be of invaluable assistance to the

criminologist. They are especially helpful because they have
tended to concentrate on low-income groups and housing settlements. Their targets have been primarily low-income
whites, farmers, and blacks. In addition to the works of
many Cuban anthropologists (Herrera, 1972; Rochon, 1967),
American-trained anthropologists have also been given access
to Cuban populations. The work of Oscar Lewis, referred to
earlier, has resulted in the publication of three books based
on his Cuban experience. These not only outline the culture
of poverty within these slum settlements, but also give the
reader a vivid picture of governmental efforts aimed at
eliminating such types of criminal activity as prostitution and
drug usage.

The work of Douglas Butterworth, a member of Lewis'
team, in examining the 400 people in the slum community of
Buena Ventura cannot be ignored. He found that there were
severe problems in the development of this area. The leader
of the local Committee for the Defense of the Revolution was
a small-time black marketeer; the organization's secretary
was a practitioner of Afro-Cuban religion who combined this
with political power, often resulting in abuse toward her
neighbors; and prostitution, drug traffic, gambling, and
other illegal activities were rampant. Butterworth concluded
that the efforts to erradicate past habits and traditions had
failed because the people "had no history of organization...beyond the family" (Butterworth, 1974). A review of
these sources is essential to the researcher attempting to
understand the development of crime.

CONTENT ANALYSIS AND
LITERARY SOURCES

With very few exceptions (see, for example, Gordon,
1971), criminologists have largely ignored content anlaysis as
a primary research tool in studying the problems of crime and
societal response. In reviewing Cuban materials, however,
one finds this to be an extremely useful tool. A revolutionary
society is not only engaged in changing traditional institu-

tions, but it also must extend its reforms into areas of values and attitudes. In this process the written media, as well as other means of mass communication, become central in all efforts to socialize the population. If one considers that all publication decisions are controlled by the government and represent a specific interest, then decisions and content bear a significant relationship to understanding the problems of that society and the manner in which they are perceived.

Newspapers and periodicals are essential to the reeducation effort. Two national newspapers are published in the island with widespread readership. Crime stories seldom appear in these publications. Indeed, at one point they were barred because a feeling existed that their publication would only tend to sensationalize crime. In recent years this policy has been modified, so that one now finds a great many stories appearing in Cuban periodicals. All of them, however, carry a moralistic message. The following story appearing in a Cuban newspaper is typical of such accounts:

FOUR YEARS OF IMPRISONMENT ARE IMPOSED FOR A CRIME OF THEFT

A door which was not properly closed allowed the theft of clothing, electrical appliances and other articles with a total value of $400 from the mixed store "El Dialogo" in the town of Amarillas, Matanzas Province.

The author of the theft, named Justino Hernández García, was sentenced to four years imprisonment by the Criminal Branch of the Provincial Popular Court of Matanzas.

The negligence of the administrator of the employees of this unit allowed this criminal act to take place. This act is an attack against the right of the workers and families in the neighborhood to acquire consumer goods as a result of their work.

The sentence imposed on Hernández García expresses the legitimate right to self-defense of the popular interests against those who assume or maintain a wrongful attitude in a society of workers.

The Popular Supreme Court ratified the sentence imposed on the accused [*Granma Weekly Review*, 1976].

This type of item exemplifies the political nature of all forms of crime within Cuban society. That causation is placed in terms of institutional failure and that collective responsibility is emphasized are also characteristic of the Cuban view of crime. The selection of this particular form of behavior for publication may be indicative of the concern with which this type of deviance is viewed. This may be especially significant in light of the fact that crime notices appear, at most, three times a month. If one also takes into account the period in which the reporting takes place, these items can clarify a great deal of information published elsewhere.

There have been two analyses of Cuban publications which exemplify the value of this research methodology. Olessen (1971) engaged in a study of women's roles based on the stories contained in *Granma*'s English weekly edition. One of the most recent and interesting efforts was an analysis of letters to the editor appearing in Cuban national newspapers (Rodríguez, 1978). Since this section of the newspaper has been relatively free to readers, voicing a variety of concerns ranging from corruption to judicial misconduct, its examination furnishes the researcher with valuable data as to attitudes and concerns.

One of the most interesting studies was performed by Lourdes Casal, who analyzed 104 novels published between 1950-1967 in order to measure changes in societal values as they referred to women and Blacks. The methodology as well as its linkages with other social sciences materials exemplify the potential this method holds for the researcher (Casal, 1975).

Of special interest to the criminologist are the efforts devoted by the regime to educate the public as to notions of socialist legality and norms of conduct. The use of the media for purposes of improving the image of the enforcement agents or educating the public is one of the most unique aspects of the government's crime prevention efforts. Film documentaries have been produced by the Ministry of the Interior detailing the activities of the police. Plays have been written, under the sponsorship of the ministry, which have explained the scope of the ministry's functions, and television dramatizations have been released describing the nature of police work as well as those factors which are conducive to antisocial behavior (Salas, 1979).

These efforts are perhaps best exemplified by the ministry-sponsored contests for writers of crime novels. The first contest was held in 1972 and since then has become an annual affair. Under the rules of the contest, anyone may submit a crime novel which will be judged not only on the basis of its literary quality but also on the image of crime and police which it presents. The novels have become increasingly popular and lead all other literary productions in terms of sales (Simposium, 1977). Short stories are routinely published in magazines depicting particular crimes or pointing out the work of police agents (Loredo, 1977). In some instances police characters have proven to be so popular as to consistently return in a form of adventure story. In other instances the novels have presented a wise character who has not only helped to solve the crime but has educated the reader in theories of causation. The following is an excerpt from a statement made by an amateur criminologist in a police novel:

> — Men are not bad by nature. The theories of Lombroso, which I am sure you know, have been discarded for some time: there are no born criminals.

> Criminals are such because of reasons which we must categorize as social. . . and in these we include a gamut of complex and subtle factors to detect them and sometimes the process is irreversible. Factors which can be attributed to the earliest stages of infancy, the family settings, the environment in general. But criminality is acquired. It is generated by society.

> — One only has to look at statistics a little bit — he continued saying — one only has to see that criminality continually rises in capitalist countries. Murders, robberies, crimes of all types are multiplied every year. And it is obvious that these societies convert many men into criminals. But this does not mean to say that once capitalism is abolished these complex and subtle factors,

which generate and are the fruit of criminality, shall immediately disappear. They will only slowly disappear. As society becomes better man becomes better also. But the road is long.

These portrayals are not only valuable as a source of popular literature, reflecting the values and beliefs predominant in the society at a particular point in time, but due to the imprimatur which they carry, they also represent regimental attitudes and policies.

HISTORICAL SOURCES

In recent years there has been a renewal among American criminologists in the history of crime and the employment of historical approaches to the examination of deviance (Inciardi et al., 1977). Gurr et al.'s work (1977) on crime and public order in Stockholm, London, Sydney, and Calcutta lends support to the argument that historical methodology can be successfully applied to the cross-cultural study of crime and control.

The recent work of Martínez-Alier (1974) on the origins of Cuban sexual legislation and mores is particularly important to the criminologist. For example, one of the most unusual forms of rape which is contained within Cuban penal legislation concerns seducation through abuse of a special relationship between the person charged and a minor. Prior legislation specified that the minor be a virgin in order for the crime to take place. In many ways this offense was "the triumph of machismo" (Martínez-Alier and Martínez-Alier, 1972). The marriage of the parties extinguishes the crime. While this legislation may seem outdated, the following statement by an official of the Ministry of the Interior is indicative of its present impact:

[Very] often a case of rape is filed as rape with a view toward getting married. Very often this type of complaint is cleared up in court and it turns out there has been no rape [*Granma Weekly Review*, 1969:9].

Another crime which presents some unusual problems to the foreign observer is that of elopement. This crime involves the taking away of a minor from the custody of her parents with the intent to have sexual relations with her or elopement for the purpose of marriage without the consent of the parents. Martínez-Alier contends that this is a crime initiated by a concern of a slave society not to have lower-class persons enter into "proper" families and to prevent intermarriage among Blacks and Whites (Martínez-Alier, 1974).

While comparison of pre- and post-revolutionary statistics is an impossible task, it is essential to the reader to understand the origins of much of the legislation and its ties to the Cuban social fabric.

OTHER SOURCES AND DATA

Some of the sources referred to most often by scholars doing research in Cuba are accounts written by vistors to the island. In most of these instances these are impressionistic versions of brief visits to the country. Statements relating to crime, including statistical data, are used in many of these publications, usually with no references made as to source or accuracy. They are useful, but the researcher should be extremely careful in reviewing the material. Two examples of this material shall be presented.

One of the most thorough accounts of present-day Cuba was written in 1967 by José Yglesias (1969), an American writer of Cuban ancestry. For three months he lived in Mayari, a small country town in Oriente province and in his writings attempted to describe the social changes which had taken place there. His approach resembles that of Oscar Lewis, but he falls far short of reaching the Lewis style. Although his work shows bias in favor of the government, it presents an interesting view of Cuba during this period.

Karen Wald focused her work on the Cuban efforts directed at children. After a stay in Cuba she published her accounts, which included an entire chapter on juvenile delinquency and reform institutions. Since it is the only eyewitnesses report on these activities, it should be reviewed by the criminologist. Her work, however, constantly makes references to statistics without any indication of sources or in-depth analysis. She is honest in declaring a strong bias in favor of the Revolution, which often clouds objective analysis of the social setting (Wald, 1976).

A great many accounts have also been written by persons who have fled the island, and the same degree of care should be utilized in reviewing these sources, since they show a similar bias and inclination toward exaggeration. The primary caution of the investigator in reviewing all of these cases is to maintain some objectivity and to rely on these sources only to support other information which has been gathered. Very often the investigator will find that Cuban reports are more accurate and far more honest than accounts from foreign visitors.

CONCLUSION

While some of the problems encountered by the researcher investigating social problems in socialist countries are unique, the majority are common in all cross-cultural research. Criminology as a separate and independent discipline is a relatively new development in the social sciences. Interest in cross-cultural research is in its infancy while other disciplines have grappled with these issues for many years. Criminologists are foolish in not learning from the mistakes and successes of their predecessors. The following guidelines are offered to the reader as suggestions in dealing with the obstacles presented by this type of research.

1. It is imperative for the criminologist doing research in socialist countries to make contact with other social scientists who have specialized in the country or area to be investigated. Their assistance is invaluable in locating sources and gaining an understanding of the problems to be encountered.

2. Contrary to popular belief, socialist countries publish a great deal of statistical data on both rates and surveys of popular opinion. Great care should be utilized in examining

this data. Wherever possible, statistical information should be interpreted in the light of qualitative and interpretative material. Figures alone may prove to be misleading and can never provide the reader with an accurate picture of the social problem being reviewed. Attempts should be made to trace statistical data over long periods of time. Often the investigator finds that after two or three years the earlier figures have been modified or rejected. Legal definitions should be well understood prior to examination of the data. This should also be done over a long period of time, since it is not uncommon to find variance in different codes. All statistical data should be crosschecked against other sources — this is the best measuring tool in determining reliability and accuracy. All possible sources should be consulted, for there is no assurance that valuable information will be contained in seemingly irrelevant publications.

3. In reviewing the information the researcher should always keep in mind that deviance and social problems in general are perceived in most socialist countries as political issues presenting to the investigator problems unique to his/her discipline and not encountered by others. Objectivity on the part of the reporter is essential to the task at hand, even though this may at times seem an insurmountable task.

Most of the cautions expressed herein are common to any cross-cultural research project, and it is hoped that the researcher will learn from the experience of others. American criminologists have become overreliant on digested and easily analyzable statistical data. They will not find this in reviewing other countries. Often the potential investigator is deterred by the lack of information and the difficulties in obtaining it. Rather than being a total barrier it should spur innovative approaches to the study of crime. The lack of information makes any research valuable. The words of Seers in conducting Cuban research are illustrative: "We debated whether under the circumstances we would be able to write anything at all valuable. What really decided the issue was that information is so badly needed" (Seers, 1964). This is not to say that the researcher should produce anything at all

— we have enough of that in so-called comparative criminology. Rather, a great deal can be done with existing information, and publication of new facts will lead to further interest and analysis.

NOTES

1. The major work in this area remains that by Walter Connor (1972). For a similar treatment of the Chinese model, see Amy Auerbacher Wilson, Sidney Leonard Greenblatt, and Richard Whittingham (1976).

2. The blockade was instituted in the early 1960s and still remains in force, although it is much more relaxed. It prevents American institutions from making payments in dollars to Cuban entities. The same procedure is also applicable to Vietnam, Cambodia, and North Korea. For an interesting discussion of these problems, see Earl J. Pariseau (1970).

3. The author found in Jamaica that the police rate was 8.1 per 100,000, compared with the U.N. rate of 1.5 for the same period.

REFERENCES

American University (1976) Area Handbook for Cuba. Washington, DC: U.S. Government Printing Office.

Asambleas Nacional del Poder Popular (1979) Actas: Primer periodo ordinario de sesiones 28, 29 y 30 de junio, 1978. Havana: Asambleas Nacional de Poder Popular.

BROHKIN, Y. (1975) Hustling on Gorky Street: Sex and Crime in Russia Today. New York: Dial.

BUTTERWORTH, D. (1974) "Grass-roots political organization in Cuba: a case of the Committees for the Defense of the Revolution," pp. 183-202 in W. Cornelius and F. Trueblood (eds.), Latin American Urban Research. Beverly Hills, CA: Sage.

CARDENAL, E. (1976) En Cuba. Mexico: Editorial Era.

CASAL, L. (1975) "Images of Cubam society among pre- and postrevolutionary novelists." Ph.D. dissertation, New School for Social Research.

——— (forthcoming). Black Cubans in the United States.

CASTRO, F. (1977) "Discurso en el primer congreso de los Comités de Defensa de la Revolución." Bohemia 69: 52-62.

CHALIDZE, V. (1977) Criminal Russia: Crime in the Soviet Union. New York: Random House.

CONNOR, W. (1970) "Deviant behavior in capitalist society — the Soviet image." Journal of Criminal Law, Criminology and Police Science 61: 554-564.

——— (1972) Deviance in Soviet Society: Crime, Delinquency and Alcoholism. New York: Columbia University Press.

——— (1973) "Criminal homicide, USSR/USA: some reflections on Soviet data in a comparative framework." Journal of Criminal Law and Criminology 64: 111-117.

Dirección Central de Estadística (1971) Censo de Población y Viviendas. Havana: Junta Central de Planificación.

DOMINGUEZ, J. (1978) Cuba: Order and Revolution. Cambridge, MA: Belknap.

DuMOULIN, J. (1969) "Santa Fe: ideología y opinón sobre problemas locales." Etnología y Folklore no. 6 (July-December).

FIERRO, L. S. and N. C. BAJOS (1977) "Epidemiología del suicidio en la Regional Matanzas." Revista del Hospital Psiquiátrico de la Habana 18: 115.

GARCIA, J. (1971) "The Olive case." Granma Weekly Review February 21: 7.

GARCIA, G. et al. (1976) "Algunos factores que inciden en los errores de la crianza en un grupo de niños de la Habana Metropolitana y la acción formadora del estudiante de medicina." Revista 17 de Abril 15: 87-92.

GARCIA HERRERA, R. (1972) "Observaciones etnológicas de dos sectas religiosas afrocubanas en una comunidad Lajera, La Guinea." Islas, no. 43 (September-December): 145-180.

GORDON, M. (1971) Juvenile Delinquency in the American Novel, 1905-1965: A Study in the Sociology of Literature. Bowling Green, OH: Bowling Green University Press.

Granma Weekly Review (1969) "As servants of the people, we have been able to achieve an even greater mutual understanding." May 11: 8-10.

——— (1971) "First National Congress on Education and Culture." May 9: 5-6.

Granma (1976) "Imponen cuatro áños de prisión por un delito de hurto." January 7:3.

——— (1978) "Síntesis sobre la actividad delictiva y su enfrentamiento durante el periodo nov. 1977 a abril 1978, leído por el General de Brigada Enio Leyva." July 1: 2.

GURR, T. R., P. N. GRABOVSKY, and R. C. HULA (1977) The Politics of Crime and Conflict: A History of Four Cities. Beverly Hills, CA: Sage.

HERNANDEZ, J., A. ENG, M. BERMUDEZ and M. COLUMBIE (1973) "Estudio sobre el divorcio." Humanidades ser. 1 (Ciencias Sociales), no. 3 (January).

HERNANDEZ DE ARMAS, N. (1977) "Las causas del delito." Revista del Hospital Psiquiátrico de la Habana 18 (April-June): 301-322.

HERRERA, R. G. (1972) "Observaciones etnológicas de dos sectas religiosas afrocubanas en una comunidad Lajera, La Guinea." Islas 43: 145-180.

HOROWITZ, I. (1967) The Rise and Fall of Project Camelot. Cambridge, MA: Harvard University Press.

INCIARDI, J., A. BLOCK and L. HOLLOWELL (1977) Historical Approaches to Crime: Research Strategies and issues. Beverly Hills, CA: Sage.

JONES, L., L. JONES and E. FALCON (1965) "Actitudes vocacionales de estudiantes de 1960 y 1965." Psicología y Educación 2, no. 5 (January-March).

LEWIS, O., R. LEWIS and S. RIGDON (1977) Four Men: Living the Revolution. Urbana: University of Illinois Press.

——— (1978) Four Women: Living the Revolution. Urbana: University of Illinois Press.

LIAZOS, A. (forthcoming) A Socialist View of Social Problems.

LOREDO, C. P. (1977) "Una sentencia recurrida." Bohemia 69: 8-9.

MARTINEZ-ALIER, V. (1974) Marriage, Class and Colour in Nineteenth Century Cuba. New York: Cambridge University Press.

MARTINEZ-ALIER, V. and J. MARTINEZ-ALIER (1972) Cuba: Economía y Sociedad. Paris: Ruedo Ibérico.

MESA-LAGO, C. (1969) "Availability and reliability of statistics in socialist Cuba." Latin American Research Review 4: 47-49, 53-91.

MORENO, J. A. (1973) "From traditional to modern values," pp. 471-497 in

C. Mesa-lago (ed.) Revolutionary Change in Cuba. Pittsburgh: University of Pittsburgh Press.

NEWMAN, G. and E. VETERE (1977) "International crime statistics: an overview from a comparative perspective." Abstracts in Criminology and Penology 17: 251-274.

NOVE, A. (1961) The Soviet Economy. New York: Praeger.

OLESSE, N. V. (1971) "Context and posture: notes on sociocultural aspects of women's roles and family policy in contemporary Cuba." Journal of Marriage and the Family 33: 548-560.

ORLEANS, L. (1965) "Troubles with statistics." Problems of Communism 14: 39-45.

PARISEAU, E. J. (1970) Cuban Acquisitions and Bibliography. Washington, DC: Library of Congress.

PÉREZ-STABLE, M. (1976) "Institutionalization and worker's response." Cuban Studies 6: 31-54.

PINEIRO LAREDO, C. (1977) "Malversación en la arrocera." Bohemia 70: 8-9.

PORTES, A. (1972) "Society's perception of the sociologist and its impact on crossnational research." Rural Sociology 37: 27-42.

ROCHON, L. (1967) "La sociededa agropecuaria Jesús Feiliú: Un caso de cambio en el medio rural bajo un régimen socialista en transición." Etnología y Folklore, no. 4 (July-December): 23-36.

RODRÍGUEZ, E. E. (1978) "Public opinion and the press in Cuba." Cuban Stuides 8: 51-65.

SALAS, L. (1979) Social Control and Deviance in Cuba. New York: Praeger.

SALZADILLO, F. L. and C. B. NARCISO (1977) "Epidemiología del suicidio en la Regional Matanzas." Revista del Hopsital Psiquiàtrico de la Habana 18 (January-March): 115-122.

SEERS, D. [ed.] (1964) Cuba: The Economic and Social Revolution. Chapel Hill: University of North Carolina Press.

SCHWARTZ, H. (1963) Russia's Soviet Economy. Englewood Cliffs, NJ: Prentice-Hall.

Simposium (1977) Universidad de la Habana 20 (April-December): 94-155.

SOLOMON, P. (1978) Soviet Criminologists and Criminal Policy. New York: Columbia University Press.

THOMAS, H. (1971) Cuba: The Pursuit of Freedom. New York: Harper & Row.

TOROELLA, G. (1963) Estudio de la Juventud Cubana. Havana: Comisión Nacional de la UNESCO.

Del VALLE, S. (1969) "Clausura del Forum Nacional de Orden Interior." Verde Olivo 10 (April 2): 7-10.

WALD, K. (1978) Children of Che. California: Ramparts Press.

WILBANKS, W. (1979) "Homicide in Jamaica." Presented at the annual meeting of the American Society of Criminology, Philadelphia, November.

WILSON, A. A., S. GREENBLATT and R. WHITTINGHAM [eds.] (1976) DEviance and Social Control in Chinese Society. New York: Praeger.

YGLESIAS, J. (1969) In the First of the Revolution: Life in a Cuban Country Town. New York: Vintage Books.

ZEITLIN, M. (1970) Revolutionary Politics and the Cuban Working Class. New York: Harper & Row.

INTERNATIONAL REVIEW OF YOUTH CRIME AND DELINQUENCY

PAUL C. FRIDAY

While crime may be considered ubiquitous, its manifestation varies by time, region, country, and state. There is, therefore, a natural curiosity about the circumstances and conditions which appear to foster crime and delinquency in one area and inhibit their development in another. This curiosity is the basis for comparative research, for it involves the search for commonalities upon which to base meaningful comparisons.

Yet, criminological theory as dominated by the Americans has emerged through time as culture-bound with limited, if any, power to actually explain the etiology of the criminal act. Despite the historical emphasis on "social facts" (Durkheim, 1938), theory as it developed in the United States has focused on the individual actor within the unique cultural context of American society.

During the 1960s there was an upsurge in interest in comparative research and cross-cultural theory testing. Unfortunately, such attempts were of limited utility.

What was done comparatively was limited to testing American delinquency models. When transported abroad, however, such theories tended to be inappropriate. Thus, after her attempt to test delinquency gang theories in Argentina, DeFleur (1969) attacked the "uncritical application" of U.S.-based delinquency theories and proposed instead the development of culture-specific explanations. Downes (1966) was unable to support differential opportunity theory in the East End of London, and Friday (1972) found none of the American models to be applicable to Sweden. However, more generalized theories such as Sutherland's differential association model did find some basic support in such diverse cultural contexts as Ghana (Weinberg, 1964), Sweden (Friday, 1972), Belgium (Junger-Tas, 1977), Mexico (Rosenquist and Megargee, 1969), and India (Rad, 1967). The result of attempts to verify the limited propositions was to reduce criminological theory to a set of diverse and often conflicting probability statements which lacked integration and synthesis or widespread applicability.

While Americans struggled with the applicability of their models abroad, European scholars, in developing their own legalistic and systems models of analysis, rejected the search for cause as futile and irrelevant. Törnudd (1971), for example, suggested the need to abandon "cause" and formulated research to provide estimates or predictions of fluctuations in the level of criminality or the process of selection within the criminal justice system.

Emerging from this development has been an emphasis on the study of crime and deviance within political, historical, and economic contexts. More explicitly, Phillipson (1971) suggests that, instead of looking for the causes of delinquency, one needs to look at the significance of the act. To him it becomes important to try to determine the process by which actors arrive at their specific conduct and the legal and structural determinants by which some actors are selected for legal sanction and others are not.

Comparative research is thus at a new point, in that it is sensitive to the failure of culture-bound theories to explain involvement, unwilling to accept as necessity the social psychological factors affecting individual pathology, and searching for more general structural and historical commonalities.

If criminology is to develop theory it needs to focus on *process*, not dichotomies or nominal legal classifications. Crime is not a dichotomy; it is not an either/or situation, it is not simply that a crime is committed or not committed. Instead, crime is an act which is a product of time and experience of the actor. It becomes necessary, then, to view the act in terms of its emergence, transmission, perpetuation, and modification within the historical context of the social system in which the actor lives. Comparative research within the context of the sociology of deviance returns criminology to analysis of "social facts" rather than "individual facts."

DELINQUENCY RATES AND TRENDS

The terms juvenile delinquency and juvenile delinquent are legal categories whose meaning and context vary considerably between and within societies. The terms are very much contingent upon the artificial age of responsibility. Legally, a juvenile is under 18 in parts of the United States, 15-17 in Sweden, 14-17 in England and Wales, and 14-20 in Japan. In Cuba the age of responsibility was reduced from 18 to 16 in 1973. One of the primary reasons for this was the belief that psychological maturity would be reached by age 15 and that the new economic conditions required 16-year-olds to assume adult responsibilities (Salas, 1978). In all societies juvenile delinquency tends to reflect special concerns. On the one hand, it represents society's failure to integrate, coopt, or socialize its young into its accepted ways. On the other hand, it represents the failure of youth to live up to or abide by the idealized conception the society has of its young. Thus, delinquency tends to incorporate two different conceputalizations — violations of expectations held only for youth (status offenses) and violations of codified norms required for all members of society (crime).

It is not easy, therefore, to draw a clear international picture of the problem of youth crime and delinquency. While the Second United Nations Congress on the Prevention of Crime and the Treatment of Offenders recommended in 1960 that the meaning of juvenile delinquency be restricted as far as possible to violations of criminal law (Lopez-Rey, 1978), antisocial behavior of youth is often viewed as a precursor to more serious acts. Consequently, much of the available research tends to operationally define delinquency as youth crime, but draws etiological generalizations from prior antisocial activity.

In most parts of the world (and there are important exceptions) both delinquency and youth crime tend to show a rapid and systematic increase. The Council of Europe (1978) recently expressed concern over the increased criminal activity of youth and the trend in urban delinquency to manifest violent behavior, drugs, alcohol, and vandalism. Lopez-Rey (1978) conservatively estimates that on the average 10 of every 100 young males commit at least one criminal offense between the ages of 15 and 20.

In Sweden, arrests of young persons aged 15-17 for serious crimes have increased nearly 10 times per 100,000 population since 1920 and an especially strong increase is evident since 1965 (Tham, 1978). In Israel the popular press reports an increase in juvenile arrests of about 25 percent over the past two years (Kotler, 1979), while other reports suggest an increasing concern with youth delinquency in the Soviet Union and China (Shipler, 1978; Butterfield, 1979). In Cuba it was estimated that by 1967 41 percent of all crimes were committed by minors (Salas, 1978). Even in Japan, where the general rate of crime is decreasing, those committed by 14-15-year-olds have increased (Clifford, 1976).

Not only has there been concern over the extent of youth involvement in crime, but also the age of peak involvement. Using official statistics, Sweden's peak age group is 15-17 (Tham, 1978), while Sveri et al. (1966), utilizing records for the under-15 age group, found the single most active age for registration of legal code violation was 14 years. This was reinforced recently by a self-report study of 519 school boys in Sweden. Ninety-six percent said they had committed at least one of 22 offenses, and the highest risk age group was 13-15 (Olofsson, 1976). In an older cohort study in Norway Christie (1960) found initial registration to be within the 14-17-year-old group. Even between the 1960s and 1970s the age of peak involvement in Scandinavia appeared to be declining. In Montreal it was found to be around 13-15 (Frechette and LeBlanc, 1978), but this varies with whether the acts being considered are status offenses or statutory violations. There is some indication, however, that the peak age varies with the legal school-leaving age (McKissach, 1973).

In general, delinquency and crime have statistically increased with urbanization and industrialization. While this generalization varies by the type of crime, time, and social conditions of the larger society, the association is found more frequently than not.

In studies in the United States and abroad (in Iowa in 1942 and Sweden in 1960), Clinard (1974) found that the greater the degree of urbanism in a community, the higher the rate of property offenses. In the United States there has been a significant positive relationship between city size and violence (Barlow, 1978). The pattern has been demonstrated in studies worldwide: it is seen in the United States (Clinard, 1974), in industrialized Europe (Christiansen, 1960; Mościskier, 1969; Szabo, 1960), the Far East (Lopez-Rey, 1978; United Nations, 1958), Latin America (Hauser, 1960), and Africa (Clifford, 1964; Clinard and Abbott, 1973).

Important exceptions to this pattern are evident, however. Japan reports a steady decrease in juvenile involvement in crime (Ministry of Justice, 1970) and studies of youth crime in the German Democratic Republic also show a steady decline and a substantially lower rate than in the Federal Republic of Germany (Freiburg, 1975). Poland is another country where the rate of delinquency is seen to be declining (Mościskier, 1976). Between 1960 and 1974 there has been nearly a twofold decrease in crime in Poland both in the country and in the towns (Michalski, 1976). However, with Poland the urban centers still have sightly higher rates characterized by property-type offenses. The rate of delinquency convictions between 1971 and 1973 in Warsaw, for example, was 128.6 per 10,000 inhabitants between the ages of 10 and 16, while the average for all towns was only 89.5 (Kossowska, 1976). Gödöny (1976), after reviewing the industrial growth and urban migration patterns in the socialist countries, concluded that the number of criminal offenses dropped by 7 to 13 percent. Looking at trends, he concludes:

> Whereas for the Western countries the high rates of delinquency and the rapidly growing trend of delinquency are characteristic, in the socialist countries even the relatively lower rates of delinquency and delinquency as a whole tend to decrease (Gödöny, 1976:98).

In the Ivory Coast where urban development has been especially pronounced, Brillon (1973) demonstrated that despite a 24 to 31 percent increase in the urban population, there has not been a noticeable increase in general crime. LeBlanc (1977) indicated that delinquency in Quebec, after an enormous increase at the end of the 1960s, decreased or at least stabilized.

The different conclusions about the association between delinquency and urbanization on the one hand and industrialization on the other are significant. They suggest that what has often been taken as a universal law (cause) of crime has meaningful variances. However, these conclusions are based on statistics, and anyone who has worked with statistics realizes the difficulty inherent in comparing rates between countries. Such statistics are based on different legal definitions, arrest priorities and procedures, as well as different national characteristics. For this reason, the statistics themselves are less important than the trends they reflect. In this sense there *is* a difference in delinquency between societies which cannot be understood independently of the structure of the state, and especially the role of youth in the society.

THE ROLE AND STATUS OF YOUTH

From a sociological perspective, then, it is important to look at the dynamics of the urban-industrial condition as it affects youth development in crime. Much of the difference between societies is reflected in the relative position on both the degree of urbanization and the level of industrialization. Christiansen (1976) suggests that while Japan has demonstrated a steady growth in the proportion of the population living in urban areas, it has not shown the development of urbanism or the urban way of life characterized by impersonality and anonymity. This he asserts is a primary factor in the lower rates of delinquency and crime.

Since urbanization and industrialization are in some way associated with crime, and since the conventional crime that does occur in these areas is disproportionately committed by the young males of the population, what, if any, factors are involved? To answer this question one must first deal with the changing status of youth in industrial societies. For while many of the traditional theories of crime and delinquency have focused on the individual, a more fruitful approach would be to assess the process by which the urban-industrial society differentially affects the probability of youths committing criminal acts.

Looking at the role and role expectations of youth, there has been a marked change in the attitudes towards children and their role as well as toward the perception of the role of the state in dealing with them since the middle of the nineteenth century. As the industrial economies develop, age in and of itself becomes a central factor. If one were to classify societies according to technological development or level of industrialization, there would clearly be seen a gradual extension of the period of time considered "youth" or childhood.

In the early stages of industrial development, youths, like women, play important economic roles; their labor is vital. But production can develop only to a certain level before a reduction in the labor force, and especially the unskilled, is required (Bell, 1973). To incorporate everyone into the labor force would result in a tremendous increase in production, production which in turn would require consumption. It is not clear if any single society can consume all it is capable of producing. In addition, increasing industrialization brings increased levels of technical competence required for participation in the economy.

The result of this is the systematic (though not necessarily conscious) exclusion of youth, women, the aged, and at times minorities from participation in the core activities of the society — work. During the Industrial Revolution in Western Europe women and children were "protected" by law from the burden of manual labor. This, in essence, isolated them from primary involvement in the society as a whole. In the United States many child labor laws and compulsory education laws were passed between 1870 and 1920. These had an effect on youths' commitments to the system itself. After the Depression the teenage labor force further decreased and the school-leaving age was increased (Greenberg, 1977). While exemption from hard labor may be considered benevolent, it may also be considered a mechanism of restricting access to the rewards of the society.

With the change in economic level also came a change in the age distribution of crime. During the nineteenth century in the United States when the peak age was higher than at present, criminal involvement tended to decline with age (Greenberg, 1977). Peak age for official contact in nineteenth-century Europe showed higher rates for agrarian countries than for industrialized England (Tobias, 1967). More recent data suggest the same decline in age with economic development (McClintock et al., 1968; Lopez-Rey, 1970).

Simultaneous with the development of the principle of exclusion based on age came an ideology of youth with slogans such as "Youth are our most valuable asset." The result was the development of status offenses which tended to reify the ideal behavior of youth. Consequently, the concern with delinquency per se tends to center the cause of crime on the psychological and interpersonal dynamics of the child rather than the structural conditions surrounding his exclusion from full participation in the society. By making delinquency an all-embracing concept with arbitrary age limits below which a person is assumed to lack maturity, rationality, or social responsibility, theories of delinquency tend to focus on individual pathology. Review of the age limits used to define delinquency shows the internationally pervasive influence of a variety of theories of psychological and physical development. Consequently, the upper age limit of 18 has been adopted by countries as diverse as

Sweden, Turkey, Ghana, Iran, Switzerland, Columbia, Malaysia, France, and Mexico.

The upper limits of delinquency reflect an extension of childhood into what has commonly been referred to as adolescence. During this period of time youths are expected to acquire the educational prerequisities to integration into the economic system and are excluded primarily on the basis of age. As Christie (1975) points out, in industrial societies youngsters are becoming older. The consequence of this is an increased segregation by age and a systematic isolation from the mainstream of the society, particularly work, and subsequently a greater involvement in and adherence to subgroups or countercultures. This isolation increases the risk for conflicts with the formal system of control.

When socially integrated, one develops commitments to the status quo. As Durkheim (1933:401) suggested,

> The individual becomes cognizant of his dependence upon society; from it come the forces which keep him in check and restrain him. In short since the division of labor becomes the chief source of social solidarity, it becomes at the same time the foundation of the moral order.

The nature of the work and the ability of the work situation to facilitate meaningful relationships are crucial.

Work, having a job, and earning an income are important parts of male social identity. Preparing for a technical career may be a structural equivalent to being employed, but being in school simply because it is required is not. It is this loss of work, defined as being unemployed or seeing no future potential for work, that probably most deeply affects the adolescent's sense of powerlessness (Marwell, 1966).

The impact of the work situation on delinquent behavior is illustrated by a study of the stages of industrialization in Poland (Mościskier, 1969). While industrialization per se did not affect delinquency rates, certain stages of industrial development — such as rapid growth and mobility in the development of the work situation — temporarily facilitated delinquency, while in situations where youths were part of the workers' councils and developed what is referred to as socialist social relations, delinquency rates did not increase.

The importance of the work situation for youths is also seen in studies from Japan. Kiefer (1970:71) concluded that

> responsible behavior is secured in Japan by developing the allegiance of the individual to the work group in such a way as to legitimate its disciplinary claims on him and intensify his feelings of obligation not to offend against it.

Since the work group seems to dominate personal life in Japan, criminality is reduced to the extent that one is integrated behaviorally into the group.

The relationship of youth to employment patterns has been shown in a variety of countries. Unemployment has been shown to correlate highly with delinquency. Hellberg (1977) suggests that in Sweden youth unemployment, criminality, school problems and alcohol and narcotic problems show a parallel increase over the years. Most notably has been the increase in youth unemployment. In the fall of 1977, 40,000 youth were unemployed (Hellberg, 1977); by August 1978 the figure had increased to 64,000 (*Aftonbladet*, 1978). While the society as a whole has made considerable technological and social progress, the young have seemed to be left behind or isolated (Daun et al., 1974). In Sweden Toby (1967) also emphasized the economic relations, as has Christie (1975) in Norway.

Sveri (1978) suggests that during the 1930s youths of 14 or 15 who finished the folk-school classes of study went directly into the labor market, helped support their families and naturally grew into the adult role. Rapid industrialization after World War II changed the economic prerequisites, requiring longer periods of time in training, so that today in Sweden only a fraction of the youth under 18 are in the labor force. He suggests that youths in such an industrial society have become "tolerated parasites."

This economic isolation has in essence lengthened childhood to the point that the social realities of integration are in conflict with the individual's physical and psychological development.

Bottoms and McClintock (1973), in an extensive assessment

of the institutional adoption of adolescent offenders in England, concluded that 40 percent of the offenders had records of lengthy periods of unemployment while others had intermittent and unstable work patterns. Interestingly, violent offenders had more stable work records than property offenders. Soviet researchers suggest that unemployed youths are 24 times more likely than secondary school students to be convicted of an offense (Gertsenzon, 1976).

Throughout Western Europe, youth unemployment has become a major problem. Figures from the nine Common Market nations show approximately 1.8 million jobless youths; they make up 37 percent of all unemployed in the region. In Britain the figure is 35 percent, 37.6 percent for France, and in Italy youth unemployment is estimated to be between 65 and 80 percent (*Time*, 1977).

In West Africa unemployment and crime is described by Brillon (1973) within the context of education. He states,

> After very little schooling, the young people from the countryside flock to the cities. Since they are not sufficiently trained to take on a well-paying job, they merely swell the ranks of the unemployed, and hence find themselves in a highly criminogenic situation [1973:22].

The meaning of the unemployment statistics and the general pattern in Western Europe to extend adolescence is the creation of extended periods of leisure for youth. In Belgium, Racine (1966) found that the role of increased leisure in juvenile delinquency is inseparable from the problems of education, mental hygiene, and social integration. This study suggests that purely restrictive measures to combat delinquency which do not account for leisure needs are dubious. Junger-Tas' (1977) study in Belgium found leisure time variables highly (and statistically significantly) related to delinquency. Most important were spending free time with delinquent friends, spending free time away from home, and feelings of boredom.

Within the Soviet Union there is a conscious attempt to deal with the problems of increasing leisure. These include after-hours music schools, chess clubs, and hobby centers with supervised model building, chemistry experiments and photography. However, these formal activities appear insufficient, as evidenced by news accounts of youths wasting time at restaurants and in impromptu groups in building entrances (Shipler, 1977).

The variance in patterns of youth crime and delinquency reflect less the absolute change in industrialization and urbanization than the internal mechanisms to reduce the isolation of youth and in turn create attachments to the established system.

SOCIAL INSTITUTIONS AND DELINQUENCY

The social isolation of youth is not simply a function of the individual's personal desires or even the economic system. It is a function of the integrating institutions in the society to effectively coopt youth. The bulk of the literature on delinquency tends to look at it in relation to specific social institutions such as the family, school, or community activity.

Family and Delinquency

The family is considered important because of its early socialization role in shaping values, morality and, consequently, behavior. The family has almost exclusive contact with children when they are most dependent and influenced, and has continued intimate contact over a subsequent period of several years. It is the first social instituton to affect behavior and to provide knowledge of and access to the goals, means, and social expectations of the wider society. But there may be deficiencies in the integration process between parent and child so that the child fails to learn appropriate behaviors (Bredemeier and Stephenson, 1962:126). On the other hand, socialization may be inadequate for dealing with societal expectations, as youths often do not learn clear definitions of appropriate norms (Toby, 1974).

Homes from which delinquent children come are frequently characterized by one or more of the following conditions: (1) other members of the family are criminalistic, immoral, or alcoholic; (2) one or both parents are absent by reason of death, divorce, or desertion; (3) there is a lack of parental control because of ignorance, indifference, or illness; (4) home uncongeniality exists, as evidenced by domination by one member, favoritism, oversolicitude, overseverity, neglect, jealousy, crowded housing conditions, or interfering relatives; (5) religious or other cultural differences, or differences in conventions and standards are present; (6) economic difficulties exist, such as unemployment, poverty, both parents working, or poor arrangement of financial affairs (Davies and Day, 1974).

The family may affect crime directly by imparting delinquent behavior. MacKay and McDonald in *Brothers in Crime* (1966) indicated that older siblings taught younger ones to steal. The Gluecks (1950) found that 70 percent of their delinquents had at least one parent with a criminal record. According to the Gluecks, drunkenness, crime, or immorality was found in 90 percent of the homes of delinquents but in only 54 percent of the control group. The McCords found that the sons of offenders had higher rates of criminality than the sons of others (McCord and McCord, 1958).

After looking at family structure and delinquency in England, Wilson (1975) found delinquency correlated with parental criminality. Children whose parents were major offenders had about twice the offense rate of those from families where the parents had no record or had only committed minor violations. Farrington et al. (1975) specifically studied the familial transmission of criminality. They searched for the records of nearly 400 males born in 1951 and found that nearly half of the boys with criminal fathers had records, while less than one-fifth of those without criminal fathers had records. Viewed another way, of the criminal fathers, 62.8 percent had one or more delinquent sons, whereas only 27 percent of the noncriminal fathers had delinquent sons (Farrington et al., 1975). This study also revealed that certain families were criminogenic. Eleven percent of the families studied accounted for almost half of all convictions within the 400 families studied. Regardless of family size, Farrington and his associates concluded, the risk of an individual acquiring a criminal record increases considerably if another member of the family has a conviction. In Poland, 31 percent of the fathers of delinquents were considered to be themselves delinquent, while 9 percent of the mothers were suspected of prostitution (Strzembosz, 1974).

The probability of recidivism is also substantially increased (Farrington et al., 1975; Buikhuisen and Hoekstra, 1974) if family members have criminal careers. Severy (1973) studied delinquent and law-abiding high school students over a four-year period. Among these youths, if there had been low exposure in early years to the deviance of family members, greater exposure during adolescence led to increasing deviance. On the other hand, when family exposure had originally been high, increasing exposure led to rejection of delinquency.

Other perspectives dealing with the family and crime have stressed the role of the "broken home." In a controversial study, the Gluecks (1950) concluded that such a family pattern was a major cause of delinquency. Several studies have tended to confirm this conclusion, but others have suggested that the broken home is but one of a number of variables that act together to generate illegal conduct. Studies demonstrating a relationship between broken homes and delinquency may be biased, since most have sampled only lower-class delinquents. On the other hand, Toby (1957) found the broken home to be more significant if the family controls were traditionally strong; if family controls were weak, the broken homes had little direct effect.

As early as 1929, Burt found no difference between delinquent and nondelinquent groups as a result of the father's death, but was of the opinion that divorce, separation, and desertion had a marked influence on delinquency. Subsequent research conducted during the decades of 1950 and 1960 revealed that while the broken home played a major role in delinquency, the effect differed considerably among children. In the working class, the effect was greater than in other social classes, and it was also greater for girls than boys.

In Norway, Christie (1960) studied all males born in 1933 and found that five percent had become registered offenders by 1958. Comparing home structure for offenders and others, he found that the home was broken 17 and 13 percent of the time, respectively, a difference which is not statistically significant. From this, one would conclude that broken homes are not necessarily linked with delinquency for adolescent males. Another study in Sweden showed a positive relationship between broken homes and delinquency only among working-class boys where other criminogenic factors were also present (Olofsson, 1971). The differential effect on females was investigated by Monahan (1957), who found that broken homes appeared to have a greater effect in generating delinquency for females and for blacks than for white males.

The structure and interaction patterns of the home are considered important factors in determining how conducive the family is to crime. West's (1969) study in Britain found that boys from backgrounds which investigators characterized as "socially handicapped" (that is, poor income, poor housing, large family, or welfare support), were more likely to be in trouble. Although these families comprised only one-eighth of the study population, they included half of the boys with "unstable" mothers, nearly half of those coming from homes with "lax rules," and over one-fourth of the homes with marital disharmony (1969:136). In Nigeria, Oloruntimehin (1973) confirmed the importance of the family interaction patterns. She found a statistically significant relationship between delinquency and the "cordiality" between parent and child. In essence, cordiality is affection and interaction which directly affects the youth's self-concept and willingness to use parental figures as role models. Likewise, Bottoms and McClintock (1973) found familial conflict in 74 percent of the serious delinquents they studied.

In general, the family may have a positive impact in insulating individuals from criminal patterns, providing it retains its ability to control rewards and effectively maintain positive attachments within the family unit. Commitments to family, or what Hirschi (1969) calls attenuated attachments, reduce the probabilities of involvement in acts of deviance. Research by Hindelang (1973) reaffirms the importance of family interaction and attachment. Delinquency is highest when family interaction and controls are weak (Rodman and Grams, 1967). Some parents do not supervise their children's recreational activities, do not enforce bedtimes, and do not perform activities as a group with their children or even eat meals together with them (Nye, 1958). For the delinquent, it is a life free of restraint, but also without guidance. Studies have shown that these weak controls and low-frequency interaction patterns are more common in low-income and ethnic minority families (Lewis, 1965). Vaz and Casparis (1971) reached a similar conclusion in their comparison of Canadian and Swiss youth. They indicate that the Canadian sample tended to be more peer-oriented and also more deviant, while the Swiss favored their parents and engaged in fewer criminal acts. Further, the Swiss boys interacted more frequently with adults than with their peers.

Kobal (1965), studying delinquency in Yugoslavia and England, concluded that there tended to be more openness and communication and general contacts between youth and adults in Slovenia than in London.

Clinard and Abbott (1973) found crime rates higher in Africa in areas less likely to have stable family relationships. A report on living conditions of delinquents, prepared by the criminological institute at Ljubljana, Yugoslavia, states that one of the characteristics of families producing juvenile delinquents is a lack of emotional ties between parents. Mackowiak and Ziembinski report a study in Poland which stressed the importance of socially positive role models (1971:27), and Bandura and Walters (1963) in the United States reported that behavior copying is more frequent when a positive relationship exists.

The importance of family role models and behavior modeling can be seen in the effects of migration in Israel (Schichor and Kirschenbaum, 1977). When a family migrates and the father, because of lack of skills, is unable to find employment consistent with his status in his home country, his status and image within the family is seen to suffer and with it control over children. This condition was seen in Israel to operate particualrly in families migrating from Moslem countries. This disintegration of the family means a reduction in the parents' ability to effectively control the behavior of their children. The Soviets, subscribing to the importance of family control, attribute 80 percent of the juvenile problems to a lack of supervision by parents (Juviler and Forschner, 1978).

The family is thus seen as important as an immediate origin of crime; not because it causes crime per se, but because relationships within the family effectively influence the exposure and importance of other norm-defining reference groups. The important point of these studies, and the issue stressed by Friday and Hage (1976), is that isolation from the family is likely to increase the child's associations with peers and/or deviant assocations.

Schools and Crime

In our highly technical, industrial society, education and schools play a key role in determining the eventual placement of the individual in society. In terms of length and intensity of exposure, education is considered, next to the family, the major force shaping youths' lives. The most general societal function of schools is to transmit knowledge, norms, and values along with their orientational and motivational underpinnings (Clausen, 1968:153). In essence, Durkheim maintained that the school functions as the primary regulator of moral education for a nation and that it is "the sole moral environment where the child can learn methodically to know and to love" (1963:67).

Domestic and international literature are replete with references to and analysis of the relationship between school performance and crime. As a primary socializing agent, school can have a positive or negative impact on youths. At its best, it can work to counteract a harmful family situation. At its worst, it can act as a stumbling block for those who have had a positive upbringing.

Studies have shown that low achievement in school is directly related to delinquent behavior (Empey and Lubeck, 1971; Gold, 1963; Polk and Halferty, 1966; Polk and Schafer, 1972; Reckless and Dinitz, 1972). Low achievers are prone to feel themselves outsiders, which in turn can decrease the probability of meaningful relationships and informal controls within the school (Olofsson, 1971). Delinquency was uniformly low among boys of all social classes who were doing well in school, while it was uniformly high among those doing poorly. In another study, Elliot and Voss (1974) found the school to be the most critical institution in affecting patterns of delinquent behavior. In Ghana, Weinberg (1964) found that 83 percent of the male delinquents who had been enrolled in school did poorly and were frequently truant. At times the truancy preceded the delinquency; at other times it was concomitant with the total pattern of behavior.

Studies elsewhere show a similar pattern. The Ministry of Interior in Cuba found that 90 percent of the juvenile offenders in juvenile homes were more than three academic grades behind their peers. These studies found school truancy and poor performance to be closely related to all forms of antisocial acts (Salas, 1978). Statistics from Poland show the same pattern. As many as half of the 100 boys aged 10 to 11 charged with theft were poor academically. At least 36 percent were poor readers and 80 percent of them were considered by teachers to be "difficult pupils" (Zabczynska, 1974). Seventy-seven percent of older youths who were delinquent were at least two years behind their peers in academic performance (Strzembosz, 1974).

Such statistics, however, do not demonstrate a causal relationship. Failure at school is often interpreted as a failure of the pupil to respond. However, it could also be interpreted as a failure of the school to stimulate interest and develop a commitment to conformity.

School performance is dependent both upon the home and the neighborhood from which children come to school and upon the way they are treated once they get there, as well as individual talents and innate abilities and temperaments. Recent teacher-writers argue that lower-class "culturally disadvantaged" children are eager to learn and are excited by the initial experience of school, but that the schooling process, reliance on IQ tests that are social-class biased, "tracking," and the physical conditions of the school and the attitudes of teachers soon deplete the initial motivation.

Schafer and Polk (1967), in a report for the Presidential Task

Force on Delinquency and Youth Crime, comment that "delinquent commitments result in part from adverse or negative school experiences" and that there are "fundamental defects within the education system, especially as it touches lower-income youth" that contribute to delinquency. Students who fail are progressively excluded by individual teachers and by other achieving students. Failure and rejection in turn make the school experience increasingly unsatisfying and frustrating.

Brusten (1974) suggests from his research in Germany that the system of tracking, in a sense, establishes a class system within a school. The ability and behavior of a child are to a certain extent determined by his social background and family class position. The school, on the other hand, represents middle-class values; and it is on these that students are evaluated. Middle-class values carry with them certain expectations of those from lower social classes; that is, teachers might expect lower-class youths to underachieve and exhibit deviant behavior (Hackler, 1971; Brusten, 1974). The result is that youths from lower social classes will end up in lower tracks which provide fewer opportunities for achievement. Those in lower tracks are likely to perceive themselves as underachievers. This has a large impact on the self-concept of students in these tracks.

School performance and delinquency cannot be viewed independently of the role youths are expected to play. School is the place where the problems of status and competition are visible for this crime-prone age group. Problems in school may be seen as a continuation of the problem created by extending the period of adolescence and keeping youths out of the labor force.

The effects of competition and strain in school on delinquency are shown in a study by Elliot (1966). He hypothesized that if school adjustment and experience are causally related to delinquency, then the latter will be lower among out-of-school than in-school youths. His findings indicate that the highest delinquency rate was among lower-SES dropouts *prior* to their leaving school (1966). He also found that the same boys had the *lowest* rate after dropping out of school. Their out-of-school rate was less than one-third their in-school rate. Elliot thus concluded that the school experience contributed to and sustained delinquency. The same conclusion was reached in New Zealand; McKissach (1973) postulated that the age variations in the level of property theft parallel the school-leaving age. Delinquency is tied to "life-style" needs legitimately unattainable while in school. As the school-leaving age is raised, the probability of delinquency in the final compulsory year is also raised.

The impact of increased educational requirements to meet the technological demands of the industrial state is clearly seen in the problems faced by the emerging states in Africa. Cusson (1972) states:

> The rapid development of the school, made necessary to prepare the youth to live in a modern society, is not without its drawbacks. Many are the young people who fail in school and who must abandon their studies. These children run the risk of becoming socially maladjusted on two counts: they are unable to adapt to the traditional life of the village because the school gave them other aspirations, and they cannot adapt to the demands of modern life because they are inadequately prepared [1972:51].

Even in the villages, the school may not be the integrating force it is expected to be. Brillon (1973:13) states:

> In the Villages, the school often indirectly plays a negative role, in that it widens the cultural gap that separates the young generation from the old, and also tends to uproot the child from his milieu. On the one hand, the children believe less and less in "fetishes," that is, the ancient customs, beliefs and values, and on the other hand, as soon as they have acquired a modicum of schooling, they refuse to do any manual or farm labour.

The school is seen internationally as an important factor in delinquency causation, since it is at both a socializing and integrating element and ultimately the source of economic rewards. A person's anticipation of success in either deviant or conforming activities is in part a function of the degree of prior success. Rewards for conforming behavior in school compete with rewards for deviant activities, and often a child can more realistically anticipate deriving feelings of competence, self-esteem, and support from delinquent peers than from conforming adults. If rewards are greater out of school, truancy will increase. The interaction process and reward structure in school are therefore critical in understanding delinquency and help to explain why truancy is one of the best statistical predictors of later delinquency (Glaser, 1962).

UNDERLYING DIMENSIONS
OF DELINQUENCY

Whether one discusses youth unemployment, the school, or family conditions as a precipitator of delinquency, the issue ultimately involves the position or role of youth. For delinquency is a temporary condition and there is reason to suggest that youths "outgrow" it as they find stable roles in the wider society. Sveri (1978) suggests that in Sweden the peak of criminal activity has already ended during the ages 16 to 18. Frechette and LeBlanc (1978) reached a similar conclusion from their study in Montreal; they found that only about 13 percent of their sample seemed to be capable of maintaining a significant pattern of delinquency over time. This longitudinal study suggests that few youths maintain their delinquent behavior over time.

The temporary nature of delinquency tends to correspond with the ability of the wider social structure to effectively integrate the young people. Delinquency tends to depend upon the manner in which young persons assume the statuses available to them (LeBlanc et al., 1978). That is, if positive or conforming roles are available through work, family, or school, the saliency of isolated peers is reduced (Friday and Hage, 1976).

Employment, school, family, and peers should not be considered independent factors in the causation of crime. Each contributes to a process which increases the probability that a given individual will engage in crime. The process involves the development of commitments to deviant versus normative patterns and to the groups that transmit those patterns. Hirschi (1969:200) argues that attachment to parents generates a wider concern for the approval of other authority figures and ultimately a belief that societal norms bind one's conduct. Hindelang 61973) empirically demonstrates an inverse relationship between attachments to parents, teachers, school, and school-related activities on the one hand and delinquency on the other. Attachment to peers, however, is related directly to involvement in crime. In essense, this is what Sutherland's differential association theory implies: delinquency increases with isolation from conventional norms. When isolation, rejections, and alienation decreases, there is a general reduction in criminality. Karacki and Toby (1962) indicate that lack of commitment to the adult way of life is at the root of delinquency. When they examined the shift of many delinquent gang members of law-abiding behavior, it appeared that these erstwhile delinquents tended to be boys who had moved from participation in the youth culture to adult roles and who successfully returned to school or work. Akers (1973) contends that a lack of attachment to conventionality means that youths are isolated from or unable to obtain sufficient rewards for conformity in the family, school, and peer groups. The lack of ties with major socializing institutions is seen to precede deviance.

Friday and Hage (1976) suggest that the family, school, community, work, and peer group interactions must be considered as a whole or totality rather than as independent factors. In so doing, the types of activities and groups tend to reinforce conforming norms. Integration is fostered when individuals interacting within a role set (such as the school) know individuals from another role set (such as the community). This tends to increase interdependence and conformity. In other words, the greater youths' meaningful or significant role relationships within all integrating institutions (family, school, community, work), the less the probability of their becoming involved in crime (Friday and Hage, 1976). Thus, it is not the significance of being unemployed, out of school, or having a broken home, but the number and importance of compensating relationships. In this sense, the important factor is not only the socialization of norms, but the controls facilitated by interaction in a variety of overlapping role sets.

The degree of overlap in relationship is a function of community. Clinard (1953) discusses the importance of neighborhood or community to integration. He refers to communicative integration as the extent to which contacts permeate the group. Neighborhood integration is seen to operate on both individual and organizational levels. On the individual level, integration involves the extent to which relationships are limited to the community that is, across role sets — the commitments individuals have to others in the community, and the number of acquaintances one has in the community. These community relationships decrease as family and school relationships become more alienating or as they disappear due to migration. In Africa, Clinard and Abbott (1973) found the low-crime area of their study to have less mobility, more tribal homogeneity, more visiting of relatives, more stable family relationships, and less individual isolation than in the high-crime area. The study suggests that internal and overlapping relations within the local community are more important with respect to norm adherence than integration into the wider society. Relationships, then, tend, to have a structural basis.

Another example of the importance of looking at the integrating function *across* sets of relationships rather than simply within the school, family, or community comes from Israel. Shichor and Kirschenbaum (1977) reviewed delinquency patterns in "new" towns where the majority of residents were immigrants to Israel after 1968. They found four major variables to explain best the differential rates of crime: extent of unemployment, quality of elementary education, year the settlement was founded, and proportion of natives born in the town. The authors suggest an explanation that confirms Clinard's findings and supports the overlapping role thesis: The more isolated the community and the more socially cohesive and more integrated the diverse socializing institutions, the more informal social control there appears to be.

Dizon (1978) in the Philippines tested the importance of overlapping role relationships. Using several measures of integration, he found that the less youngsters were integrated in the family, the school, and work situation, the higher they scored on frequency and seriousness of self-reported offenses. Youngsters with delinquent friends reported more as well as more serious offenses than those without such friends. In the Philippines peer attachment had a significant inverse relationship with adult attachment or involvement in other roles. In Belgium Junger-Tas (1977) also found a lack of social integration in such important subsystems as the family and the school, which seemed to lead to attachment to other marginals, who then tended to support and reinforce deviant norms.

Other studies have also supported the thesis that the pattern of interaction across socializing institutions is as significant as the pattern within any single structure. Shoham et al. (1970) found the length of stay in Israel to be significantly more highly associated with delinquency than urban-rural differences. This implies that the shorter the stay, the less is the likelihood of integration into diverse social groups. Weinberg (1964) concluded that the extracultural effects of family, school, and peers were effectively interrelated in Ghana. The study found that not only did delinquents experience more familial stress than nondelinquents, but they were also more alienated at school and isolated from other community or integrating activities.

Factors facilitating overlapping role sets must not be viewed as a function of the individual, but a product of the wider political, economic, and demographic societal characteristics. Rahav (1978) conducted an ecological study of delinquency in Israel and found that the major explanatory variable was the number of youths in a particular community. This suggests that a "critical mass" is needed before the development of the processes which lead to the formation of subcultures of youth. The study concludes:

> Delinquency, as a systematic response to structural strains, appears only when the local juvenile groups is large enough to develop a delinquent subculture. When the group is too small social control is too tight to allow any systematic deviation [Rahav, 1978:14].

The implication of this finding is that the larger the cohort of juveniles, the less the probability that any one group — work, school, or community — can integrate individuals or in turn provide consistent reinforcement of norms or overlapping social controls. The crime rate in turn will vary by the amount of time required before all of the members of the large cohort can become part of integrated role sets. Thus, cessation of criminal activity most frequently corresponds in time to the development of employment, marriage, and other social responsibilities. Even large cohorts of youth may be easily integrated if the economic and social conditions of a society are in a growth phase. One subsequently finds lower rates of criminality under such conditions, as is evident in many of the socialist countries; that is, when either the economic or social conditions absorb rather than isolate youths. When segregated from meaningful participation and a variety of responsible roles, youths will tend to deviate.

Criminality is not reduced simply by the formation of attachments to a given set of relationships, but by a function of the interaction of attachment and control by the overlap of groups themselves. Internationally, then, when delinquency and youth crime are high, youths tend to have an isolated pattern of role relationships which is created and fostered by external, structural conditions in the society.

REFERENCES

Aftonbladet (1978) August 18: 1.
AKERS, R. (1973) Deviant Behavior: A Social Learning Approach. Belmont, CA: Wadsworth.
BANDURA, A. and R. A. WALTERS (1963) Social Learning and Personality Development. New York: Holt, Rinehart & Winston.
BARLOW, H. D. (1978) Introduction to Criminology. Boston: Little, Brown.
BELL, D. (1973) The Coming of Postindustrial Society: A Venture in Social Forecasting. New York: Basic Books.
BOTTOMS, A. E. and F. H. McCLINTOCK (1973) Criminals Coming of Age. London: Heinemann.
BREDEMEIER, H. C. and R. M. STEPHENSON (1962) The analysis of social systems. New York: Holt, Rinehart & Winston.
BRILLON, Y. (1973) "The evolution of crime in the Ivory Coast," in Urban and Rural Crime and Its Control in West Africa. Abidjan: Abidjan Institute of Criminology.
BRUSTEN, M. (1974) "Soziale Schichtung, selbstberichtete delinquenz und prozesse der stigmatisierung in der schule." Criminologisches Journal 6: 29-46.

BUIKHUISEN, W. and H. A. HOEKSTRA (1974) "Factors related to recidivism." British Journal of Criminology 14: 63-69.

BURT, C. (1929) The Young Delinquent. London: University of London Press.

BUTTERFIELD, F. (1979) "Peking is troubled about youth crimes." New York *Times* March 11: 13.

CHRISTIANSEN, K. O. (1960) "Industrialization and urbanization in relation to crime and juvenile delinquency." International Review of Criminal Policy 16: 3-8.

——— (1976) "Industrialization, urbanization and crime," pp. 46-37 in Crime and In-dustrialization. Stockholm: Scandinavian Research Council for Criminology.

CHRISTIE, N. (1960) Unge norske lovovertredere. Oslo: Universitetsforlaget.

——— (1975) Hvor tett et samfunn? Oslo: Universitetsforlaget.

CLAUSEN, J. [ed.] (1968) Socialization and society. Boston: Little, Brown.

CLIFFORD, W. (1964) "Crime and criminology in central Africa," pp. 210-232 in T. Grygier, H. Jones, and J. C. Spender (eds.) Criminology in Transition. London: Tavistock.

——— (1976) Crime Control in Japan. Lexington, MA: D. C. Heath.

CLINARD, M. B. (1953) "Urbanization and crime," pp. 238-246 in C. B. Vedder (ed.) Criminology: A Book of Readings. New York: Drydon.

——— (1974) The Sociology of Deviant Behavior. New York: Holt, Rinehart & Winston.

——— and D. J. ABBOTT (1973) Crime in Developing Countries. New York: John Wiley.

Council of Europe (1978) Information Bulletin on Legal Activities. Strasbourg: Council of Europe (June).

CUSSON, M. (1972) "Observations on the problem of juvenile delinquency: the case of Abidjan," pp. 49-66 in First West African Conference in Comparative Criminology. Abidjan: Abidjan Institute of Criminology.

DAUN, A., B. BORJESEN and S. ÅHS (1974) Samhallsförändringar och brottslighet. Stockholm: Folksam.

DAVIES, L. and E. C. DAY (1974) "The criminal and social aspects of families with a multiplicity of problems." Australian and New Zealand Journal of Criminology 7: 197-213.

DeFLEUR, L. B. (1969) "Alternative strategies for the development of delinquency theories applicable to other cultures." Social Problems 17: 30-39.

DIZON, D. P. (1978) "Explaining youth crime: a proposal for a crosscultural pers-pective." Presented at the World Congress of Sociology, Uppsala, Sweden, August.

DOWNES, D. (1966) The Delinquent Solution. New York: Free Press.

DURKHEIM, E. (1933) The Division of Labor in Society (George Simpson, trans.). New York: Free Press.

——— (1938) Les regles de la methode sociologique (S. A. Solvay and J. H. Mueller, trans.), in G. E. G. Catlin (ed.) The Rules of Sociological Method, Chicago: Univer-sity of Chicago Press.

——— (1963) Education and Sociology. New York: Free Press.

ELLIOT, D. S. (1966) "Delinquency, school attendance and dropouts." Social Problems 3: 307-314.

ELLIOT, D. S. and H. L. VOSS (1974) Delinquency and Droptouts. Lexington, MA: D. C. Heath.

EMPEY, L. T. and S. G. LUBECK (1971) Explaining Delinquency. Lexington, MA: D. C. Heath.

FARRINGTON, D. P., G. GUNDRY, and D. J. WEST (1975) "The familial transmission of criminality." Medicine, Science and the Law 15: 117-186.

FRECHETTE, M. and M. LeBLANC (1978) La Delinquance Cachee des Adolescents Montrealais, vol. 1. Montreal: G.R.S.I.J., University of Montreal.

FREIBURG, A. (1975) "Zur jugendkriminalität in der DDR." Kölner Zeitschrift zur Soziologie und Sozialpsychologie 27: 489-537.

FRIDAY, P. C. (1972) "La verifica delle teorie della struttura differenziale delle opportunity delle associazioni differenziali nella societa Svedese" (The applicability of differential opportunity and differential association theory in Sweden). Quanderni di Criminologia Clinica (September) 14: 279-304.

FRIDAY, P. C. and J. HAGE (1976) "Youth crime in postindustrial societies: an integrated perspective." Criminology 14: 347-368.

GERTSENZON, A. A. (1976) Kriminologiia. Moscow.

GLASER, D. (1962) "The differential association theory of crime," in A. M. Rose (ed.) Human Behavior and Social Processes. Boston: Houghton Mifflin.

GLUECK, S. and E. GLUECK (1950) Unraveling Juvenile Delinquency. New York: Commonwealth Fund.

GÖDÖNY, J. (1976) "Criminality in industrialized countries," pp. 91-109 in Crime and Industrialization. Stockholm: Scandinavian Research Council for Criminology.

GOLD, M. (9163) Status Forces in Delinquent Boys. Ann Arbor: University of Michigan Institute of Social Research.

GREENBERG, D. (1977) "Delinquency and the age structure of society." Contemporary Crisis 1: 189-223.

HACKLER, J. C. (1971) "A development theory of delinquency." The Canadian Review of Sociology and Anthropology 8: 61-75.

HAUSER, P. [ed.] (1960) Urbanization in Latin America. New York: International Documents Service, Columbia University Press.

HELLBERG, I. (1977) "Ungdomsarbetslöshet och Kriminalitet." Bra Apropa No. 3: 3-10.

HINDELANG, M. J. (1973) "Causes of delinquency: a partial replication and extension." Social Problems 20: 471-487.

HIRSCHI, T. (1969) Causes of Delinquency. Berkeley: University of California Press.

JUNGER-TAS, J. (1977) "Hidden delinquency and judicial selection in Belgium," pp. 70-94 in P. C. Friday and V. L. Stewart (eds.) Youth Crime and Juvenile Justice. New York: Praeger.

JUVILER, P. and B. E. FORSCHNER (1978) "Juvenile delinquency and the Soviet Union" (unpublished).

KARACKI, L. and J. TOBY (1962) "The uncommitted adolescent: candidate for gang socialization." Sociological Inquiry 32: 203-215.

KIEFER, C. W. (1970) "The psychological interdependence of family, school, and bureaucracy in Japan." American Anthropologist 72: 66-75.

KOBAL, M. (1965) Delinquent Juveniles from Two Different Cultures. Ljubljana: Reviga za Kriminalisto in Kriminologijo.

KOSSOWSKA, A. (1976) "Delinquency in the Warsaw area," pp. 141-264 and 347-357 in Polska Akademia Nauk. Archiwum Kryminologii (vol. VII). Wroclaw: Zakland Narodowy im Ossolinskich.

KOTLER, Y. (1979) "Israel's juvenile crime war." Atlas World Press Review (February): 53.

LeBLANC, M. (1977) La Delenquance Juvenile au Quebec. Montreal: Ministere des Affaires Sociales.

LeBLANC, M., L. BIRON, G. COTE, and L. PRONOVOST (1978) La delinquance juvenile: son developpement en regard du developpement psychosocial durant l'adolescence. Montreal: Groupe de Recherce Sur L'Inadaptation Juvenile. (unpublished)

LEWIS, H. (1965) "Child rearing among low income families," pp. 342-353 in L. A. Ferman, J. L. Kornbluh, and A. Harber (eds.) Poverty in America: A Book of Readings. Ann Arbor: University of Michigan Press.

LOPEZ-REY, M. (1970) Crime: An Analytical Appraisal. London: Routledge & Kegan Paul.

——— (1978) "Youth and crime in contemporary and future society." UNAFEI Resource Material Series No. 14.

McLINTOCK, F. H. N. H. AVISON and G. N. C. RESE (1968) Crime in England and Wales. London: Heinemann.

McCORD, J. and W. McCORD (1958) "The effects of parental role model on criminality." Journal of Social Issues 14: 66-75.

MAKAY, H. D. and J. F. MacDONALD (1966) Brothers in Crime. Chicago: University of Chicago Press.

McKISSASH, I. J. (1973) "Property offending and the school leaving age." International Journal of Criminology and Penology 1: 353-326.

MACKOWIAK, P. and S. ZIEMBINSKI (1971) "Social aspects of sources of criminality and its prevention and control." International Review of Criminal Policy 29: 25-31.

MARWELL, G. (1966) "Adolescent powerlessness and delinquency." Social Problems 14: 35-47.

MICHALSKI, W. (1976) "Phenomena in the field of the dynamics and structure of crime in Poland," pp. 129-135 in Crime and Industrialization. Stockholm: Scandinavian Studies in Criminology.

Ministry of Justice (1970) The Trends of Juvenile Delinquency and Procedures for Handling Delinquents in Japan. Tokyo: Ministry of Justice.

MONAHAN, T. P. (1957) "Family status and the delinquent child: a reappraisal and some new findings." Social Forces 35: 250-258.

MOSCISKIER, A. (1969) "Delinquency in regions under intensified industrialization and the relation between the dynamics of delinquency and the dynamics of socioeconomic processes (1958-1960 and 1964-1968)." Archives of Criminology 4: 223-228.

——— (1976) "Delinquency in Poland and the processes of industrialization and urbanization." The Polish Sociological Bulletin 33: 53-63.

NYE, I. F. (1958) Family Relationships and Delinquent Behavior. New York: John Wiley.

OLOFSSON, B. (1971) Vad var det vi sa! Stockholm: Utbildningsforlaget.

——— (1976) "On delinquency and conformity among school boys," pp. 1-15 in National Council for Crime Prevention. Swedish Studies on Juvenile Delinquency. Stockholm: Brottsforebyggande Radet.

OLORUNTIMEHIN, O. (1973) "A study of juvenile delinquency in a Nigerian city." British Journal of Criminology 13: 157-169.

PHILLIPSON, M. (1971) Understanding Crime and Delinquency. Chicago: AVC.

POLK, K. and D. HALFERTY (1966) "Adolescence, commitment and delinquency." Journal of Research in Crime and Delinquency 3: 82-96.

POLK, K. and W. E. SCHAFER (1972) Schools and Delinquency. Englewood Cliffs, NJ: Prentice-Hall.

RACINE, A. (1966) "Role des loisirs dans l'etiologie de la delinquance juvenile," pp. 41-45 in Loisirs et Delinquance Juvenile, Publication No. 15. Bruxelles: Centre d'Etude de la Delinquance Juvenile.

RAHAV, G. (1974) Middle-Class Juvenile Delinquency in Israel. Ann Arbor, MI: University Microfilms.

——— (1978) "Culture conflict, urbanization and delinquency: an ecological study." Presented at the American Society of Criminology Meeting, Dallas, Texas, November.

RAD, S. V. (1967) Facets of Crime in India. Bombay: Allied.

RECKLESS, W. and S. DINITZ (1972) The Prevention of Juvenile Delinquency. Chicago: University of Chicago Press.

RODMAN, H. and P. GRAMS (1967) "Juvenile delinquency and the family: pp. 188-221 in LEAA U.S. Task Froce Report: Juvenile Delinquency and Youth Crime. Washington, DC: U.S. Government Printing Office.

ROSENQUIST, C. M. and E. I. MEGAGREE (1969) Delinquency in Three Culutres. Austin: University of Texas Press.

SALAS, L. P. (1978) "Juvenile delinquency in the revolution: Cuba's response." (unpublished)

SARNECKI, J. (1978) Vad skall vi gora at ungdomsbrottsligheten? Bra Apropa, No. 3.

SEVERY, L. J. (1973) "Exposure to deviance committed by valued peer groups and family members." Journal of Research in Crime and Delinquency 10: 35-46.

SCHAFER, W. E. and K. POLK (1967) "Delinquency and the schools," pp. 227-277 in LEAA Task Force Report: Juvenile Delinquency and Youth Crime. Washington, DC: U.S. Government Printing Office.

SHICHOR, D. and A. KIRSCHENBAUM (1977) "Juvenile delinquency and new towns: the case of Israel," pp. 95-108 in P. C. Friday and V. L. Stewart (eds.) Youth Crime and Juvenile Justice: International Perspectives. New York: Praeger.

SHIPLER, D. K. (1977) "A problem for Soviet's young: what to do with leisure." New York *Times* December 16: A2.

——— (1978) "Rising youth crime in Soviet troubles regime and public." New York *Times* March 5: 1.

SHOHAM, S., N. SHOHAM and A. ABD-EL-RAZEK (1970) "Immigration, ethnicity, and ecology as related to juvenile delinquency in Israel," pp. 77-97 in S. Shoham (ed.) Israel Studies in Criminology, vol. 1. Tel-Aviv: Gomeh Publishing.

STRZEMBOSZ, A. (1974) "Extent of recidivism among juvenile aelinquents and their later careers," pp. 149-155 and 220-224 in Polskiej Akademii Nauk, Archiwum Kryminologii, vol. VI. Wroclaw: Zaklad Narodowy im Ossolinskich.

SVERI, K. (1978) "Ungdomsbrottsligheten i perspektiv." Bra Apropa No. 3: 30-36ff.

——— G. RYLANDER, T. ERIKSSON and A. ASP (1966), Kriminaliteten och samhallet. Stockholm: Aldus/Bonniers.

SZABO, D. (1960) Crime et Villes: Etude Statistique de la Criminalite Rurale en France et en Belgique. Paris: Editions Cujas.

THAM, H. (1978) "Ungdomsbrottsligheten engligt den officiella statistiken." Bra Apropa, No. 3.

Time (1977) "Danger: not enough young at work." May 30: 64-65.

TOBIAS, J. J. (1967) Crime in Industrial Society in the 19th Century. London: B. J. Batsford.

TOBY, J. (1957) "The differential impact of family disorganization." American Sociological Review 22: 505-512.

——— (1967) "Affluence and adolescent crime," pp. 136-137 in LEAA U.S. Task Force Report: Juvenile Delinquency and Youth Crime. Washington, DC: U.S. Govenrment Printing Office.

——— (1974) "The socialization and control of deviant motivation," pp. 85-100 in D. Glaser (ed.) Handbook of Criminology. Chicago: Rand, McNally.

TORNUDD, P. (1971) "The futility of searching for causes of crime," pp. 23-33 in N. Christie (ed.) Scandinavian Studies in Criminology. Oslo: Universitetsforlaget.

United Nations (1958) Urbanization in Asia and the Far East. Proceedings of the Joint U.N./UNESCO Seminar, Bankok, August 8-18, 1956. New York: United Nations — 55.57.V7A.

——— (1966) Report on the Inter-regional Meeting on Research on Criminology: Denmark, Norway, Sweden, 18 July-7 August, 1965. New York: United Nations.

VAZ, E. W. and J. CASPARIS 61971) "A comparative study of youth culture and delinquency: upper class Canadian and Swiss boys." International Journal of Comparative Sociology 12: 1-23.

WEBER, M. (1949) "Social science and social policy," in The Methodology of Social Sciences (E. Shils and H. Finch, trans. and eds.). New York: Free Press.

WEINBERG, S. K. (1964) "Juvenile delinquency in Ghana: a comparative analysis of delinquents and non-delinquents." Journal of Criminal Law, Criminology, and Police Science 55: 471-481.

WEST, D. J. (1969) Present Conduct and Future Delinquency. New York: Internastional Universities Press.

WILSON, H. (1975) "Juvenile delinquency, parental criminality, and social handicap." British Journal of Criminology 15: 241-250.

ZABCZYNSKA, E. (1974) "The follow-up studies of 100 boys charged with theft at the age of 10-11," pp. 128-139 and 216-220 in Polskiej Akademii Nauk. Archiwum Kryminologii. Wroclaw: Zaklad Norodowy im Ossolinskich.

**DELINQUENCY AND
MINORITY STATUS:
A Psychocultural Perspective**

GEORGE DeVOS

A psychocultural approach in anthropology is not simply "comparative sociology." It is my contention that a proper "anthropological" perspective involves concern both with a sociological or social structural analysis of deviancy, whatever the culture, and an analysis of the psychological or attitudinal selectivity of those within a culture who become deviant. In other words, we are not only looking for universals in social conditions related to deviancy; we must also examine the psychological motivations that give rise to what is unsanctioned behavior in a given cultural setting. For purposes of focus I shall not attempt here to examine the widest possible anthropological definitions of deviant behavior, but concern myself specifically with what is considered deviancy in youth. I shall draw most heavily for comparison from my research activities in contemporary Japan and some comparative data gathered in a collaborative effort with Italian social scientists.

Elsewhere (DeVos, 1973:

11-326) I have attempted to summarize historical changes within Japan in social definitions of deviant behavior. For example, I have pointed out that the concept of "delinquency" itself is a fairly modern one, since the Japanese had in their premodern society no concept comparable to our modern concept of adolescence. I subsequently did a survey of the extant anthropological literature on deviancy and found that this concept was generally lacking in illiterate societies. For most premodern societies one went from "childish" behavior, whether it was deviant or not, to "adult" behavior. There was no concept of "delinquency" interposed between that of childish misbehavior on the one hand and criminal behavior on the other. Generally speaking, the age level at which an adult sanctioning system was imposed was far earlier than that found in modern societies. Therefore, one cross-cultural note to be made is that "adolescence" as a traditional stage does not appear in many societies in any form resembling that found in the modern industrial world. The concept "delinquency" is derivative of the concept "adolescence." Hence we must consider the concept "delinquency" itself as a fairly modern one.

In Japan today, delinquent behavior is defined by specialists in the field of corrections much as it is in the United States. There are some differences, but they are of a minor nature. Over the past 18 years I have been reviewing the Japanese literature on delinquency and have noted various changes related to the general trends taking place in Japanese society.[1]

My principal research concerns have been (a) the relationship of social indices of delinquency to urbanization and modernization, (b) selectivity of delinquency-formation within given family interaction patterns, and (c) problems of delinquency related to minority status. Perhaps the easiest way to present some research conclusions and the theoretical contentions derived from them is to begin with the social issues with which I was first concerned during initial contact with Japanese Americans in 1947 in Chicago.

ACHIEVEMENT, CULTURE, AND
PERSONALITY: THE CASE OF
THE JAPANESE-AMERICANS

By 1947, over 17,000 Japanese-Americans had come to the Chicago area after their release from the relocation centers in which they had been interned during World War II. I joined a research team of several social scientists who were interested in problems of adaptation as they might influence Japanese-Americans making their home in Chicago for the first time. Charlotte Babcock was a psychoanalyst working with the Chicago Institute of Psychoanalysis. She began therapeutic interviews with several individuals seeking psychological and psychiatric counseling. William Caudill, Adrian Corcoran, and I were graduate students in anthropology. Setsuko Nishi, Lee Rainwater, and Alan Jacabson were graduate students in sociology. We collaborated using various methods of approach from the perusal of social agency case records, psychotherapeutic procedures, psychological tests, interviews, and community observations. We quickly came to the conclusion that there were almost no visible social maladaptations or personal malajustment related to the ordeal of being interned in the relocation camps during the postwar period. Moreover, as subsequent events confirmed, Japanese-Americans moving into the transitional sections of Chicago which were noted for their high rate of delinquency among adolescents did not, in turn, conform to the expected pattern previously noted for these specific areas studied in the 1930s by Shaw and McKay (1931, 1932). Japanese youths did not become delinquent.

Japanese on the west coast from the early thirties up to the present time manifest a rate of delinquency in police statistics that has hovered about one-eightieth that of the majority population of the state, while Mexican-American and black youths in California have rates that hover between four and six times that of the majority "white" category in California statistics.

I was intrigued by this unusual resistance to delinquent behavior and the very positive attitude evidenced by Japanese youths in regard to education. William Caudill and I began to look for meaningful explanations to help understand why the behavior of Japanese-Americans goes counter to many of the sociological predictions related to the effects of discrimination and minority satus of populations migrating into American urban centers. In the conclusions, I shall return to these findings in examining how cultural background interacts with patterns of social discrimination over several generations.

Subsequently, from 1960-1968, with several Japanese colleagues (principally Keiichi Mizushima and Hiroshi Wagatsuma), I made an examination of family, community, and delinquent behavior in Japan itself. We found that the Japanese are somewhat unique in urban statistics related to delinquency. The crime and delinquency rate in Japan is much lower than those reported for other modern states. The fact that a city such as Tokyo is relatively "safe" can be observed firsthand as confirming the fact that Japanese statistical differences are not simply an artifact of reporting. However, a more careful breakdown of social grouping in Japan demonstrates very quickly that there are some socioeconomic and minority status variables within Japanese society that operate to some degree in a similar fashion to those reported in the United States. Indeed, variables such as broken homes and past records of truancy among what could be defined as lower-class Japanese replicate patterns reported in American studies. And the two large minorities within Japanese society—the former outcastes or "Burakumin" and the Koreans—have very high rates of delinquency among their youth.

This latter finding was determined by a research plan we devised to study the city of Kobe where minorities constitute over seven percent of the population (DeVos, 1973:369-389). Although there were no official statistics available, by using family court records, we were able to determine the delinquency rate of Koreans and Japanese by spotting the residences of those being arraigned in the family court on special maps which contained the known boundaries of the Korean and outcaste ghettos. By this method we were able to determine a delinquency rate among outcastes which was four and a half times that of the majority. These figures confirmed the informal impressions of probation officers and other agencies working with juveniles in the area. It was safe to assume that the rates would be the same if similar studies were applied to the nearby cities of Kyoto, Nara, and Osaka.

Our more intensive study of delinquency was conducted in Tokyo. We picked a ward in Tokyo which, for a number of years previous, had the highest delinquency rate among the 23 wards comprising metropolitan Tokyo. We were interested not simply in the relative incidence of delinquency in this ward but in the selectivity of those who, given similar social, economic, and environmental conditions, became delinquent in contrast with those from the same area and socioeconomic background who manifested no delinquency.

Urban Migration in Cross-Cultural Perspective

During the time of our actual fieldwork (the early 1960s) we noted an interesting general decline in the incidence of delinquency in Japanese cities. We could watch the nature of this decline firsthand in Arakawa ward, a ward that had been showing a very high rate of urban immigration over the past three generations. By utilizing our family case history methods, we were able to reconstruct urbanization patterns and how they influenced with relative success or failure the social integration of the individual and the family within this ward. We were struck with the fact that the general pattern of urbanization into a Japanese city from a rural countryside was, by and large, nontraumatic. Through apprenticeship traditions as well as kin networks, the inmigrating individual readily became part of an already existing social group. There are only very small segments of a Japanese metropolis in which one finds indigent labor and unattached families. While such an area existed on the periphery of Arakawa ward, the relative numbers of immigrants who moved into a slumlike or flophouse-like environment were notably small given the overall rate of movement of people into the urban environment.

We found in our intensive sample of 100 individuals (50 husbands and 50 wives) that roughly half of the total already had some urban background. But only seven of the husbands and three of the wives were born within Arakawa ward itself, and if we went back one generation (which we did in reconstructing their family histories), we found that almost all of the grandparents or stepgrandparents were of rural origin. Search as we might, we found no material to indicate that marital or social malajustment was related to differences between rural and urban background in either generation of the delinquent or nondelinquent segments of our sample. Most of the inmigrating men had come to Tokyo by age 16. The women tended to be slightly older at the time of arrival. The age of inmigration was related to finding vocational training. Of 31 fathers, 17 came to obtain work or for an apprenticeship. The women migrants (14 of 32) came to work as domestics or maids; five to join urban relatives or to be married. It is notable that six mothers in the delinquent sample reported coming to Tokyo specifically to get a job so as to live independently. There were no such cases of seeking an independent livelihood among mothers of the normal control families. We noted throughout that the mothers of the delinquent sample took a more negative or critical attitude about the traditional women's role in regard to both work independence and marital compliance (DeVos and Wagatsuma, 1972).

Generally, the housing of this area would have to be considered slumlike. Tiny rooms housed many people. However, once inside the area, talking with people, seeing how they lived day by day, we found no evidence of what Oscar Lewis has termed the "culture of poverty" (Lewis, 1965). The attitude among these individuals was quite different from what one would find in an American ghetto-slum. This difference in attitude, which was demonstrated not only in the delinquent part of our population but in our nondelinquent controls, shows a general optimism about the future revealed directly in interviews or indirectly in the Thematic Apperception Test.

These findings in Arakawa, which we are in the process of comparing with later findings being obtained from Koreans living in the city of Osaka (results with the same Thematic Apperception Test cards), demonstrate a vast difference in fantasies about social achievement. Material obtained from the Arakawa Japanese reveals high achievement drive. In this respect the material obtained from this poor area was quite similar to materials obtained from middle-class American families (Caudill, 1952) and from a sample of 800 Japanese gathered by members of Nagoya University from two cities and three rural villages as part of a large-scale psychological survey (Muramatsu, 1962).

We shall return to discuss some of the psychological variables later. Suffice it to say here that our observational as well as interview findings about urban inmigration point to the conclusion that the pattern of urban migration into Japanese cities is *not* traumatic. Therefore, one does not find indices of social disruption related to the process of urbanization in Japan. On the contrary, manifest in contemporary Japan is evidence of social disruption in rural communities that have become depopulated due to a decrease in Japanese agriculture. The younger generation of rural folk are now working in factories, leaving farm work to a remaining older segment of the rural population (Sofu, 1976).

The Japanese urbanization experience is very much in accord with the conclusions arrived at by Inkles (Inkles and Smith, 1976). Inkles finds in the six cultures in which he has studied urbanization intensively (Argentina, Chile, Bangladesh, India, Nigeria, and Israel) that urbanization per se leads to no increased psychological or social stress. On the contrary, among the rural migrants working in the urban environment one finds less evidence of psychological tension than among those staying in the rural villages in each setting. These conclusions are similar to those of Edward Bruner (1976), who has done a very detailed anthropological study of the Toba Batak of Sumatra, who have been moving in large numbers from villages to urban centers. Again, Bruner finds that urbanization is not a disruptive experience for the Batak. They settle into communities which are comfortable for them psychologically. These urban settlements afford continuity of traditional cultural practices in family interaction as well as in social regulation. In short, there is no evidence that "anomie" results from urbanization in a number of recent cross-cultural studies of this process. It may be the American urban experience which is fairly unique.

Evidence from Italy, however, seems to run parallel to that reported from the United States. In the northern cities of Italy with a large influx of southern populations, one finds increasingly high delinquency rates among the children of migrants, although crime is generally low among the adult migrants themselves (Klineberg and DeVos, 1973). However, the southern Italian is treated in the north with disparagement as an undesirable minority. He is seen as an inferior alien in the northern urban setting. He does not find supportive community institutions or integrative patterns of interaction which help maintain his self-respect. Already an adult, with fixed modes of thinking, the migrant may not exhibit criminal or deviant behavior. However, there is statistical evidence that the children of migrants manifest delinquent and other deviant responses. In this respect, the migratory situation in the cities of northern Italy and the United States bear comparison. In both instances cities are settings in which the inmigrants are very often entering a situation of degraded minority status *as well as* experiencing social changes related to urbanization. Some southern Italians come from regions of extreme poverty where their concept of government and authority makes them suspicious of and resistant to social agencies. They have in some instances developed patterns of economic survival that involve unsanctioned activity as part of their social environment. Evidence in both instances would indicate that it is the disparaged minority status of the urban dweller and his reaction to it, not the urbanizing process itself, that contributes to social indices of dislocation. We shall return to this discussion later, for, again, the reaction to minority status is somewhat predetermined by social attitudes already developed in the communities of origin.

Our intensive observation of Arakawa ward gave us some impressions of how and why cultural patterns related to general economic conditions influence the patterns of community formation taking place in the ward. Historically, Arakawa ward was a rather marshy area in the unpropitious northeast direction radiating out from the center of premodern Edo. In this area were located the execution grounds of the Tokugawa shogunate, where records indicate that over 200,000 were executed during a 250-year period starting sometime in the 1600s. In premodern Edo this was the area where the endogamous outcaste communities performing ritually impure occupations were placed. Nearby also was the notorious Yoshiwara — the gay quarters where the townsmen of Edo mingled with off-duty samurai and other frequenters seeking the sexual pleasures and gambling taking place there. Crossing the Arakawa River was a bridge that gave exit to the major highway leading north and east. South of this bridge were numerous small teahouses and an area of prostitution for travellers entering or leaving the city. With the early advent of industry during the initial period of Japanese modernization at the turn of the century, this area, as part of the renamed Tokyo, was the first to use the riverbanks for the location of spinning mills and the river for transport. The area also became known from this period as the "wastebasket" of Tokyo: Waste collectors would bring their materials from the other areas of Tokyo to reprocess old cloth or paper. Interestingly enough, this new area was to emulate the pattern of the old artisan and merchant traditions of the inner city. Initially, the merchants and artisans served the castle lords and attendant samurai; therefore, they were located close to the northeast of the central castle area. As Tokyo grew, these merchant areas expanded and incorporated what became Arakawa ward.

In our retrospective life histories we picked up rich material of how these merchant traditions were newly imparted to youths arriving from various rural areas. Urban growth continued with the spread of small house-factories of less than five workers who turned out new products to be sold cheaply outside of Japan. These were cottage industries with working housewives. The population flowing in eagerly picked up the lifestyle of the already existing merchant-artisan traditions. This pattern of city growth is quite different from that taking place to the west of Tokyo, where one finds a pattern radiating out resembling that found in some American cities. To the northeast, however, one still finds a continuing pattern of urban growth resembling more the older European cities in which one also finds a tenacious hold on central city property by merchants or artisans still utilizing the central city area for trade. New arrivals to the city's merchant-artisan areas find property in more distant suburban areas where land remains cheaper. Should there be financial failure of a particular family, these inmigrants would be forced to move out and more successful individuals would attempt to move in closer to the city center. Very often an individual moves into this area as an apprentice, and he may marry into a family and inherit the business. Both formal and informal adoption is relatively frequent despite official emphasis on primogeniture in the Japanese family. The oldest son may not inherit if he is not capable. We found that roughly one-fourth of the heads of households in Arakawa inherit by marrying a daughter. In effect, family interaction patterns quickly set up networks within a growing community in a Japanese city. There is no pattern of the unemployed or underemployed poor moving into the center city as is evidenced in the concentric growth of American cities such as Chicago. Such a pattern, which has been well studied in American sociology, does not appear in any of the contemporary Japanese cities. Moreover, in times of economic recession, individuals could move back to live with rural relatives.

What one observes, therefore, in the relatively poorer merchant-artisan areas of Tokyo is how a Japanese community gradually organizes itself. Communities manifest organization rather than disorganization. The results of city growth are not ghettos from which the more affluent leave for a suburban life; successful settlers, rather than depart, improve their property, building better housing for themselves and seeking to remain in an area in which they have settled. What goes on in communities such as Arakawa differs greatly from what can be observed to occur in lower-class neighborhoods in the United States. In Japan these communities become more and more intertwined in a complexity of occuaptional and voluntary networks. One does not find a relative lack of internal voluntary community structures so evident in American lower-class urban areas. The tendencies to maintain ethnic neighborhoods in the United States in general give way to socioeconomic forces in which the wealthier members of the ethnic community partake of the general pattern of moving out of the central city, whereas American middle-class groups tend to form voluntary networks. These networks are continually weakened by the exigencies of residence changes that occur among the middle class in the United States. Such frequent changes of residence do not occur in Japan. Generally, what is so notably different in comparing Japan with the United States as far as urban living is concerned is the rapidity of mobility found in both middle-class and lower-class Americans. In American neighborhoods there is much less continuous face-to-face contact through most of the life cycle. In Japan one is more apt to die in the area in which one was born.

The overall effects of economic conditions on rates of crime and delinquency in an industrial society are as evident in Japan as they are in the United States. From the close-up perspective that we gained by studying an individual ward we could see how increasing prosperity had an indirect effect on increasing voluntary community activities which led to neighborhood betterment and social involvement with what were perceived to be community problems. In this community we saw how increased prosperity meant less mobility rather than more. What we could see going on was a diminishing overall incidence of local delinquency on the one hand and a rate of increased time devoted to voluntary community involvement on the other. If one looked at the effects of economic conditions as they influence the day-by-day behavior of individuals in Arakawa ward, one could see an increase of family member participation in voluntary organizations. Some of these organizations were directly related to the supervision of problem children and to formal systems of social control, such as the police.

The Japanese police are organized in a manner totally different from their American counterparts. The Korean system in urban districts gives direct responsibility of several blocks of a ward to several officers stationed in a police box (Ames, 1976). These officers by statute are required to make personal contact twice a year with each residence and its members. The policemen are known by name. They know who belongs and who is a stranger to their area. Moreover, the ward has special police units dealing with juveniles in subdistricts. These police are familiar with many of the teachers in the junior high and high schools. There is discussion of students with special problems. There is also the traditional informal surveillance of volunteers who report to the police on the "delinquency-prone" activities of particular juveniles.

The probation department is staffed by professional probation officers who supervise the activities of a select group of local volunteers who act as Hogoshi — volunteer probation officers who take responsibility for two or three youths put in their charge. The volunteers are selected from a group of well-placed individuals of respected social status from the same neighborhood who know well the area in which they live. The rate of recidivism in Japan of those placed on probation in this manner is quite low.

In sum, looking at the intermeshing of formal systems of social control with informal systems operating in Japanese neighborhoods one is struck by the high degree of social communication at both formal and informal levels among professionals and volunteers who create a system of surveillance over youth as well as one another. Domestic privacy is relatively lacking in a Japanese lower-status neighborhood. The lack of transients makes it possible to know a great deal about one's immediate neighbors. The number of voluntary activists binds housewives together. The men are involved in networks organized around occupations.

It is obvious that there are very large differences in cultural patterns between Japan and the United States in urban growth and the internal organization of cities. It is apparent that small Japanese entrepreneurs have survived much better in the Japanese economy than is true for counterparts in the United States. These petty entrepreneurs, when they manage some leisure time, devote some of it to forms of community service. This usually occurs only within middle-class segments of American populations. Since American communities tend to be homogenized by income, one does not find the development of a heterogeneity that one finds in a growing urban Japanese community. In Japan, since the more affluent citizens do not move, they become more available to devote some time to community "betterment." They take more pride in their area, however poor, since they do not plan to leave. Such is not the case in American neighborhoods with high rates of mobility. Moreover, Americans generally seek more leisure activity outside of their immediate neighborhood compared with Japanese.

We studied some of these voluntary organizations, associations, committees, councils, and clubs. Their purposes vary: Some are for social welfare purposes, some for business interaction, and some for recreation. Each ward office in Tokyo annually publishes a directory of such organizations, listing the names and addresses of officials and representatives of each group. These directories can run over 100 pages.

Central to this difference of the Japanese and the American community is the manner in which residential property can or cannot be bought and sold. Japanese cannot, even should they wish to, emulate the extremely high rate of residential turnover one witnesses in American cities. The problems inherent in buying and selling property or changing residence are quite different. The economics of residential change contribute to how people will think about remaining in or changing their neighborhood. The relative occupational heterogeneity of the Japanese neighborhood stems, therefore, both from a social reluctance to change residence and the economic difficulties of doing so.

One does not find occupational or professional segregation to the degree it is found in the United States. However, as we shall discuss below, there are minority ghettos with special problems.

We have also mentioned that there are cultural patterns that determine how people migrate into the city and where they find residence. In brief, the Japanese economic and social patterns combine to make the Japanese neighborhood community heterogeneous in social class and in community commitment. Even in newer communities, residents assume they will become permanent. Everyone living in an area becomes known to others. There is less possibility of anonymity than in the United

States, even in the more prevalent lower-class districts that have some residential turnover.

The overall cultural homogeneity of Japanese society in Tokyo creates residential patterns in which ethnic divergence or minority status are relatively absent. Tokyo lacks the large minority ghettos of Koreans and the Burakumin descendants of the former pariah caste found in the cities of Osaka, Kobe, Kyoto, and Nara. It is in such minority districts that one finds relatively high crime and delinquency rates, as we shall indicate. The general cultural homogeneity and the patterns of low residential mobility within the city tend to integrate rather than alienate city dwellers from one another. Moreover, as we have indicated, the rural-urban movement in Japan generally takes place within shared sets of cultural expectations.

It is the unique cultural pluralism of American cities related to ethnic diversity that creates special difficulties for some ethnic groups, but not others, within the American urban environment. Hence, one finds in American cities not only higher rates of delinquency for specific ethnic groups but differentials in the rate of mental breakdown and other symptoms of social dislocation.

The social networks existing within a Japanese community are part of their cultural tradition. It would be indeed difficult, given not only the economic circumstances of American city life but the continuing problems of ghetto segregation and residential selectivity according to income which occurs in American patterns of urban mobility, to produce the type of informal, voluntary organizations and informal social control that characterize the wards of Japanese cities. The total social pattern of Japanese urban life is sufficiently different from that occurring in contemporary American society to warrant the differences in overall rates of delinquency that contrast the urban environment in the United States as compared with urban Japan.

Family Life and Delinquency in Japan
Turning from community patterns as the influence on overall rates of delinquency to family patterns affords us another op-

portunity to test conclusions arrived at in American research on delinquency. There have been a number of issues raised concerning family interaction and the selective appearance of delinquency in particular children when the community variables are held constant — What can we find out about family patterns in Japan related to delinquency formation?

In our attempts to study family life intensively we carefully matched 50 Japanese families. Through the cooperation of several junior high schools, we eventually selected 31 families each containing a youth 13-15 years of age who had developed some difficulty that had come to the attention of the police. These youths were matched from the same classrooms with 20 youths in whose families there was no known incident of delinquency.[2]

Our major concern was finding out as well as possible why a particular youth became delinquent. We conducted intensive interviews and psychological tests for at least six hours with each parent. By design we selected only families having two available parents (or a stepparent and a parent). If we had not done so, we would have had a good proportion of delinquent youths from broken families — since the Japanese, as reported elsewhere, also manifest a considerable proportion of delinquents coming from broken families. Wagatsuma and I have prepared a large volume noting our research results in detail (DeVos and Wagatsuma, n.d.).

Research on delinquents in Japan has been extensive,[3] and some sociological parallels are readily apparent. Middle-income groups showed a higher incidence of family stability and a lower incidence of delinquency than either higher-income groups or poor families. However, family impoverishment overlaps with other variables such as family instability, neglect of children by working mothers, and the actual living conditions found in particular households. The Japanese studies manifest the same problems of selectivity in sampling in many instances as do American studies. Other results are based on studies of *institutionalized* delinquents as compared with noninstitutionalized delinquents on probation. We find that adjudication of delinquent cases is governed very strongly by availability of an intact

TABLE 6.1 Marital Disruptions and Irregularities Over Two Generations in Arakawa Delinquent and Nondelinquent Sample Families

	NONDELINQUENT (19)						DELINQUENT (31)					
	Parents		Grandparents				Parents		Grandparents			
			Paternal		Maternal				Paternal		Maternal	
	Fa	Mo	FaFa	FaMo	MoFa	MoMo	Fa	Mo	FaFa	FaMo	MoFa	MoMo
Intact families (1 marriage)												
1 generation	14 (74%)		15 (79%)		16 (84%)		13 (42%)		13 (42%)		15 (48%)	
2 generations	8 (44%)						2 (6.5%)					
Broken first marriage												
Death	3	2	0	1	0	3	8	5	6	3	3	1
Divorce/separation	2	3	3	3	3	3	8	11	11	14	10	12
No legal marriage	0	0	1	1	0	0	2	2	1	1	3	3

family and the nature of home conditions which are taken into account when the judge makes a judgment of a case. Such judgments, of course, are not limited to judges, but are taken into account by probation officers and others coming into contact with the youths and their families. The question of broken homes has been studied extensively in the Japanese statistics; some are on large samples and in great detail (Yoshimasu, 1952); Highuchi, 1953. Yoshimasu cited statistical research from which he concluded that homes broken when a child is less than five years old produce a higher incidence of delinquency when the mother is not present. However, homes broken when a child is more than five years old show a higher rate of delinquency when there is no father. Similar results to those of Yoshimasu were reported independently a year later by Higuchi.[4] It was interesting for us in turn to find significant evidence of family disruption in our small delinquent sample. Although we avoided including any delinquent from a presently broken home, when we compared our delinquent subjects with controls, we found considerable evidence of past family disruption in their background. Of the parents of our delinquents, 58 percent had a previous marriage, in contrast to 26 percent among the parents of the nondelinquents. Many of the disruptions were caused by war deaths in both groups. However, there were considerably more disruptions due to divorce or separation in the delinquent sample. We became interested in family disruptions found in the present generation of the parents, and from our interviews we were also able to ascertain that, according to the retrospective reports of parents, there were many more disruptions in the grandparents' generation among the delinquent subjects compared with the nondelinquents. In comparing the grandparent generation and the present generation, only two of the 31 families studied showed no disruption over two generations, contrasted with 44 percent of both parents in the 19 nondelinquent families who had lived in intact families until at least 12 years of age. Our data, therefore, on a small scale would support the contention that a history of family disruption is related to the appearance of delinquency in children even when the present family is technically considered an intact unit (see Table 6.1).

Family Cohesion and
Delinquency Formation

There is general consensus among those studying parental attitudes as related to delinquency formation that among the key factors to be considered are (1) the expression of love within a family, and (2) how parents maintain discipline and supervision in socializing the child as well as how they relate to one another in their marital roles. We were therefore interested in obtaining detailed information about love and affection versus neglect and rejection, as well as possible forms of discord and the types of supervision and discipline employed with children. We interviewed and tested each parent for more than six hours over two or three interviews separately. We also interviewed and tested each subject to gain some consistent or inconsistent impressions of their family lives. We utilized the Glueck's overall criteria (Glueck and Glueck, 1950) of paternal love, maternal love, family cohesion, paternal discipline, and material supervision as five general ordering concepts for our very extensive data. Our case summaries, derived by categorizing our various field notes, run over 150 pages. Scoring our cases according to Glueck criteria, we found glaring differences between our delinquent and nondelinquent samples.

In respect to father's discipline, for example, we concluded that 58 percent of the fathers in our nondelinquent sample showed adequate consistent discipline compared with *none* of the fathers of delinquents. Conversely, 18 out of the 31 fathers of delinquents evidenced withdrawal and/or laxity in their discipline. Only one father of a nondelinquent could be so categorized. In respect to the supervision of mother, only two mothers of the delinquents obtained an optimal rating. Half, or 15, showed definitely unsuitable maternal supervision. Of the mothers of nondelinquents, 18 out of 19 were rated good in this respect.

The ratings of affection or love in nondelinquent fathers in only two instances were unsatisfactory, compared with 16, or

over half, of the delinquents' fathers. No mothers of nondelinquents were rated unsatisfactory in this regard, compared with
19 (63 percent) of the mothers of delinquents who we considered
showed insufficient maternal affection in one way or another.

In respect to family cohesion, no nondelinquent families were
rates as unintegrated or totally lacking in cohesion, whereas we
were constrained to rate 35 percent of the families of delinquents as totally unsatisfactory in this regard. Conversely, 12
families of nondelinquents (or 63 percent) were considered to
show evidence of strong cohesiveness compared with only one
such family among those delinquent children. There was no
question in our minds, therefore, that in spite of the obvious
rigidities entailed in having to rate the families overall either in a
trichotomous or dichotomous classification as used by the
Gluecks, in respect to their criteria we could point up very
significant differences between the families of our delinquent
and nondelinquent subjects. Our results led us to agree very
strongly with those of the conclusions of Bennett (1960), who
conducted an intensive comparison in England of 50 delinquent
and 50 neurotic children.

She considered, in general, that broken homes were related to
personal instability in parents rather than having a direct causal
relationship to delinquency. In her English sample, Bennett
found a great deal of mutual incompatibility as well as immaturity and instability in one or both parents. In addition to
the general findings postively relating unstable and discordant
homes and delinquency in England, she found antisocial
tendencies latent if not manifest in a number of parents of delinquents in contrast with the social attitudes of the neurotic
children's parents.

We also agreed with her, when looking at a psychological
dimension, that the category "delinquent" is a heterogeneous
one rather than one which points to any specific personality patterns. Again, Bennett's results stressed inconsistency in
discipline, which we found true for our Japanese delinquent
sample. We would have to state, therefore, that despite totally
different cultural traditions, our findings in Japan are conso-
nant with intensive family studies such as that conducted by

Bennett. (We report similar results with the somewhat less intensive Italian family studies below). Despite cultural variations, when one has intensive enough materials, one can readily assess the presence or absence of discord and affection as well as consistencies, inconsistencies, or inadequacies in parental discipline and supervision.

In comparing a number of the variables that we could safely assess from our data, we found one specific Japanese pattern worth noting: consistent evidence that the sibling position of parents is apparently related to the later appearance of delinquency in a child. In Japan it is the common observation that eldest sons are indulged more than other children in the family. It has been said often that in the pattern of urban inmigration in Japan it is more often the second sons and daughters of rural families who go into the city. We were therefore interested in the relationship of sibling position to possible manifestations of delinquency, since one would presume the possibility of relative degrees of neglect or rejection related to young sibling positions in Japanese families. We examined carefully the sibling position of both parents and the children of our sample and found some differences which reached significance even given our small numbers. There was a lower average number of children (2.9 percent) in the families of our normal controls, compared with the delinquent groups (3.75 percent). In the sibling position of the delinquent sample we found the position of middle or second son overrepresented. Eleven (32 percent) of our delinquent subjects were in this position compared with one out of 19 of our nondelinquent subjects. In the nondelinquent sample the subjects tended to be either the oldest child or oldest or youngest son in contrast to the delinquent subjects.

Going back to the parents' generation to examine their sibling positions, we found that half of the fathers of our nondelinquent subjects were first sons, compared with one-quarter of the fathers of delinquents. Fifteen percent of the fathers of nondelinquents were second sons, compared with 60 percent of fathers of delinquents. Finally, among the fathers of nondelinquent children, fathers who were fourth sons or younger sons of even larger families occurred in 25 percent of cases compared with only six percent of fathers of delinquents. This would appear to be a highly significant trend.

Turning to mothers, we found also some significant differences. First and second daughters were slightly less represented among the mothers of delinquents, whereas 11 out of 31 mothers of delinquents in our sample are third of later-born daughters in their own families. This comprises over 35 percent of the mothers or stepmothers of delinquents compared with only 10 percent of the mothers of the nondelinquent sample. Figures suggest, perhaps, that the position of relative neglect due to sibling position found in the parents of the delinquent subjects may contribute to the relative neglect of one or more of their own children, a sense of resentment over deferential treatment toward one's own children. Given other convergent experiences, resentment over unequal treatment may lead to the appearance of delinquency in a specific child.

Role Behavior and Marital Dissatisfaction

A necessary but sometimes neglected consideration in studies of parental interaction and parental behavior toward children is the effect of social status and internalized attitudes about how one should fulfill one's social role. This consideration is extremely important in looking at family behavior in Japanese culture.

In examining the Japanese tradition one is made aware of how the father is very often respected for his social role position rather than for himself as an individual. Later, when we discuss minority status in Japan, we will return to this point to consider the effect of being a minority member on the status of the father in Japanese culture. In the past, the father's position was considered unassailable within the family. This attitude of deference and respect would prevail even should the father, considered from a personality standpoint, be insufficient in the requirements of his role. Formal behavior in the family was defined by roles: The growing male child would witness what to expect in deference to a "father." Upon reaching maturity, he could expect to be afforded similar recognition no matter what he felt subjectively about his own inefficiencies. However, in our Arakawa sample we judged a number of cases among our delinquent sample in which a tradition of disparagement directed toward parental figures was evident in retrospective accounts of relationship occurring within the grandparents' generation. In the perception of the mothers of delinquents, for example, we found a number of instances where their own fathers often seemed equated with their present husbands and all were judged as inadequate or "weak." Some would state directly that in their family experiences males generally tended to be "weak."

Such husbands tended to be pictured as isolates, spending much time away from the family and in a number of instances manifesting patterns of problem drinking. There were a few reports of periodic outbursts on the part of the men, sometimes resulting in physical violence directed against the wife or child. Such a pattern is not infrequently reported for certain American ethnic groups, especially in lower-class settings where drinking is part of a tradition brought from Europe. Characteristically, in these groups the social status of the father in terms of the mother's judgment manifests antagonism and/or disparagement. (We shall note later how this relates to the position of the Korean father in Japan.)

Looking at majority Japanese, even those of lower-class status, one notes that there is a strong tradition to uphold the dominant status of the father. We found in our particular sample that when this status was not maintained by women in their formal attitude there would more likely be the appearance of delinquency in a child. One must note here that these are sometimes subtle judgments to make; but when one examines behavior in a Japanese family one notes very quickly how formal differences in relationships are taken seriously or whether by peculiar inflections or by use of slightly improper language (too high or too low a level of politeness) the status of the individual can be disparaged. Our taped transcriptions were very helpful in this regard. Such subtle disparagement was also noticeable in the language used to depict parental or authority figures in the Thematic Apperception Test stories obtained from all three members of each family.

The breakdown of status and role maintenance noticed in some of our Arakawa families may not simply be a new phenomenon. However, with increase in social mobility, the traditional definitions that a bride should support the occupational role of the father (be it ever so lowly), may come eventually, in Japan as well, to find less social support than was true in the past. Where occupational role is considered hereditary, there tends to be less conflict in respect to social status. The bride brought in is considered appropriate to the status of the father. In contrast, in the ideology of mobility current in American families, there is no comparable traditional position protecting a male's status. The only guide for perception of male adequacy available to women is the highly visible success pattern of middle-class achievement. We will discuss this point more later on.

Being aware of the strong emphasis on role behavior in a traditional Japanese family, we were somewhat surprised by the readiness of Japanese women in our sample to express rather direct dissatisfaction with their husbands and their marriages. Such expressions of dissatisfaction were not limited to the mothers of delinquent subjects, but the degree and the strength of the expressed dissatisfaction was much more severe in these women. We believe that some of this dissatisfaction was related to the fact that all of these women find themselves in a relatively low status within Japanese society, married in many instances to husbands who had, by the time of our interview, experienced some form of occupational failure.

One of the questions we asked of each of our 50 husbands and wives was: "Would you or would you not again marry your present spouse if you were to repeat your life over?" We probed further into the reasons either positive or negative for expressing attitudes about the marital partner. We obtained fairly detailed descriptions of family life by seeking out illustrative materials from our subjects. As a result of these interviews we attempted a classification of each husband and wife according to overall estimated degrees of marital dissatisfaction or satisfaction. In general, in all of our groups, husbands were either more guarded or tended to express mild satisfaction with their spouses, whereas wives tended to be more frank and open and more expressive of difficulties. The parents of nondelinquents were generally more positive in tone than those of delinquents. In the delinquent sample, however, we could clearly rate only five mothers as satisfied as opposed to 23 clearly dissatisfied with their marriage. We thereupon examined the differences between those married only once as compared with remarriages. Out of our 50 couples, 20 were remarried. There were five remarriages among the parents of normals and 15 remarriages among the parents of delinquents. We noted a general tendency for less satisfaction on the part of both spouses in a remarriage situation; it is particularly apparent in the wives. One is struck with the fact that, although these families are officially intact, the manifest attitudinal evidence directly suggests a relative lack of cohesiveness in the families of delinquent subjects.

In attempting to gain a two-generational picture we applied the best possible rating scale to the attitudes held of each spouse toward his or her own parents. In many respects this evidence was comparatively fragmentary, and some of our ratings may be of questionable validity. However, we present our findings because they are in line with our other results. The attitudes of the nondelinquent control families toward their own parents were generally more positive than those of the families of delinquents. The husbands in the nondelinquent control families in 10 out of 19 instances gave generally positive descriptions of their own fathers, compared with three who were generally negative. In the remaining six cases the statements were either so bland or so ambiguous that we could make no determination. These husbands rated 11 of their mothers definitely positive and three negatively. The mothers in these families rated their own fathers positively in 10 cases and negatively in two. Their mothers were rated positively in 13 out of 19 instances, negatively in five. Combined, the ratings were approximately three times as many in a positive direction as in a negative direction in the nondelinquents. This contrasted with the fact that the fathers in the delinquent families rated their own fathers positively only in 10 cases, negatively in 14. Of those who had definite ratings for mothers, they rated 11 mothers positively as compared with 13 mothers rated negatively. The wives in the delinquent sample were even harsher in their ratings: They rated their fathers positively only six out of the 31 cases and definitely negative in 15 instances. Their mothers were rated positively in only nine instances and definitely negative in 17 instances.

We considered ourselves fortunate, in that those working with us doing the interviews were able to reach levels of rapport which allowed us to gain such ratings. We must stress the fact that these interviews were conducted on three or four occasions in each instance by professionally trained psychologists which permitted a continuity and intensity that is seldom reported in interview material concerning the family members of delinquents in this country. It is due to the generally adequate training of Japanese professional personnel that results in this nature could be obtained.

FAMILY PROBLEMS AND DELINQUENCY IN ITALY

We have indicated that the statistics of delinquency in Italy suggest a disproportionate number of young delinquents coming from families of southern migrants to the northern industrial cities. We were able to obtain a series of matched case histories of families with delinquents in the cities of Genoa and Cagliari in Sardinia.[5] We were interested in obtaining an intensive picture of family interrelationships, and we sought to gain sufficient materials to be scored for the Glueck criteria in a fashion comparable to that obtained from the Japanese families in our previous intensive study.

In Cagliari we obtained 40 family case histories — 20 with delinquent subjects and 20 controls from the same living area. Similarly, in Genoa Professor Bandini conducted intensive interviews with 25 families with delinquents and a control group of 15 families. Unfortunately, one of the cases was incomplete in this latter group and was discarded. Thus, we had for comparison with our Japanese materials a series of 45 delinquent subjects and their families and 34 controls.

Migration, Occupation, and Delinquency

We matched our cases as well as possible from the same living areas. However, in comparing the occupational backgrounds of the fathers, we found some minor discrepancies. These were matched in the non-delinquent sample by two boys from professional families. In the poorer neighborhoods where these cases were obtained we also picked up some nondelinquent families who were on the commercial, shopkeeper, or technically trained level. The most significant difference that appeared with respect to occupational background, however, was that among the delinquent experimental group there were 23 fathers who could be classified as unskilled compared with only five in the nondelinquent controls. Conversely, in the skilled level of occupation we found only one delinquent father compared with 10 from the nondelinquent control sample. There were no appreciable differences in those employed, ill, or retired between the two samples. As for place of origin, the Cagliari samples were, for the most part, born within the city of Cagliari — there were only nine who came from the rural mountainous areas. Conversely, both the delinquent and nondelinquent Genoese samples were predominantly individuals who had come up from southern Italy. The one fact that seems to stand out in our data is that a preponderance of fathers of delinquents are found in the unskilled worker category regardless of origin. In the case of Cagliari, 11 out of 12 were city-born. In the case of Genoa, nine out of 11 came from southern Italy. One could tender the generalization that the fathers who migrated either to the city in Sardinia or from southern Italy into Genoa who did relatively well as far as occupation is concerned would tend not to have a delinquent son. Conversely, a father who remains unskilled or unemployed may come to have problems with a son (see Table 6.2). It may not be simply an economic problem, however, but some interaction with personal traits, as we discover when we look at personal problems within these families.

TABLE 6.2 Occupational Background and Place of Birth of Italian Family Samples

	Origin	Families with Non-delinquent Son Cagliari	Genoa	Families with Delinquent Son Cagliari	Genoa	Nondelinquent	Delinquent
	N	20	14	20	25	34	45
1 Professional, Engineer, Teachers	Outside City	1	0	1	1	2	3
	City	1	0	0	1		
2 Commercial-Shopkeeper	Outside City	1	1	0	0	3	0
	City	1	0	0	0		
3 Technically Trained	Outside City	0	0	0	0	1	0
	City	1	0	0	0		
4 Skilled, e.g., blacksmith, mason, mechanic, bricklayer	Outside City	1	3	0	1	10	1
	City	4	2	0	0		
5 Semi-skilled, e.g., jailguard, truckdriver, shipworker	Outside City	1	3	2	2	8	10
	City	4	0	2	4		
6 Unskilled, e.g., janitor, daily laborer, fisherman, peddler	Outside City	0	3	1	9	5	23
	City	2	0	11	2		
7 Unemployed, ill, or retired	Outside City	1	2	1	5	6	8
	City	3	0	2	0		
	Rural or outside	5	12*	4	18**	17	22
	City born	15	2	15	7	17	23

Place of birth: *Sardinia (2), Naples (2), Calabria (3), Sicily (3), other (2).
**Sardinia (5), Naples (4), Calabria (4), Sicily (3), other (2).

Personal Problems and Delinquency

We noted systematically the abuse of alcohol, mention of sexual irregularities, violent behavior, mental or physical illness in either parent, and a history of some separation from family on the part of the child before the age of 11.

We paid attention to problems of physical illness, since we assumed that they could be both economically and interpersonally disruptive for a family. We must note that parents in the Sardinian families seemed much more prone to some form of physical illness than what was reported for the Genoese: 16 out of 40 of the fathers and 13 out of the 40 mothers in Sardinia had some form of physical problem — in total, 18 parents of delinquent sons compared with 11 parents of nondelinquents. In Genoa, the health level seemed much better, but again, more instances of physical illness appear in the parents of delinquents than in nondelinquents. These physical problems in many families are compounded by behavioral problems (mental illness is included in this category).

Mental problems were mentioned in four fathers in the nondelinquent group and nine mothers in the delinquent group. Three of the four fathers in the nondelinquent group were described as having episodes of depression, another as having had a "nervous breakdown, but now okay." Among the mothers, one was described as being schizophrenic, two as being mentally disturbed or having mental illness, two as neurotic, three as depressed, and one as having attempted suicide. These results suggest that mental problems such as depression in fathers are not related to the appearance of delinquency in a son. (Note that such a problem does not tend toward "acting out" behavior, but to forms of withdrawal). Conversely, mental problems in a mother selectively appear in the delinquent sample. Mental illness probably interferes more with the expected closeness of a mother in the Italian cultural setting; in addition, it makes proper day-by-day supervision of a child more problematical.

Violent behavior or physical abuse was mentioned in the case of 13 fathers, 12 of them in the delinquent sample. Alcohol abuse was mentioned in eight fathers and two mothers in all in-

TABLE 6.3 Personal Problems in Italian Families

	Sardinian Families				Genoese Families				Totals					
	Nondelinquent		Delinquent		Nondelinquent		Delinquent		Nondelinquent			Delinquent		
	Fa	Mo	Fa	Mo	Fa	Mo	Fa	Mo	Fa	Mo	Tot	Fa	Mo	Tot
Mental Problems	2*	0	0	4+	2**	0	0	5++	4	0	4	0	9	9
Alcohol Abuse	0	0	3	2	0	0	5	0	0	0	0	8	2	10°°
Violent Behavior	0	0	6	0	1	0	6	0	1	0	1	12	0	12°
Sexual Irregularities	0	0	0	2	0	0	0	0	0	0	0	0	2	2
Physical illness	6	5	10	8	2	0	5	2	8	5	13	15	10	25
Total — Physical and behavioral	8	5	14	15	5	0	11	6	13	5	18	25	21	46

	Sardinian Families		Genoese Families		Totals	
	Nondelinquent (Tot)	Delinquent (Tot)	Nondelinquent (Tot)	Delinquent (Tot)	Nondelinquent (Tot)	Delinquent (Tot)
Problem in one or another parent	11	20	5	15	16	35
Son separated for at least several months before age 11	1	10	1	7	2	17
Families with no problems	8	0	8	8	16	8

*Occupation of fathers with Depression — Skilled (2), unskilled (1).
**Occupation of fathers with "Nervous Breakdown" — unskilled (1).
+Mothers mental illness — Neurotic (2), Depressed (1), "Mentally disturbed" (1).
++Mothers mental illness — Attempted suicide (1), Depressed (2), "Mental illness" (1), "schizophrenia" (1).
°Occupation of fathers with violent behavior — Professional (1), semi-skilled (1), unskilled (7), unemployed (4).
°°Occupation of fathers with alcohol abuse — Professional, semi-skilled, unskilled (6), unemployed (3).

stances in the delinquent sample. Sexual irregularities were mentioned only in two cases. We may not presume, therefore, that it was absent in other families, but simply that our interviewers perhaps found it more difficult to elicit material of this nature. One of the cases involved adultery and divorce and the other a history of prior prostitution in a mother of the Sardinian sample that remained a source of quarreling between parents.

In Table 6.3 I attempt to summarize the number of families showing a parent with one of the above-mentioned behavioral problems. The results are highly suggestive. In the Sardinian delinquent sample, eight fathers and eight mothers out of 20 manifested one of the above problems; in the Genoese sample, eight fathers and five mothers out of 25. In the nondelinquent controls only two fathers and no mothers out of the 20 families manifested one of the above problems, and only three fathers and no mothers out of 14 in the Genoese sample. In addition, the large majority of fathers displaying problem behavior were classified as unskilled or unemployed. Violent behavior on the part of the father in 11 out of 13 instances was by men so classified. Alcohol abuse in 10 out of 11 instances was reported for individuals in the unskilled or unemployed categories.

When we add up the appearance or absence of physical or behavioral problems among the parents of delinquents we find a very high proportion showing one or another form of complaint.

To summarize from both samples, alcohol abuse and/or violent behavior appeared significantly in the fathers of delinquents and mental illness in the mothers of delinquents. Both parents showed a tendency toward more physical illness in the delinquent sample.

What was most crucial of all our ratings was how these special problems influenced cohesion, supervision, and discipline within these families.

Interaction Patterns:
Affection, Family Cohesion,
and Child Rearing

Table 6.3 also displays another type of problem related to

family cohesion — the physical separation of the subject during a certain period of childhood. We found that in the nondelinquent subjects there were only two separations of more than two months reported for sons in the nondelinquent samples, compared with 17 in the delinquent families. There were 10 out of 20 instances in the Sardinian sample and seven out of 25 in the Genoese. The case material suggests that physical separation in childhood may be related indirectly to expressions of love and family cohesion. Separations from the family related rather specifically to some form of negative social attitudes held by a son.

The differences in family interpersonal attitudes and behavior between the delinquent and nondelinquent samples were graphically apparent when the families were scored formally in accordance with the five Glueck criteria of discipline by father, supervision by mother, affection of father, affection by mother, and general family cohesion. As in the case of the Japanese, the results were highly significant. Only two out of 20 of the Sardinian fathers and two out of 25 of the Genoese fathers could be rated as manifesting suitable discipline toward their sons. A total of 23 in both samples were rated either overly strict or erratic, in comparison with only three of the nondelinquent fathers so rated.[6]

Only nine out of 45 delinquent mothers were rated as showing suitable supervision, compared with 20 ranked as unsuitable. Ratings of affection of father and mother indicated far more negative attitudes on the parts of fathers than of mothers, since 28 fathers of delinquents were rated as basically negative compared with five fathers of nondelinquents, and the affection of mother was rated as basically negative in 17 cases as compared with no cases in the nondelinquent sample. The discrepancy between fathers and mothers in a negative direction as far as affection is concerned is more noticeable in the Italian family than in the Japanese. In fact, in the Japanese ratings 15 out of 31 fathers were rated as basically positive in their attitude towards their sons in comparison with only six out of 45 among the fathers of Italian delinquents.

In rating family cohesion, our ratings of noncohesion occurred in 31 out of 45 of the delinquent families compared with only one of the nondelinquent families. This compared with 11 out of 31 families in Japan rates negatively among the families with a delinquent. There are no notable differences between Sardinian and Genoese families, with the possible exception that the affection of the mother was more negatively rated in the Sardinian sample compared with the Genoese.

These results are graphic and impressive. In going through the individual cases we were struck with how the interpersonal relationships of the family were a very telling differentiator. Whatever the economic circumstances or other forms of difficulty encountered by these families, where there was strong family cohesion one would tend to find expressions of affection toward the children and more proper forms of discipline and supervision. In other words, family cohesion is perhaps the most telling criterion related to the selective appearance of delinquency in the families considered. Granted that these families in many instances live in extremely poor housing and have encountered great financial hardships periodically; when an individual finds sufficient capacity to draw strength from his family relationship, he will not tend to partake of negative social attitudes or develop hostile attitudes, nor will he be as likely to develop deviant behavior to the extent that eventually he becomes ajudicated for it.

We tried to rate for some sensitivity of social discrimination in the Italian materials. However, either the topic was a difficult one to elicit or we could not gain sufficient rapport with individuals to have much of this material presented in our cases. We did notice some tendency for families of delinquents to complain more about experiences of discrimination, but the results were so inconclusive that they do not bear presentation. We will return to the topic of minority status in the Italians in the general discussion following the presentation of our more intensive materials from Japan.

MINORITY STATUS AND
DEVIANCY IN JAPAN

Having found points of comparison in family interaction patterns and parents' relationships with delinquent sons in Italy and Japan, let us return to the issue of minority status itself.

In Japan there are two major minority groups: the Burakumin, who comprise, according to various estimates, over two million or about two percent of the Japanese population, and the Korean minority, who are inmigrants from Korea to Japan of three generations past. At present, there are estimated to be about 750,000 Koreans, including those whose status in Japan is illegal and unregistered. The Burakumin compose a stable population that has lived in various ghettos, both rural and urban, for a number of generations. The Koreans, on the other hand, have been moved around both before and during Japan's war effort against the United States. Those presently remaining in Japan are the remnants of the groups that totaled close to three and one-half million by the end of World War II; for the most part, they speak no Korean. Three-quarters of them were born in Japan of inmigrant parents or grandparents. Although they remained classified as Koreans, they are as acculturated to Japanese culture as would be any second- or third-generation Americans from Europe or Asia.

In both cases these minority groups face serious discrimination within present-day Japanese society. They manifest social indices that can be seen as indirectly related to their minority status. Among these indices are higher rates of family instability, relatively poor performance in schools, higher rates of alcoholism, and what we are concerning ourselves with here — higher rates of delinquency. As we have mentioned, the evidence indicates a delinquency rate among the former outcastes of at least four times that of the majority population and a rate among Korean youth which seems to be somewhere around seven times that of majority Japanese youth. By examining these two groups we can assess to some degree the difference between individuals who are of obvious foreign extraction compared with indigenous Japanese who are the inheritors of caste disparagement. Our in-depth research reveals that similar social processes are working in both cases, although their legal status is quite different in each instance. The Burakumin are now accorded full civil rights. There are presently city programs to provide better public housing. In effect, the Japanese government has taken responsibility for their social plight. This is not true in the case of the Koreans.

Let us sketch in some of the findings of our previous research on the Burakumin and the results of our present ongoing study of the status problems of the contemporary Korean minority. It is difficult to obtain any meaningful statistics in either case. What we shall be doing is reporting a more qualitative, intensive study of their situation. We must note here that our contact with the Korean minority is more recent than the material on which I report taken from our previous studies of Buraku deviancy.[7]

Social Alienation and Burakumin Status

The caste status of the Japanese pariah caste had been firmly fixed by the Tokugawa shogunate. Four years after its overthrow in 1872, the new modernizing Japanese government under the Emperor Meiji passed an emancipation law declaring the "Eta" caste abolished. This official document did nothing to change the social attitudes. Most Japanese considered outcastes literally "a special breed" of people of alien origin. Up until World War II there were even periodic unsuccessful attempts by physical anthropologists to find measurable differences. The conviction remained that the inhabitants of urban outcaste ghettoes and "special" rural villages were somehow inferior aliens — not proper Japanese. Today there are no longer attempts to maintain such opinions openly. There is some general recognition by more educated Japanese that the development of caste in Japanese society was based on attitudes of ritual impurity, not on differences of racial origin. But, as we well documented, the psychological and social consequences of racism were evident in their effects on *Japan's Invisible Race* (DeVos and Wagatsuma, 1966). The title of our book was used ironically, to indicate that actual differences in racial or cultural origin are not necessary to afflict growing children with the negative psychological and social effects of racism.

We reported in detail the extant material on the educational deficiencies of Buraku children, some research on truancy and absenteeism, and our own attempt to determine a rate of delinquency among the Buraku youth. We also reported on attitudes toward health and welfare authorities and the type of antagonism directed toward social agencies by members of outcaste ghettos. To summarize, we found that wherever there were studies made comparing the IQs on either individual or group tests conducted in public schools, Buraku children showed up relatively poorly. In some of these studies the average IQs reported were in greater contrast than similar studies reporting differences between majority white and black children in the United States. We cited such evidence as a good example of the early effects of racism on the self-concepts of young children. We further contended that there is an interactive relationship between a social self-concept and cognitive development. Our major contention was that one must look at the effects of negative social attitudes over several generations to document their effect in particular social situations.

In other chapters of our book we gave brief case histories illustrating the self-hatred which was internalized within some Buraku individuals. We attempted to document how these attitudes are passed on from one generation to the next within the Buraku. The attitudes of social depreciation initiated in the dominant majority, directed either toward oneself or to other members of one's family. Mutual disparagement was one of the major problems found in the Buraku ghetto. Some militant groups aware of this problem were struggling at the time of our study with how to develop self-respect. Militant leaders were attempting to mobilize the Buraku communities in political and social activities which would lead to more affirmative self-images.

Attitudes of self-defeat and defensive antagonism continue to make for differences in relative performance on the nationwide examinations which direct students toward higher education, toward vocational schools, or, early on, into work of a relatively unskilled nature. There is, however, increasing community recognition that militant self-help is necessary. During a recent visit to Japan I was told of the following incident by a militant leader of one of the major Buraku communities in Osaka: Fourteen youths were due in six weeks to take the examination for preparatory middle school. It was obvious that these boys and girls were ill-prepared and were going to fail the examination. Mr Yamamoto decided to try something radical. These youths were housed together in a community house and special tutors were brought in. For six weeks they were not permitted to leave the building. Food was brought to them by their mothers. They were drilled by teachers morning, noon, and evening. They cried. They were angry, but to no avail. They were forced to go through the ordeal of preparation for the examination. It was a very trying experience for them. All 14 passed the examination. The follow-up has been startling. One of these youths has gone on to medical school, another has become a lawyer. Two have gone into nursing.

This story was told to me with great pride. There is enthusiasm and a sense of purpose about the future. One senses in communities such as those I visited in Osaka vital concern with community betterment coming from within the community itself. The youths in the community are not just defending themselves from the outside. They are part of community revitalization, spurred on by the optimism of local leaders who carry on with a sense of determination and dedication.

I have seen no objective test measurement on members of this community, but I would judge that, were test results available, we would not find — as we found in one of the previous assessments — that over a third of the children were graded below 76 in IQ (DeVos and Wagatsuma, 1966:261). This is not to say that the problems with truancy, absenteeism, and delinquency have been eliminated in Buraku communities. The rates problably remain higher than those for majority Japanese. Some communities, however, have become involved intensively in changing this pattern.

In earlier studies dropout rates were recorded during the

obligatory education period of 23 percent among Buraku children compared with three percent among non-Buraku children in the same schools. We found not only widespread difficulties in education in the 1960s, but that, as might be anticipated, the type of delinquency itself and the amount of recidivism was greater in children from Buraku areas (DeVos and Wagatsuma, 1966:263). In our study in Kobe we found that in a sample of delinquents among Buraku youth there was a high rate of threat, intimidation, and extortion. In a number of cases of threat and extortion, the age of the delinquent boy was much lower than the age of the individuals threatened. It was not unusual to find a weaponless boy 15 years old threatening a group of two or three older boys. In some cases the boy would simply tell the other children that he was from a feared Buraku. He thus evoked fear in the majority children and by doing so could obtain from them either money or goods on the basis of simple intimidation.

We found that the rate of recidivism was 29 percent among majority children compared with 41 percent among residents of the Buraku ghettos. When we examined the reported delicts, we found almost none occurring within the Buraku area itself. It was widely agreed among our informants that violence and other forms of antisocial behavior rarely took place within outcaste communities, although the children will be verbally aggressive toward one another. Physical aggression within the Buraku itself is usually stopped by an interceding adult.

Should any child be accused of delinquent behavior, Buraku people in the early 1960s would support the child rather than the outside authority. It was more important that the children obey their parents than show allegiance to the majority society. In court cases, obedience was cited by the parents as a mitigating factor. As elsewhere, children in the Buraku were put on probation under the supervision of voluntary probation officers within their own communities. In most instances it is interesting to note that the child had manifested no delinquent acts within the community itself. The recidivism rate was higher among Buraku youths because of acts committed on the outside.

As in minority communities in the United States, the Buraku

community is not supportive of court decisions to place a child in a correctional institution. Hostile protests have been staged at court buildings over some decisions. Occasionally such appeals are successful: a youth is put on probation and compelled to remain in the outcaste community.

We reported in our earlier work (DeVos and Wagatsuma, 1966:268) how public buildings housing prefectural offices, police, or courts were periodically the focus of protest or subject to acts of hostility by members of Buraku communities. There were often scenes of protest about what was considered to be unfair treatment.

A career in professional crime has been the deliberate choice of some Buraku youths. If a boy was successful in joining a professional criminal gang or "Yakuza" group, his outcaste background would be discretely forgotten because professional criminals do not scrutinize their associates' origins. Buraku youths feel ready for cirminal activity and can, by joining a criminal group, avoid facing the types of discrimination that still occur in regular occupations. In a similar manner, although it is imposible to document the relative numbers involved, Buraku women frequently become prostitutes as a way to "pass" and remove themselves from the Buraku community and its ghetto life.

A major problem common to minority groups in the sense of devious hostility indirectly expressed toward agencies and authorities coming from the outside to "help" them. Japanese Buraku communities developed a long tradition of handling "outsiders." Not only did they develop a defensive attitude toward dominant groups, but they were likely to develop ways of expressing ambivalent attitudes of dependency toward the economically dominant majority group members. The dependent feelings toward the majority group were expressed by devious ways of "taking." These allowed individuals to maintain self-respect, since they would not feel completely helpless vis-à-vis the outside. It is not surprising, therefore, that individuals from the minority groups who had genuine intentions to help were sometimes angered when they discovered various forms of cheating or what would be called in American society "ripping off" on agency or a person. These actions confirmed underlying prejudice concerning a "worthless nature" of individuals who would not appreciate being helped through the efforts of a benevolent government.

It is not surprising that Burakumin developed certain expectations of economic assistance from the majority society. They tended to see it as a right that went with their minority status. Evidence from our study in the 1960s of the Buraku communities suggested to us direct functional parallels between deviant trends in traditionally disparaged minority groups in the United States and Japan. An aggravated delinquency rate is but one symptom of a total situation influencing the internalization of social values. However, this internalization pattern in minority groups is influenced not only by the external pressures of discrimination but also by the nature of response of minority families and the community generally. Comparing our impressions of 15 years ago with the present situation, we would say that the mobilization of political action and the development of militant leadership within some communities have been positive forces. Although we have no statistics to demonstrate our impressions, we could indicate that the situation that we perceived in the past has been alleviated somewhat and energies refocused toward betterment of community and family life.

The ameliorative effects of the new public housing now provided by the government are not simply due to the provision of funds for new housing, but to the militancy and mobilization of efforts which direct energy into more focused social activities involving all age levels of the community. This is not to say that the situation in outcaste ghettos does not remain serious. Too large a proportion of Buraku youth continues to be debilitated both psychologically and socially by minority status and its influence on family life within the ghetto.

Koreans in Japan — An Ex-Colonial Minority

The present minority status of Koreans in Japan is due to historical circumstances different from those of the Burakumin at the turn of the century. The modernizing Japanese self-consciously modeled themselves on the economically, militarily, and socially dominant European colonial powers. They too, sought imperial expansion by taking over what they perceived a "less developed" sphere of influence. Their modernized military readily defeated the Chinese and, later, the Russians. By 1910 they had officially annexed the kingdom of Korea, a backward, Confucianist state which had been for some time a satellite of the Manchu dynasty of China. The country was governed by the Yanban — a group of hereditary nobility whose members spent most of their time in the capital, periodically going to the provinces as administrators but having no identity with the people they were governing. The large majority of Koreans were destitute agriculturalists whose level of literacy was low. The youth of the elite Koreans were aware that modernization was necessary; some of them hoped that Japan would come to their assistance. Instead, they were colonized and treated with condescension and disparagement.

The Japanese colonial administration constituted about 3.5 percent of the Korean population. They assumed most of the administrative positions in the colonial government. Japanese merchants dominated the Korean economy, and colonial administrators put through a land reform program whose ultimate result was to divest many landowners of their tiny holdings. The elite Koreans began to send their children to Japan for advanced education. Educated Koreans were aware of the end of World War I and the principle of self-determination advocated by Wilson, leading to the formation of independent states for the national minorities of eastern Europe. They, too, sought independence from Japan, but their activities were brutally suppressed by the Japanese. Some of the youthful Koreans joined leftist political movements that sprang up in Japan after the Russian Revolution.

For the most part, however, Koreans were uneducated and unconcerned with international politics. An increasing number of unskilled Koreans began to seek labor opportunities in the main Japanese islands. The Korean migrants were subjected to overt prejudice on the part of the Japanese. Their comportment and their food habits were disturbing to the Japanese, who were used to self-control and deference on the part of subordinates.

The more open, emotionally expressive Koreans were considered distasteful by many Japanese.

In a forthcoming book, Changsoo Lee and I describe in detail the history of the social conflict and animosity that characterize minority Korean relationships in Japan (Lee and DeVos, in press). Perhaps the most dramatic episode of the colonial period took place in 1923 when over 6,000 Koreans were killed in a hysterical aftermath to the Tokyo earthquake. Unfounded rumors had spread that Koreans were planning to overthrow the emperor and that they were running wild, looting the damaged, burning city. As a consequence, young women, children, and men were killed indiscriminately both by Japanese troops and by ordinary civilians.

After 1939 the Japanese forcefully brought in many more Korean laborers to replace Japanese who had been drafted into the armed forces. By 1945 there were over 3.5 million Koreans in the Japanese main islands — most working in unskilled capacities in factories and mines. After the war the vast majority of Koreans repatriated either to North or South Korea. A few hundred thousand Koreans were naturalized, but there remain today close to 700,000 who, for complex reasons, are classified as noncitizens although at least 80 percent of them speak no Korean and are culturally Japanese except for the maintenance of some aspects of a traditional Korean diet. The ghettos in which most of these Koreans reside are worse than those of the Burakumin. Since they are not officially citizens, they are not automatically accorded welfare or health benefits given to ordinary citizens, nor are they eligible for public housing. Many are under-employed or unemployed. The Japanese regard them as a different "race." Children of a Japanese and a Korean parent are called "mixed blood," as are children of Caucasian or Black and Japanese parents. On the Guttman-type "social distance scales" used by Japanese social scientists to measure relative degrees of social acceptability of differing national and racial groups, Koreans are consistently listed at the bottom of the least socially acceptable of all national groups. In effect, even more than the Burakumin today, the Korean-Japanese are subjected to what must be considered a form of severe "racial" discrimination.

Conversely, the social attitudes of the Koreans are quite similar in many respects to those we have just discussed as characteristic of the Burakumin. There are various militant movements seeking to better their position in Japanese society. The Korean community politically is fractionated by ideological cleavages. Those loyal to North Korea are divided in their support of either Chinese or Russian communism. Those loyal to South Korea are divided by support for or antagonism toward the regimes of former President Park and his successors. As already mentioned, the incidences of delinquency and general difficulties at school are higher in Korean communities than in the outcaste groups. A good number of Koreans are involved in criminal and marginal occupations. They tend to be hostile toward Japanese officials and agencies. Many consider themselves harassed by police in regard to regulations that they must at all times carry their alien identity papers. Justified or not, many Koreans react with hostility whenever they have contact with Japanese officials.

At present there are movements within Japan on the part of liberal Japanese to ameliorate the difficult circumstances in which Korean-Japanese find themselves. There are efforts in the schools to educate majority children away from the prejudicial attitudes of the past. The effects of such programs today are not visible.

As part of our research we have been gathering psychological materials, principally the Thematic Apperception Test and the California Psychological Inventory. We are planning systematic comparison of normative samples of Koreans in Japan with those obtained from recent immigrants from Korea to the United States, and with a normative sample of Koreans who have repatriated from Japan to Korea. This work has not as yet been completed. However, some definite impressions are forthcoming from both the Korean-Japanese sample as well as from a sample of Korean immigrants who have recently arrived in California. There are striking differences between results obtained in the Korean minority sample and those from majority Japanese. Contrasted to the majority Japanese on whom we have over 800 records (DeVos, 1974), majority Koreans in our sample give almost no optimistic stories envisioning a successful future achieved as a result of hard work. The fantasy of minority Koreans in Japan portrays their protagonists in stories as frozen to present circumstances with a sense of uncertainty and incapacity. In particular, the men express a deep sense of futility and refusal to deal with the future consequences of the situations in which they picture themselves. Korean minority women, on the other hand, tend to focus on problems of interpersonal control or domination, or on questions of submission or rebellion. Neither the men nor the women pay much attention to problems of self-motivated achievement. There are even indications of sex role reversal in which women in some stories are envisioned as more socially assertive than men.

These results differ strikingly from those obtained from recent immigrants coming directly from Korea to the United States. We have recently completed a report (DeVos, 1979) in which we compared the Korean-American sample of 50 Koreans of all ages with the previous work done by Caudill (1952) with Japanese-Americans some 30 years before. This contemporary sample of immigrant Koreans who arriving in the United States in the 1970s was remarkably similar in respect to achievement themes to the previous sample of immigrant Japanese gathered by Caudill, who came to the United States before 1924. Comparing the two Korean samples — one in Japan and one in the United States, we notice a striking contrast between those who have come to the United States voluntarily seeking a future here and those who have now become a third generation of "alien" residents in Japan where very little hope is seen in their futures. In brief, Koreans in Japan exemplify Robert Merton's characterization of "alienation" as the personal dimension of social anomie (Merton, 1949). A great deal of discussion in Japan has been devoted to the fact that many Koreans are constrained by prejudice and lack of alternative opportunities to enter occupations of an irregular or criminal nature. Much less attention has been paid to the psychological debilitation evident in more passive forms of retreat and alienation suggested in the stories of many of the young people in our Japanese-Korean sample. There is internal psychological debilitation as well as a sense of career impasse resulting from the minority status accorded Koreans in Japan. Over the course of three generations Korean-Japanese manifest what Kardiner and Ovesey (1951) termed the "mark of oppression." They are psychologically vulnerable, giving evidence of self-hate, as well as occupationally and economically deprived.

In contrast, the Korean immigrants to the United States, as voluntary arrivals, still manifest a sense of optimism about the future. They recognize hard work as a means to success. This optimism has been fostered in the postwar independent Korean social climate. Korea, as a whole, is manifesting a vital surge of economic development on the one hand and political frustration on the other. Some Koreans are dissatisfied, frustrated, or impatient with political or social conditions at home. They have come to the United States to find what they perceive are greater opportunities and a freer social climate. The Koreans in Korea have taken on perhaps more than they consciously admit, many of the patterns of their former Japanese colonizers. Now, with independence in their own industrial development, they have become intensely competitive with the Japanese.

Interviews as well as test results confirm that these new American immigrants bring with them traditional concerns about Korean family life and worries about family harmony. Both in their sponataneous fantasy on the TAT as well as in their conversations they reveal how they grapple with figuring out how traditional roles are to be carried out in a new American setting.

The materials obtained from the Korean sample from Japan, in contrast, show an avoidance of family themes in their fantasy. Instead they manifest a sense of retreatist isolation and alienation. What one finds in the fantasy material of the Japanese-Korean is a sense of social fragmentation and isolation from the nuclear family as well as from the social group. While stories given by the Japanese majority in Japan occasionally envision discord within the family, they usually resolve such stories in a positive direction. In the Japanese-Korean TAT stories, however, there are more highly individuated concerns that at the same time blank out perceptions related to close family relationships.

These data obtained from the Korean minority in Japan are unique in comparison to other samples of Asians or Americans with which I have worked in several research ventures. I would assert, therefore, pending our final analysis that there is considerable disruption of family cohesion characteristic of the Koreans residing in Japan.

The preliminary, yet unpublished, material obtained by Robert Sakai from the California Psychological Inventory survey used in Japan, comparing Koreans with the normative sample of Japanese, shows depressed scores on the socialization scale related to the internalization of social values. This result is particularly apparent in females under 25 years of age. There is also direct indication in Sakai's observational results from the Osaka area of strains in Korean family living which makes assimilation to Japanese norms more difficult. For many, some form of alienated social life seems most probable.

Generally, our observational material on ghetto living patterns in Osaka and Kawasaki, an industrial satellite city of Tokyo, bear out the social and personal difficulties experienced by minority Koreans. In effect, the Koreans give evidence in some settings of the "culture of poverty" so well described by Lewis (1965) in respect to minority Puerto Ricans in New York City.

Conclusions

A Generational Perspective on Social Responses to Minority Status

Having briefly sketched some of the material we have gathered over the course of years from Japanese, Japanese-Americans, the minority group of Burakumin and Koreans in Japan, as well as our brief case history evidence from Italy, I would like to propose some generalizations concerning how minority status acts as a significant variable in delinquency formation. It is obvious to me from the evidence with which I have been working that the effects of minority status differ with cultural-historical circumstances. There is an interactive process at work. Unfortunately, much sociological research is implicitly univariant in assessing causality. That is, the emphasis is often solely on the patterns of discrimination encountered rather than on how discrimination produces different responses depending on the cultural background of those encountering discrimination. If one takes a psychocultural approach, however, one is constrained to examine in greater detail how childhood socialization is involved in establishing patterns of ethnic identity or social self-identity. These patterns differ in the succeeding generations of individuals experiencing social discrimination.

Differing patterns of deviancy cannot be separated out from differing patterns of social assimilation or the relative maintenance of a separate ethnic identity in given societies. It is particularly important in assessing immigrants to consider the potential vulnerability of their children to deviant behavior. To do so one must understand how family interaction maintains or fails to maintain status definitions inherited from the past culture.

To illustrate, roughly 85 percent of the Japanese-Americans who came to the United States were from rural areas. In most instances, these individuals were motivated to leave by conditions of poverty at the time of departure. However, they may not have become degraded by generations of poverty or oppression; on the contrary, they brought with them a fixed, firm concept of the relatively high status of farmers generally in Japan. Also, they had a strong tradition of family cohesion and conformity to community standards. In short, they brought with them a sense of having been of "middle-class" background in Japan despite their present economic duress. This sense of relative social status is very important in understanding the adaptation of Japanese-Americans to the United States. As we have indicated, we found that the status of the male parent as head of family was maintained in patterns of role playing within the family. The man as head of household was emotionally and behaviorally supported in that capacity regardless of his relative success or failure in occupations in the outside American society (DeVos, 1978). A strong achievement drive was internalized by most American-born Japanese children. Also internalized as part of the past were cultural experiences passed on as deference to authority, a capacity to be permeable to teachers as "teachers" rather than dominant strangers pressuring them to change their thoughts and behavior. One might say in the case of the Japanese-Americans that their own culturally derived social class definitions were more salient in helping them adapt to American society than any difficulties that arose out of differences in culture or attempts at derrogation on the part of the host society. The Japanese did not envision themselves as an "oppressed" minority regardless of the negative attitudes directed toward them by a racist American society. They were relatively "immune" to the potentially deleterious effects of social discrimination. If anything, the frustrations they experienced stimulated compensatory efforts as a means of overcoming the handicaps placed upon them. What occurred as a consequence was that teachers and others coming in direct contact with them began to perceive Japanese favorably. They were perceived as possessing "middle-class" virtues of cleanliness, diligence, and politeness by middle-class Americans. They were accorded rewards of appreciation for their accomplishments, if not total social acceptance.

The records of the Japanese schools and reports of psychologists testing Japanese children in the late 1920s and early 1930s attest to the type of adaptation that was occurring at the time. We witnessed in the Japanese children at the time a response to educational opportunities very similar to that of the Jewish minorities coming from Eastern Europe.

The present-day migration of Koreans to the United States is a voluntary one. They come in with attitudes quite similar to those motivating the Japanese and the Jews of the past era. They are very strongly motivated to "make it" in American society. Although this wave of what has now become over 350,000 Koreans has mostly occurred in the last eight years, one already sees evidence of a type of striving very characteristic of the Japanese of the earlier period. One must note that these new arrivals are coming from a resurgent Korean state in which past policies of universal education have borne fruit and a sense of hard-earned independence has produced individuals who have developed a strong positive self-regard. The younger immigrants from Korea have never experienced the colonial domination suffered by their parents. They bring with them into a pluralistic American society a protective sense of self-regard that will be sustaining. One can well predict that Koreans in the United States will show few of the social stigmas of those growing up in minority status in Japan. The Koreans in Japan settled there in far different historical and social circumstances. They were at best secondary citizens within the Japanese empire only to be subsequently deprived of formal citizenship when Korea itself regained its independence.

The Korean peasant who came to Japan in the 1920s and 1930s did not conceive of himself as of middle-class status. He had gone through generations of grinding poverty in a Korean state run by a hereditary nobility totally disinterested in his lot. He was in most instances illiterate. Education was for the elite. There was little regard for his status nor little to help him feel that he was a capable individual. Therefore, by the time the Korean rural folk migrated to Japan they had already experienced generations of social depreciation. Now living in an alien culture, they were subjected to even more stringent negative attitudes and social derogation. Although the family was traditionally "Confucian," the type of community and family life reconstituted by Koreans in Japan in many instances did not protect the individual from disrespect. Fathers lost status in their own households. Mothers' attitudes were often derogatory rather than supportive, as witnessed in some of our case history materials. They were subject to "caste" as well as class and ethnic depreciation in a racist Japanese culture that did not consider the Koreans as innately capable. There were no supportive community networks developed which maintained the Korean individuals status. This was quite different from what we found true for the Japanese communities within the United States. The more individualistic Korean rose or fell according to his own prowess. Group support was less forthcoming.

Our materials on Italian migrants are less sustained by detailed ethnographic observation. Yet, if we draw on the contemporary writing of Italian social scientists generally, we note well the severe derogation experienced by the southern Italains in the northern Italian cities. They are looked down upon with contempt. One can see this expressed even in the cinema where the stereotypes of knife-wielding Sicilians or female prostitutes are a butt of humor in numerous comedy films. It is not surprising, therefore, that there is a high incidence of delinquency in the children of southern migrants in the northern cities. Neither should it have been surprising that the Sicilians that have moved into high delinquency neighborhoods in the city of Chicago as reported in the studies of Shaw and McKay in the 1930s also produced a high delinquency rate. As we indicated in our introduction, the Japanese, moving later into these same neighborhoods, broke the pattern. Their children in the late 1940s did *not* become delinquent.

We hope we have been able to show in some degree that the effects of discrimination and minority status are related *selectively* to situations in which the youth suffers from a lack of sustaining social self-identity as well as a lack of sustaining family cohesion, a sufficient degree of affection, and satisfactory supervision and discipline by involved parents.

It is obvious that the communities formed by "foreign" migrants in American or northern Italian cities in many instances do not make up for the interpersonal inadequacies of particular families. Hence, youths from less cohesive families and less self-respecting communities become more vulnerable to the economic and social difficulties experienced as minority persons.

Finally, I hope it is clear from the foregoing that our work does not espouse a unitary sense of determinants, be they sociological, psychological, or cultural. Questions of deviant behavior can only be answered from a comparative perspective that sees social forces operative through several generations. One cannot simply look at the effects of minority status on the individual or the group. This gives implicit weight to one set of determinants. Rather, one must understand behavior as a result of interaction between social pressures of individuals who react to these pressures, with patterns of behavior shaped by past cultural, historical circumstances.

NOTES

1. I have previously published how changes in roles of criminal and delinquent behavior are related to socioeconomic variables (DeVos, 1973 :327-368). I shall not repeat here any of these findings. What I shall concern myself with are some of the social variables with which I have been directly dealing in research on delinquency in Japan. I shall also refer to some comparative materials on Italy gathered in a comparative research project involving Edwin Lemert, Franco Ferracuti, Hiroshi Wagatsuma, and Arnold Meadow.

2. After we initiated our investigation we found that a youth in one of our control cases had become invoved in delinquent activities — hence, we ended up with 31 families in our experimental sample — and 19 in our control sample.

3. One must note to those not familiar with recent social science activity in Japan that, at present, Japan has the second largest membership of psychologists in professional organizations and the second largest membership of sociologists — in each instance second only to the United States. The field of criminology in Japan, therefore, has available a very large number of research workers that produce a variety of studies yearly. Naturally, the work varies in cogency and adequacy but one can draw some conclusions on the basis of a survey of this entire body of material (see DeVos and Wagatsuma, 1972).

4. It is interesting to note that these materials were presented by psychiatrists who were somewhat antagonistic to psycholanalytic interpretations of child development. Certainly these results relate to the work of Bowlby and others in England concerning the effect of separation on the later appearance of delinquency (Bowlby, 1947).

5. In our collaborative research with Italian social scientists we were able to gain the cooperation of Professor Tullio Bandini at the University of Genoa and Professor Narida Rudas at the University of Cagliari.

6. In some instances neither rater felt the material was sufficient to give a rating — in those instances the records were scored with a question mark.

7. Recently, I have had some contact with outcaste communities and can see an ameliorative process in action. However, I would deem it necessary to make a more intensive reinvestigation before commenting on the possible results of this community action.

REFERENCES

AMES, W. (1976) Police and Community in Japan. New Brunswick, NJ: Rutgers University Press.
BENNET, I. L. (1960) Delinquent and Neurotic Children. New York: Basic Books.
BOWLBY, J. (1947) Forty-Four Juvenile Thieves. London: Balliere, Tindall and Cox.
BRUNER, E. (1976) "Tradition and modernization in Batak society," pp. 234-252 in G. DeVos (ed.) Responses to Change: Society, Culture and Personality. New York: Van Nostrand Reinhold.

CAUDILL, W. (1952) "Japanese-American personality and acculturation." Genetic Psychology Monographs 45: 3-102.

DeVOS, G. (1973a) "Adolescence and delinquency in cross cultural perspective," in Socialization for Achievement. San Francisco: University of California Press.

——— (1973b) Socialization for Achievement. San Francisco: University of California Press.

——— (1978) "Selective permeability and reference group sanctioning: psychocultural continuities in role degradation," in J. M. Yinger and S. J. Cutler (eds.) Major Social Issues: A Multi-disciplinary View. New York: Free Press.

——— (1979) "Some psychological characteristics of recent Korean immigrants to the United States." Presented to the Center for Korean Studies Conference, University of Hawaii, January.

——— and H. WAGATSUMA (1972) "Family life and delinquency: some perspectives from Japanese research," in W. Lebra (ed.) Transcultural Research in Mental Health. Honolulu: University of Hawaii Press.

——— (1966) Japan's Invisible Race. Berkeley: University of California Press.

——— (n.d.) The Heritage of Endurance.

GLUECK, S. and E. GLUECK (1950) Unraveling Juvenile Delinquency. Cambridge: Harvard University Press.

HIGUCHI, K. (1953) "Psychiatric study of juveniles after the war." Judicial Report 41: 1.

INKLES, A. and D. SMITH (1976) "Personal adjustment in modernization," pp. 214-233 in G. DeVos (ed.) Responses to Change: Society, Culture and Personality. New York: Van Nostrand Reinhold.

KARDINER, A. and L. OVESEY (1951) The Mark of Oppression. New York: W. W. Norton.

KLINEBERG, O. and G. DEVOS [eds.] (1973) Migration, Ethnic Minority Status and Social Adaptation. Rome: United National Social Defense Research Institute .

LEE, C. and G. DeVOS (in press) Koreans in Japan. Berkeley: University of California Press.

LEWIS, O. (1959) Five Families. New York: Basic Books.

——— (1965) La Vida. New York: Random House.

MERTON, R. (1949) Social Theory and Social Structure. New York: Free Press.

MURAMATSU [ed.] (1962) Nippongin — bunka to pasonarite no jissho-teki Kenya (The Japanese — An empirical study in culture and personality). Tokyo; Reimei Shobo, Nagoya: Remei Shobo.

SHAW, C. N. and H. D. McKAY (1931) Social Factors in Juvenile Delinquency. Washington, DC: National Commission on Law Observance and Enforcement.

——— (1932) "Are broken homes a causative factor in delinquency?" Social Forces 10: 514-524.

——— (1942) Juvenile Delinquency and Urban Areas. Chicago: University of Chicago Press.

SOFUE, T. (1976) "Psychological problems in Japanese urbanization," pp. 253-268 in G. DeVos (ed.), Responses to Change: Society, Culture and Personality. New York: Van Nostrand Reinhold.

YOSHIMASU, S. (1952) Criminal Psychology. Tokyo: Toyo Shokan.

BEYOND THE SUB-CULTURE OF VIOLENCE
An Evolutionary and Historical Approach to Social Control

CHERYL HAFT-PICKER

The term "subculture of violence" has become a cliché in modern criminological literature. Despite an obvious preoccupation with the concept, criminologists no longer agree on what the subculture of violence actually is or whether it even exists at all. Wolfgang and Ferracuti (1967) developed the subculture of violence theory to explain the "appearance of explosive, aggressive crime in a variety of places, times and cultures." Recognizing high levels of violence in certain isolated areas of the world, they tried to mesh psychology and sociology into an integrated theory of criminology to explain this phenomenon. But the subculture of violence theory has proved to be an anachronism in criminology. In today's world, very few societies are monocultural islands. Although we can still locate geographically isolated areas where people engage in high degrees of violence, one might still question the relevance of researching villages in Sardinia when the American criminologist is more concerned with explain ing violence in his or her own polycultural society. American criminologists find themselves in a theoretical dilemma when confronted with subculture of violence theory and then asked to explain disproportional rates of violence among blacks in the United States.[1] Since Wolfgang and Ferracuti used geographical isolation as an important criterion for selecting their case studies, it would, therefore, seem illogical to generalize their propositions to a poly-cultural society where subcultures cannot easily be isolated. Thus, it would be ridiculous to even suggest that poor, young black males form a subculture of violence.

Although violence has been witnessed and experienced throughout history as a resilient force in the world, its existence still perturbs man. Like political theories and sociological and religious thought, explanations of violence are subject to the changing thought paradigms of the times. For example, the modern interdisciplinary trend has now ushered the study of violence into the realm of criminology. Although considered to be an interdisciplinary mixture of social sciences, criminology is really only a blend of psychology and sociology, and lately some political science.[2] Probably because of its antiquantitative methodology, anthropology has been excluded from the mixture. Thus, despite much discussion about subculture, the criminological glossary excludes the concept of culture, a term so interwined with anthropological concerns. It is my belief that the confusion surrounding subculture of violence theory is attributable to the lack of consensus concerning an acceptable theory of culture. Criminologists have never even confronted such questions as: What is the purpose of culture? Why are there so many varieties of cultures throughout the world? Why have certain cultures met with extinction despite centuries of prosperity, yet others faced with persistent obstacles have continued to survive? Such questions must be at the core of any inquiry into such a universal phenomenon as violence. How can we, as criminologists, even aspire to explain the "sub" when the greater entity "culture" is not understood?

Theodosius Dobzhansky shrewdly recognized that two rival trends vie for influence in ideas — specialization and synthesis. Although the former tends to predominate, attempts to synthesize knowledge are indispensable. He prophesized that a failure to synthesize knowledge would support Albert Schweitzer's remark:

> Our age has discovered how to divorce knowledge from thought with the result that we have indeed a science which is free, but hardly any science that reflects [Dobzhansky, 1962].

It is therefore the objective of this essay to reflect upon an alternative framework for the study of violence by expanding beyond a criminological realm of specialization and synthesizing knowledge from the natural sciences, linguistics, history, and anthropology. In accomplishing this objective, a framework will be established from which criminologists can define and distinguish cultures, the purpose of culture will be conceptualized, and groundwork will be laid for a theory which portrays violence as the tool of social control in the evolutionary development of justice systems.

After briefly discussing the limitations of the subculture of violence theory, I will try to accomplish the above by assessing the importance of reestablishing conceptual links between evolution and culture.[3] Man's bioligical capacity for culture, which endows him with the faculties to symbolize and conceptualize, has been an expedient adaptive mechanism to environmental change. Although survival is of universal concern, the processes developed to maintain and achieve it vary among cutlures. Man's need for a system of justice that regulates, organizes, and controls his behavior — whether exemplified in a sophisticated legal code, through oral tradition, or even with the primitive principles of reciprocity that Malinowski claimed once pervaded all social behavior — has always been the source of group survival. The evolution of cultures may require the evolution of justice systems throughout the world. This possibility will be explored as a framework for the study of violence.

LIMITATIONS OF THE
SUBCULTURE OF VIOLENCE THEORY

The recognition accorded Wolfgang and Ferracuti's *Subculture of Violence* (1967) and the resulting debates sparked off by the theory have revealed an inquisitive interest in a culture explanation of violent behavior. Unfortunately, blind ambition to theorize about the violent crime rate in the United States has led to gross misinterpretations of the subculture of violence theory. Reviews of the *Subculture of Violence* incorrectly assume that the theory was derived to explain the black, poor youth preponderance of violent crime exhibited in all United States research since Wolfgang's homicide study in 1958. However, close examination of the development of the theory reveals that the subculture of violence has its origins in explicitly comparative research that draws evidence from all over the world. It was only after the publication of the *Subculture of Violence* in 1967 that researchers tried to utilize the theory as a way of explaining the consistent violent crime variables that where showing up in study after study.[4]

For example, attempts were made to test the hypothesis of a "deep south" subculture of violence. Researchers found that the violent crime rate was significantly higher in the South than in the North even when variables of urbanization, median income, race, education, medical care, and unemployment were controlled (Hackney, 1969; Gastil, 1971; Pettigrew and Spier, 1971). When a significant difference in violent crime rates was linked to other indicators of a positive valuation of violence [e.g., a higher percentage of gun owners in the South (Hackney, 1969) and favorable attitudes toward violence (Blumenthal et al., 1972; Stark and McKenvoy, 1970)], the existence of a Southern subculture of violence was confirmed. There are serious problems with this research as it relates to subculture of violence theory. First, Newman (1978) suggests that a historical analysis of the Southern violent crime rate is crucial before the conclusion of an existing Southern subculture of violence can be reached. Although the South has, since 1958, had a clearly higher violent crime rate, its rate of increase since 1970 has been much slower than that of the North, especially the Northeast. The second difficulty with the theory of a Southern subculture of violence is the assumption that, because certain differences in violent crime rates may be ascertained between the South and the North, a subculture of violence necessarily follows. The sheer size of the south would appear to preclude it from being classified as a subculture, especially given the knowledge that Wolfgang and Ferracuti's concept of subculture was explicitly derived from subcultural theories of delinquency.

Throughout the delinquency literature stemming from the 1920s we find a dearth of theoretical and empirical research in which the gang has been used as the microcosm by which researchers have identified the existence of a subculture (Newman and Haft, 1977). For example, Cloward and Ohlin (1960), on the first page of *Delinquency and Opportunity*, state "This book is about delinquent gangs or subcultures." Given the fact that the concept of subculture has evolved from the theoretical gang literature, which directed its attention on the social relationships within which delinquency occurs, one would have to unrealistically stretch the imagination to adapt Wolfgang and Ferracuti's notion of subculture to a region such as the South.

It is not the objective of this chapter to cite all the data that might lend credence or disbelief to the existence of a subculture of violence in the United States. Research that has tested the subculture of violence has already attempted this by beginning with impressive amounts of what Newman (1978) labels "phenomenological data" and then working backwards to the subculture of violence hypothesis (Curtis, 1975; Scherer et al., 1975). This type of research has led to the racist charges against the subculture of violence theory, since it implies that all poor blacks are, or are potentially, violent. Furthermore, Wolfgang and Ferracuti never adapted their concept of subculture to an American setting. Thus, when Ball-Rokeach (1973) attempted to test the existence of an American subculture of violence by comparing self-reported values toward violence between violent and nonviolent groups, an utter disregard for the definition of subculture was displayed. Can any group be labeled a subculture of violence? Could a family? Would the infamous

Kallikaks form a subculture of violence? Given the evidence that there seem to be extremes in the application of the term subculture — some suggesting half the United States, others just gangs of young boys — where does one search for the meaning of subculture?

Although Wolfgang and Ferracuti (1967) stated that the major works on delinquent subcultures did not address themselves to the "problem of defining the meaning of subculture more precisely," they never alleviated this problem. Their subculture of violence theory may have built the framework for understanding the transmission of violent values, but it never linked up to Albert Cohen's (1955) statement that

> a complete theory of subcultural differentiation would state more precisely the conditions under which subcultures emerge and fail to emerge and would state operation for predicting the content of subcultural solutions.

The theory left the historian searching for the origins and antecedent events of the subculture of violence and the psychologist still trying to understand the dynamics of value transmission, a task left unfinished by Sutherland. Conceptualizing the dynamics and origins of a subculture of violence is a task too difficult to accomplish without a solid understanding of culture — its purpose, its function, and its evolution.

EVOLUTION AND CULTURE: THE CAPACITY TO SYMBOLIZE

From an evolutionary perspective, the enviroment presents adaptive challenges to which a living species may respond to alteration of its genetic composition. Dobzhansky (1962), a world-renowend geneticist and evolutionist, argued that in addition to a genetic response, man has the option of responding to adaptive challenges in this environment through the alteration of his culture. Because of the time element involved in adaptation, culture is obviously a more efficacious means of response than any biological device.

Culture is acquired and transmitted in every generation by learning and training. Cultural modifications can therefore be passed to potentially any number of individuals, irrespective not only of their descent relations, but also of space and time. Genetic modifications can be conveyed only to direct descendants and the unmodified genes can be eliminated only by the slow process of extinction [Dobzhansky, 1964].

It is Dobzhansky's claim that the genetic base that has made culture possible has developed in human evolution because it conferred upon its possessors an adaptive advantage of unprecedented potency. The fact that culture has a gentic base is generally well accepted by biologists and anthropologists (Dobzhansky, 1962; Coon, 1954; Jerison, 1964; Alland, 1967; Garn, 1964; Wallace, 1961; Hallowell, 1950; Henry, 1959). Sociologists and criminologists have unreasonably refused to accept this fact because of the possible social policy implications (Campbell, 1975). What must be clarified is the idea that culture is not the direct product of biological evolution; but the capacity to develop and maintain culture is.

Wallace (1961) cited two major concurrent events, outstanding in the development of man over the last few million years that support a genetic basis for culture: (1) A rapid and vast increase in the size of the brain in certain hominid lines, and (2) a similarly rapid and vast increase in the complexity of culture in the same hominid lines.

After studying physiological data on Sinanthropus-Pithecanthropus and Neanderthal fossils, Garn (1964) and Weidenreich (1951) concluded that there was no major taxonomic gap between hominids then and modern man. This finding is important because, despite the fact that it is now scientifically accepted that all hominids belong morphologically to a single species, how does one explain that subsequent human evolution raised cranial volume from below 1000cc to approximately 1400cc, or roughly one-half? Scholars (such as Wallace, 1961) have recognized these cerebral increases as valid indices of "those enlargements of hominid cognitive capacities that have accompanied the evolution of human culture." Evolutionists believe that the enlargement of the brain directly correlates with man's ability to conduct symbolic comunication and conse-quently to create culture (Dobzhansky, 1962). Emerson (1958) even went so far as to say that most social behavior of man is culturally determined through symbolic communication.[5]

Much research and speculation has been stimulated in modern linguistics by a hypothesis that Sapir (1949) suggested and Whorf (1956) later advanced. They postulated that human language is not only a vehicle, but a molder of thought. Far from just being a communication technique, language directs and molds the perceptions of the effector and receptor in addi-tion to providing for them habitual modes of analyzing ex-perience into significant categories. Human languages denote complex cultural codes through which symbolic behavior is transmitted. Language is thus not merely a verbal code with an accepted syntax and grammatical structure; language establishes a consensus of shared signs.

In 1690, John Locke's conclusion in his *Essay Concerning Human Nature* sowed the first seed for the science of semiology; the study of "the nature of signs the mind makes use of for the understanding of things or conveying its knowledge to others." Linguists, such as Umberto Eco (1976), Ferdinand de Saussure (1968), and Roland Barthes (1968), devoting lifelong efforts to the study of semiology, contend that cultures are distinguished from each other by symbolic systems and shared patterns of orientation that shape behavior. Succintly stated,

> Members of a particulart culture share certain classifications of the world. Such classifications are a prerequisite for com-munication, for meaningful behavior, for competent judging of appropriateness of that behavior and that these classifications are involved in the semantic system of the language [Eglin, 1976].

To the extent that members of different ethnic groups speak dif-ferent languages, dialects, or patois, they develop different ways of looking at the world. People who live in the same community may experience identical events quite differently if they are oriented toward their environment with different vocabularies, which structure the selection and interpretation of sensory cues.

When Wolfgang and Ferracuti postulated their subculture of violence theory, they suggested that there is a potent theme of violence in the values that make up the lifestyle and the socialization process of the subculture, thus implying that it was the subculture's value system that set it apart from the larger culture. To test this idea, Ferracuti et al. (1970) proposed that those most committed to the subculture of violence would be more violent and display less guilt concerning their homicides. When homicidal offenders from the subculture of violence in Sardinia were compared with those from the dominant culture, only weak support was found for this hypothesis.

In another study, this time in Puerto Rico, Ferracuti and Wolfgang (1973) conducted intensive psychological testing and found that those from the subculture of violence displayed higher clinical scores on aggression than did those from the dominant culture. Newman (1976) compared respondents' assessments of the seriousness of robbery and other crimes between a violent Sardinian subculture and a matching nonviolent subculture. Considerable differences were found, but these differences had to be understood to operate under very specific condtions. While it was found, for example, that over half of the Sardinian subculture respondents would not report a robbery to the police (compared with 10 percent of other respondents), nevertheless, they would punish such an act just as severely as anyone else. The hypothesis advanced by Newman, therefore, was that respondents from a subculture of violence may not value violence any differently from those from a nonviolent subculture, but they do differ considerably concerning the conditions under which it may be employed and the societal response to it that they see as applicable.

There are a great many theories of human nature, and one of the most plausible is a recurrent doctrine emphasizing that human beings throughout the world manifest the same instinctive reactions to survival threats (Lorenz, 1966; Kwan and Shibutani, 1965; Malinowski, 1926). Violence *is* an instinctive reaction to survival threats, but the perception of what constitutes a survival threat differs among cultures. Given the fact that the symbolic capacity of man contributes to diversified and other varying phenomena, a survival threat in one culture may be merely a nonthreatening obstacle in another. Thus, if we accept that the genetic base of culture is the capacity to symbolize, then the approach to understanding culture should be from a semiological perspective. Isolating cultures according to geographical boundaries is a futile task in a polycultural society. But developing a methodology whereby cultural groups can be distinguished according to members who are capable of sustaining and understanding shared symbolic experiences is much more realistic. This type of approach incorporates the spine of culture: symbolization.

EVOLUTION AND CULTURE: INSTRUMENT OF ADAPTATION

Evolution has provided us with our first link between biology and culture: the capacity to symbolize. Recognition of the genetic base for culture provides an alternative framework from which criminologists can begin to define culture. But there is a second link between evolution and culture which must be discussed in approaching the initial question "What is the purpose of culture?" It has been stated that culture is an efficient instrument of adaptation. In addition to theorizing that culture has a genetic base, Dobzhansky (1964) hypothesized that the various cultures of homo sapiens can be regarded as means of adapting to the environment and of exploiting various ecological niches. From an evolutionary perspective, common biological needs can be met by parallel but different bodily features or behavior patterns.[6] For example "binocular vision is a homologous structure in most primates, whereas the different kinds of eyes or wings of insects, birds, bats, etc. are analogous or parallel developments in different evolutionary lines. What is important about these analogies among species is that evolutionary selection can satisfy a given function like sight or flying in different, albeit parallel, ways. Since the evolution of parallel but distinct solutions to common problems or biological functions follows the pattern of a nondirected trial-and-error process in all other organisms, it is hard to see why human cultures

should be unique in this respect (Masters, 1976). Washburn
and Avis stated in 1958 that culture was an unplanned response
to the problem of survival and adaptation — thus, if survival
can be considered a universal problem, cultures could also exhibit parallel but distinct solutions.

Malinowski (1926) recognized the organization of human beings into permanent groups, related by traditional law, custom,
or agreement, as an essential fact of culture, vital to man's survival.[7] When he wrote *Crime and Custom in Savage Society*, he
cautioned his readers not to look at the various forces which
make for order, uniformity, and cohesion in a savage tribe as
mere subjects of curiosity. Instead, he hoped that the study of
primitive man would provide the foundation for understanding
the law of modern man. Unfortunately, many legal scholars and
criminologists have searched for the origins of law only within
written legal codes. Whether it be expressed by the feuding
villages of Appalachia, the secret societies of Camorra, the
Mosaic Law, the Hannurabi Code, or the primitive laws of the
Torbiand Islands, man's need for establishing some form of
social contract, transcending spatial and temporal boundaries,
has been met by different though parallel systems of justice. A
rigorous examination of how a culture's system of justice adapts
to its environment could possibly explain that culture's solution
to the survival dilemma.

For example, somehow, the Jews managed to escape the
cultural death of many of the civilizations within which they
dwelled (Babylonian, Persian, Philistine, Roman). To explain a
4000-year-old story of survival on four continents and in six major civilizations, the presentation of an ethnic identity among
foreign cultures despite a 3000-year history without a country of
their own, one must understand the Mosaic Law. This body of
oral law, later documented in the Talmud, created a judicial
system which has enabled the Jews to survive 4000 years of a
tumultuous history. The Mosaic Law has evolved from simple
retributive principles to a complex code of law ethics and
morality, enabling Jews to adapt to the ever-changing demands
of new environments. Because the Jews were able to transport
their laws wherever they went and adapt them to diverse

cultures, they were able to survive the demands of different environments. Thus, even the simplest principles of retribution have the potential to evolve into sophisticated written legal codes.

If a culture does not have a judicial system that has become an integral institution in that culture's tradition, violence will be the institution around which the culture organizes itself and establishes a hierarchical ordering of relationships. Violence thus becomes a form of social control and the tool of informal justice in the evolutionary development of a legal system. When a culture resorts to violence in settling internal disputes, the culture is resorting to a feuding response as the means of establishing an informal justice system. The feuding response is the reaction to a given set of historical phenomena: ecological scarcity of resources and threat to existence by a distrusted group of people (that is, central government, dominant culture, foreign enemy, and so on). In the absence of these conditions, the feuding response will dissipate and evolve into a more formalized justice system.

THE FEUDING RESPONSE

The *Oxford English Dictionary* defines feud as "a state of perpetual hostility between two families, tribes or individuals, marked by murderous assaults in revenge for some previous insult or injury." The feud, being one of the most ancient procedures of dispute settlement, is also one of the most ancient systems of "doing" justice (Ianni, 1972; Black-Michaud, 1975; Bloch, 1961; Campbell, 1964; Dozier, 1966; Durham, 1909; Goebel, 1976; Hardy, 1963; Hasluck, 1954; Peters, 1967; Seagle, 1941; Sonichesen, 1962; Wallace-Hadrill, 1959). The fact that the feud performs both these functions makes it a fascinating study for the criminologist: It is where the origins of the criminal law and the origins of criminal violence intersect.

Feuding has been identified in various forms in an enormous variety of societies and cultures from the beginning of time to the present. It is probable that all of Europe at some time during the middle ages was dominated by feuding as the main form of

carrying out justice, either through a peaceful dispute settlement or a violent resolution (Ives, 1941; Newman, 1978). The
remnants of feuding societies have been preserved to the present
day in two ways: they have provided many of the basic features
of the modern criminal law; and due to a number of reasons,
but primarily geographic isolation, small pockets of feuding
societies have endured. The best known of these are in Albania
(Frasheri, 1964; Hasluck, 1954; Durham, 1909); Turkey (Campbell, 1964); Texas, Kentucky, Colorado, and Appalachia
(Richardson, 1943; Sonnichesen, 1962); Scotland and Ireland
(Arensberg, 1937); Corsica, Calabria, Sicily, and Sardinia (Ianni, 1972; Hess, 1970; Hobsbawn, 1959); Egypt and surrounding
Arab nations (Abu-Zeid, 1960; Black-Michaud, 1975; Peters,
1967; Hardy, 1963); the Philippines (Dozier, 1966); and the list
goes on.

The "pure feud" is usually taken to be that in which collective responsibility predominates: If an individual commits a
wrongful act, his whole tribe, family, or clan is held responsible
for avenging the act. This was the situation that prevailed during Norman and Frankish times, and the tradition that was
transported to England after the Norman Conquest. During this
period from roughly the sixth through fourteenth centuries,
feuding ebbed and flowed according to change in economy,
government, religion, and kinship structure. Sources from the
history of the ninth and tenth centuries tell us of the

> dissolution, of perversions of power, of the reorientation that'
> invasion and starvation made necessary in the pattern of govern-
> mental administration, of spasmodic instead of measured
> government action [Goebel, 1976].

Throughout this period the State gradually gained more power,
and the shift from the private revenge of the feud to public arbitration was slowly achieved. Feuding underwent many
transformations, of which the major one was the shift from collective to individual responsibility for violence — whether as a
crime or a punishment for a crime.

Most basic to a discussion of wrongdoing in early medieval
times was the theory of peace — whether this be a folk, a

king's or a public's peace (Goebel, 1976). The origin of this conception stemmed from the fact that a group had been formed on the basis of kinship, and that any breach of peace law was a matter for group action. The individual acquired legal importance only by virtue of his association with and continued membership in the group, which has been described as *mannhelgi*, a word symbolizing a man's honor (Goebel, 1976). In the event of a breach of the peace, the reaction toward the offender was not merely that of an unattached individual, but of the whole association. Individuals committing breaches of peace within the group were deprived of group protection immediately. It was not enough to simply expel them from the association, but their "peace" was taken away. Thus, they were deprived of all legal protection — their existence completely wiped out. It is in this manner that outlawry was conceived.

The shift from the private feud of the Germanic tribes to public and royal arbitration and intervention began to take place when the Franks settled in Gaul in the Merovingian Age and a complex society emerged, whereby the age of mercantilism was dawning. The tendency and purpose of the new folk laws of the Frankish empire were toward restricting the blood feud and furthering the process of emendation. Surprisingly, the feud continued despite conditions which made collective responsibility more difficult.

If it can be stated that revenge and feud represent the lowest stratum or organized action against wrongdoing, then the second stage is the growth of compensation. The notion of demands for injury may be regarded as a considerable advance in the direction of a nonviolent settlement of wrongs, but it would be a mistake to suppose that any of the measures aimed at the discouragement of the feud were the fruit of a new and extensive social objective intended to substitute for kinsmen's revenge. The notion of compensation was embraced because it offered pecuniary advantages to the State. When the State began to enter as an arbitrator between two conflicting parties, part of the compensation was given to the arbitrator as a payment for services redendered (Goebel, 1976).

It is important to mention at this point why the feud itself was no longer desirable to the Frankish kings. The intense loyalty that kinship members shared with each other threatened the developing concept of the divine right, which demanded unqualified obedience and allegiance. Thus, in offering alternatives to the feud, especially when the State would manipulate these options, the Frankish Kingdom was able to shift loyalty from the kinship group to the kingdom. The king, the only legitimate avenger in the eyes of God, began to weave a thread of unity among the divided principalities.

The royal policy followed two lines of action. On the one hand, it sought to direct or modify the process of private prosecution: a policy devoted essentially to the amendment of procedural forms (Seagle, 1941). On the other hand, it sought to develop a State initiative in the prosecution and punishment of offenses. In its infancy, a crown law consisted of a few procedures instituted to cope with two situations: the thief and the professional malefactor, both obviously a threat to the emerging existence of the State (Wallace-hadrill, 1962). These two problems the State began to make its own and thus embarked on a long series of experiments with administrative and procedural devices. Slowly, the scope of its activities widened to encroach upon matters that were once the subject of the feud and private compensation. Since the new procedures largely still existed by way of supplement to old, traditional, folk peace procedures, they still did not grow to sufficient proportions to displace the compensation process itself.

The attempt to lay the foundation for such an interest was undertaken fervently by the concept of infidelity; the threat of greatest magnitude to the State. Sworn allegiance to the kinship group as a primary loyalty became the root of infidelity and a sore contention for the king. Loyalty must first be to the king, who embodied the divine right of God. The king was therefore to be God's only avenger. But the decay of the jurisdictional unity of the Frankish empire put a halt to the development of public authority, and amidst the chaos of the tenth-century feud the progeny of violence reigned again.

We now come to a point in history when feuding is revived and has resurged enough to formulate an "ambiance sociale totale'' (Bloch, 1961). Changes in Frankish law were induced by very disturbed conditions which prevailed in Northern France for over a century after the cession of Normandy. Decentralization brought about basic changes in the treatment of wrongdoings. It is precisely the process of the decay of jurisdictional unity that sparked off the reenactment of the feud. The charters of the late tenth and early eleventh centuries indicate that the compensation was no longer considered a substitute or a means of ending the feud. This situation can be attributed to the decay of material wealth which could not support a system of compensation involving material commodities. A system of law which looked to settlement by fixed payments of some tangible value could not be maintained under these conditions.

From the year 970 to 1040, 40 years of famine engulfed Europe. Norman invasions dragged on for over three-quarters of a century and the destruction was devastating. The reemergence of feuding was the response to these troubled times. One might inquire into the reasons why feuding was particularly rife during the middle ages, a period which followed such disorder. Historians have generally isolated a number of factors (Bloch, 1961): (a) There were periods of extreme famine and economic hardship (also a common trait of modern feuding societies). (b) It was a period of disruption and chaos, with constant battles and threats to the small societies from outside. Europe was attacked from three sides at once, in the south by the devotees of Islam, in the east by the Hungarians, and in the north by the Scandinavians. The theme of disruption and chaos gave birth to the feudal state. Albania and Yugoslavia were hardest hit by these invasions, which endured many centuries longer. These countries epitomized the resort to feuding as if in a desperate attempt to establish an inner sense of order. (c) In the midst of this chaos, close social bonds developed, especially in relation to the feudal lord and vassal relationship. Reciprocity based on obligations to authority, not equals (as was the case in the pure feud: Newman, 1978), was a central element of social life. Unquestioning submission to the group on the basis of a mutual obligation to maintain the group's cohesive nature was typical during the later phases of feuding in the middle ages (Bloch, 1961).

Blood feud in the Middle East has displayed an incredible resilience to change despite the influence of foreign systems of law. The origins — or perhaps more explicitly, the sacredness — of the blood feud stems from religious obligations imposed on the victim's next of kin. However, in order to understand this principle, it is necessary to briefly view the concept of responsibility as it was understood in pre-Islamic Arabia. The general picture which emerges is that of a nomadic tribal society interspersed with a few settled mercantile communities, notably at Mecca and Medina, with no central authority to curb the autonomy of the various tribes.

The tribal structure was based on a blood relationship derived from a common ancestor. Since a single two- or three-generation family could scarcely survive desert life in isolation, the basic kinship group often extended into nonblood agnates. Each member was responsible for the group and in return received assistance. The blood feud had its roots in the need for survival in the desert. Protection of what little resources one had was a vital obligation of tribal existence. While one source of encouragement for the institution of blod feud lay in survival mechanics, another source of fundamental potency lay in religion. The idea of revenge or "thar" came to take form, not so much as the expression of an animal instinct but of a religious obligation from which a juridicial construction evolved. For instance, an avenger could not kill a man in his sleep because the soul was not present. At the moment of striking the mortal blow, the avenger had to cry aloud that he was taking vengeance for this murdered kinsman so as to inform any witness that this was a judicial killing and not an unjustified attack. Although in theory one man paid for the death of another, thus extinguishing the blood feud, unbridled revenge often reigned. Therefore, certain religious and social customs were observed n order to maintain restraint under the onus of community survival. During four months of the year, it was accepted that absolute peace should reign. During the spring month of "rajab," murderers, safe from execution of the blood feud, would often try to claim protection of another powerful tribe when the four months were over. The sheikh or head of this protector tribe was often called upon to help arrange an eventual settlement. If proof of the original act was uncertain, the two parties might agree that the avenger should bring a formal accusation against the suspect, who in turn would take an oath and perform purificatory acts before the assembled notables. Under this procedure of a certainly rudimentary legal character, as many of the accused's kinsmen as possible (probably 50 in number) swore solemnly that the accused had not committed the act. If any of them refused to do so, the accused was found guilty (Hardy, 1963). The choice between exacting vengeance and accepting compensation always lay with the offended kinsmen. Blood money provided a functional means to acquisition of goods one normally did not possess. The payment of blood money was a collective remuneration and therefore the offender's kin were also responsible for the "diya."

Similar factors identified in relation to feuding in medieval Europe were also operative in pre-Islamic Arabia: the existence of external threat; the problem of survival in a desert of scarce resources; and the existence of very intimate social bonds. It was not until Mohammed that the idea of *personal* responsibility became a concept in the *quid pro quo* of crime and punishment. With the coming of Mohammed, the Prophet made crime a matter for the whole community and not merely one of blood relation. As small empires gradually arose, so did the anonymity of individuals, and thus the difficulty of establishing collective responsibility for violence. In strikingly parallel fashion, the feuding societies of Arabia moved from collective to individual responsibility. Vengeance was wrought in the name of Mohammed, not kinship or tribe. It was not long before the right to execute vengeance became the right merely to request the public authority to do so (Hardy, 1963). But further foreign invasions delimited the State's power over customary law. People of the Middle East today often regard punishment levied by the State as extraneous to the tradition of the blood feud. The true judgment in people's minds is still rendered according to the old notion of private vengeance. Shari's law still exists as a decisive judicial legal body paralleling that of the State's.

The notion of collective responsibility was historically central to the feud. Because of this collective orientation, invariably the questions of fidelity and honor have assumed great importance and commonly a conflict between fidelity to one's clan or kin and fidelity to an outside force (such as a king or government). The importance of the reciprocity involved in kinship ties in this instance cannot be denied. Values or traditions of feud are transmitted via the intimate reciprocity of social relationships based on the model of kinship. Even where the exterior forms of kinship appeared to be dissolved, the norm of reciprocity ensued. Attention must also be drawn to the fact that there are many different forms and structures of feuding, ranging from the "pure and simple" (for example, kinship feuds) to the highly complex feuds which verge upon guerilla and civil war. Inherent in the development from collective to individual responsibility lies the intermediary stage of dispute settlement, whereby the State assumes the function first of negotiator, then arbitrator, and finally plaintiff. It is most significant that the major historical themes that have been discussed so far — economic scarcity, threat of force from foreign or outside source, fidelity, collective responsibility, oath-taking, kinship and reciprocity, and religious beliefs — have been similar for both the Arabic and European feuds.

Wherever feuding has been a phenomenon, certain themes have been universal in its development. Although feuding is not always exhibited as a constant with invariable characteristics, the following various themes are represented consistently.

(1) Survival threats. Societies that exhibit feuding have undergone historical turmoil. The roots of contention stem from two sources: the ecological factor of scarcity of resources and the threat or existence of foreign invasion. Throughout the histories of the Middle East, Italy, Albania, and Texas, the struggle for survival has always been omnipresent wherever both ecological scarcity and foreign invasion existed. The course of the feud within these societies may be reflected in an in-

vestigation of the ways individuals unite to supercede these survival threats.

The presence of feud in the societies of the Middle East and the Mediterranean is associated with the phenomenon which Black-Michaud (1975) has entitled "total scarcity." The concept may be summarized as "the moral, institutional and material presence of a certain type of society in which everything felt by the people themselves to be relevant to human life is regarded by those people as existing in absolute inadequate quantities." The feud, being a response to conditions of total scarcity, produces a surrogate social system that amerliorates institutional deficiencies caused by a constellation of ecological and historical variables. By fostering the interplay of three basic social components, mutual aid, conflict, and leadership (the last component substituting a hierarchy of honor), under the conditions of ecological scarcity or foreign invasion the feud can constitute an ongoing social process.

Total scarcity can occur in any society and at any time depending upon the availability, production, and exploitation of material goods and resources. It develops in societies whose material scarcity has reached such an intense pitch that social organizations are affected in every aspect by this precarious subsistence economy. It maintains a decisive influence upon patterns of social organization designed to facilitate group survival. Survival, during conditions of material scarcity, becomes a group-endeavored struggle (Black-Michaud, 1975).

The notion of scarcity has deep roots in the everyday existence of individuals living under these conditions, for it extends beyond the external, physical world to include the more abstract sphere of cultural values. Prestige, honor, and manliness come to be regarded as commodities which, like land and water, are limited in supply. In conditions of total scarcity, the struggle for survival embraces a competitive fight for that which is available; prestige, honor, and the like. Violence and physical assertion become the means to override the struggle (Horowitz and Schwartz, 1974; Black-Michaud, 1975).

As we have stated, areas that exhibit feuding have undergone historical turmoil. We discussed one source — ecological scarcity — leaving the second — threat or existence of foreign invasion — still unexplored. The histories of both Albania and Italy exemplify descriptive backgrounds caused by foreign invasion (Nagluck, 1954; Durham, 1909; Frasheri, 1964; Ianni, 1972; Hobsbawn, 1959). Feudalism, as depicted in the overall historical view, arose out of chaos and disorganization caused by foreign invasion. Feuding in Albania and Italy had been the reaction to either the collapse of extant institutions or the reaction to alien influence. It is a phenomenon that has consistently arisen after periods of abnormal hardships, especially when invaders tried to seize and then enforce adherence to alien cultural norms through coervice means.

The role of the Mafia as a self-help institution can be analyzed against the backdrop of a weak state, foreign invasion, and consequently a tradition of dual morality (Hess, 1970). Sicily's political structure has always been marked by a very definite situation — an extraordinary weakness of the formal government machinery, popular mistrust, and hostility toward all State organs and subsequent withdrawal into an informal system of self-help institutions characterized by a very definite philosophy of life.

> Mafia is a trait of character, a philosophy of life, a moral and a particular sensibility predominant among all Sicilians. They are taught in their cradle that they must help one another, stand by their friends and fight their common enemies even when friends are in the wrong and enemies in the right. Every man must defend his dignity under all circumstances and must not let the slightest disrespect or affront go unavenged. They must not divulge secrets and always keep clear of official authority and laws. The mafioso wants to be respected. When offended, he does not rely on the law. If he did so, he would be displaying weakness and offending omerta, which brands despicable any man who turns to an official in order to get his right [Hess, 1973].

This lack of loyalty to formal organization is not, according to a historical perspective, some irrational factor. Instead, it must be understood as an extremely purposeful, rationally motivated behavioral response to the intense distrust and hatred of the central government. Mafia organizations, always emerging during period of social disorganization or political upheaval, have established parallel systems of law throughout Southern Italy. The Mafia, after the collapse of Sicilian feudalism in 1812, assumed the intermediary role as dispute settler between the aristocracy and mass of peasants. Since the central government was too weak to establish a strong political order, the Mafia emerged as the one well-established and organized social network capable of maintaining order. The Mafia became the mediator between the two social strata, which otherwise could not have interacted without violent conflicts (Ianni, 1972). Thus, the Mafia was the source of order within the Sicilian social system.

Albania has also developed the Mafioso type within its boundaries. Although ecological scarcity has been a strong contributing factor in the development of feuding relations, foreign invasion has most certainly had its impact. In the course of her long history, Albania has been invaded by various civilized, half-civilized, and barbarian races. The Gauls, the Romans, the Goths, the Slavs, the Normans, the Venetians, and, finally, the Turks successively set their foot on Albanian territory. To ensure for all protection from invasion and a fair share of grazing, arable land and irrigation, a corpus of unwritten laws has grown up. Feuding was an attempt to maintain an internal order of justice while community boundaries were constantly being threatened.

The feud has been an ever-present phenomenon in Texan history. Even today, the word feud in this country is immediately associated with the South and the West. Historians have often wondered why questions of personal and family honor should be so much more sensitive in Houston than in Boston (Hobsbawn, 1959). It has been argued that feuding is not evidence of lawlessness coupled with a favorable attitude toward violence, but rather a reasonable substitute for legal redress when written law either has not yet arrived to the area or where legal remedies are not embraced because of a disorganized situation. Feud occurs not among "the unrestrained, but among highly conservative people who cling to ancient folkways" (Sonnichsen, 1962). Vigilante committees are the expression of a highly developed belief in America of the "right of the governed at all times to instant and arbitrary control of the government. The committee's aim is to assist the law and to accomplish its purpose, even if it means resorting to unlawful means" (Sonnichsen, 1962). The vigilante principle therefore does not spring from disrespect for law, since the extralegal justice of frontier communities is really a return to the oldest code of man — the law of private vengeance. As legal historian Seagle (1941) stated, "The matrix of all law is the blood feud."

(2) Fear. We have seen that many feuding societies develop a substitute system of social control in order to defend themselves from foreign invasion or from a government whose policies are perceived as threatening. This has certainly been the case (though in differing degrees and circumstances) in Sicily (Hess, 1970); Sardinia (Pigliaru, 1970); Yugoslavia and Albania (Hasluck, 1954); and in Texas (Sonnichsen, 1957), where self-help institutions arose. From a historical perspective, the rise of a substitute system of self-government, which often resorts to violence as a major solution to social conflict, must be seen as an extremely purposeful, motivated solution to survival.

The dominant element in all such feuding societies is fear: of starvation, of foreign invasion, of choas. Feuding societies often rise from the ruins of a series of invasions and wars which have destroyed the basic social structure and organization. In segmentary societies which are basically acephalous and equalitarian, the motive for alliance is almost definitely fear (Black-Michaud, 1975). Fear of aggression promotes equalitarian alliances which create a balance of forces in the face of potential anarchy. If fear of aggression were removed in societies of this type, organization into a series of evenly matched coalitions would no longer be necessary and the system would then fall apart (Bryson, 1935). If, on the other hand, aggression knew no limits and no alliances were formed to check the spread of violence, chaos would ensue. Seen in this light, feud constitutes the main organizational principle of all the feuding societies in the Mediterranean, the Middle East, and nineteenth century Texas (Bancroft, 1866; Seagle, 1941). Fear maintains a social system while at the same time constituting a permanent threat to peace and order. "Fear of incurring a blood-feud...is the most important legal sanction and the main guarantee of an individual's life and property" (Pitt-Rivers, 1966).

(3) Honor and shame. Peters (1951), defining feud as a relationship between feuding parties, emphasizes the equalitarian aspects of feuds. To Black-Michaud (1975), however, the feud is also a means of affirming authority in the absence of an institutionalized power structure. It was pointed out that members of a feuding group only share an equalitarian outlook as far as distribution of material resources is concerned. Leadership necessarily arises in the face of outside threat, and a hierarchy develops based on the distribution of honor and shame, courage, and many other "intangible" attributes.

To resolve the apparent contradiction between an equalitarian model and the existence of leadership in feuding societies, it is necessary to investigate the nature of the internal hierarchy that develops. It was already stated that a situation of scarcity arises out of ecological and historical circumstances. This situation creates an endemic insufficiency of material goods and resources and therefore prevents the acquisition and long-term accumulation of wealth by individuals or groups. This in turn hampers the development of social stratification and an attendant power structure based on economic differentiation. By minimizing opportunities from one generation to the next of inheritable wealth, an equalitarian ethos reinforces the mandate for survival. What is transmissible, though, are notions of honor, prestige, manliness, and shame. What are these intangible commodities that so heavily underlie extreme uses of violence?

Honor and shame have often been described as the two universal poles of social evaluation. "They are the reflection of the social personality in the mirror of social ideals as well as being the apex of the pyramid of temporal social values. They condition a hierarchical order" (Black-Michaud, 1975). Cutting across all other social classifications, honor divides social beings into two fundamental categories: those endowed with honor and those deprived of it. Like material acquisitions, honor becomes a commodity that is strived for in order to achieve a status step on the hierarchical ladder of society. It becomes especially important when material resources are scarce and thus cannot be a means to status attainment. Mediterranean and Middle Eastern peoples as well as Italians and Texans are constantly being called upon to use the concepts of honor and shame in order to assess their own conduct and that of their fellows.

The anthropologist Peristiany (1965) explained that honor and shame are the constant preoccupation of individuals in small-scale, exclusive societies where face-to-face personal as opposed to anonymous relations are of paramount importance (Black-Michaud, 1975). Embodied within this evaluative system is the insecurity and instability of the honor-shame ranking, which actually is its perpetual, motivating force. Because of the constant threat to the individual's or group's mental and physical survival, instability forms the foundation for human interaction. Within the cultural sphere, this instability is emphasized by the constant need of individuals to assert and reassert their honor. Hobbes once spoke about the existence of a pecking order of honor in societies of equals, such as in an agricultural or pastoral community. Within these societies there exists constant competition for the bestowal of honor. The victor in any competition for honor finds his reputation enhanced by the humiliation of the vanquished.

Honor is closely related to power, which in turn is related to the physical person. The rituals by which honor is formally bestowed involve a ceremony which exploit its birthright of natural resources. Through the exercise of physical violence, which causes fear and serves as a catalyst for construction of a network of alliances, each group ensures survival. The individual's defense of his own honor and that of his group provides an opportunity for self-aggrandizement and the acquisition of prestige. In an economically very homogenous society, a man's prestige is the only quality he possesses to differentiate himself from other members of the same society. In conditions of total scarcity, the translation of conflicts over materially limited goods into conflicts in which the prize at stake is said to be honor prevents extreme material scarcity from resulting in wide-scale destruction (Hobsbawn, 1959).

(4) The resilience of feuding. Feuding establishes relationships between hostile groups because of survival threats. This is achieved only in the absence of conditions conducive to a respected centralized authority and through the only means available: violence. Violence creates a balance of power as well as an internal hierarchy dominated by prestige, honor, and manliness. As a social system in its own right, feud operates successfully to control the relations between groups and coerce conformity to norms. Violence, being an integral part of the system, is the only instrument of social control; a means of communication and a language for the expression of temporary relations of dominance and submission. Thus, where scarcity reigns, feud and violence become synonymous with society and institution.

SUMMARY

It is premature to venture upon a discussion of subculture, since the definition and purpose of culture still remains vague. By reestablishing a conceptual link between culture and evolution, further efforts can precisely define culture from a semiological perspective and approach the purpose of culture as an alternative adaptive mechanism to survival. It has been suggested that the evolution of parallel but distinct solutions to the survival dilemma has been met by the evolutionary organization of human beings into social control systems. The feuding response, one form of social control, has been consistently evoked throughout history as a response to external threats, such as chaotic conditions and ecological scarcity. This phase of the evolutionary development of justice systems utilizes violence as the intangible commodity around which a hierarchical ordering of relationships is established and justice maintained.

NOTES

1. Violence refers to those violent crimes cited by the Uniform Crime Reports: murder and nonnegligent manslaughter, forcible rape, robbery, and aggravated assault. Disproportional rates can be reflected by the fact that in 1976, 11 percent of the U.S. population was black and 45.5 percent of those arrested for a violent crime were also black. It is argued that arrest data reflect other variables besides the actual offense behavior, but victimization surveys substantiate the disproportional involvement of blacks in violent crime.

2. The radical criminology movement incorporates Marxist ideology into interpretations of crime and criminal justice.

3. Evolutionism has been a very durable paradigm since the 1800s. Since Spencer, Tyler, and Maine, scholars are still studying the relationship between biological and cultural evolution (Dobzhansky, 1962; Alland, 1967; Garn, 1964; Hallowell, 1950; Wallace, 1961; Campbell, 1975).

4. Data that are believed to support the subculture of violence theory emphasize the preponderance of poor, youth, male, intraracial variables portraying violent crime (Wolfgang, 1958; Amir, 1971; Normandeau, 1968; Mulvihill and Tumin, 1969; Pittman and Handy, 1964).

5. Because studies (Etkin, 1954; Kellogg, 1968) claim that chimpanzees can develop a vocabulary in sign language, it can be argued that symbolic communication does not necessarily create the capacity for culture. Hallowell (1950) suggested the concept of protoculture to denote the systems of socially learned behavior among the primates below man. Protoculture is distinguished from culture by the lower level of symbolic communication.

6. The process of adaptation is much more complex than presented in the article. Although space does not permit elaboration, it still must be understood that

> change does ot occur in response to need. Without mistakes there could be no evolution, and evolution, therefore, is an accidental process. An evolutionary change can only occur if some of the variation already present within the population has a certain value as far as adaptation to new conditions is concerned [Alland, 1967].

7. Malinowski thought that the fundamental purpose of law was to curb

> certain natural propensities, to hem in and control human instincts and to impose an nonspontaneous compulsory behavior to secure a type of cooperation which is based on mutual concessions and sacrifices for a common end...different from the innate spontaneous endowment [Malinowski, 1926].

REFERENCES

ABU-ZEID (1966) "Honor and shame among the Bedouins of Egypt," in J. G. Peristiany, Honor and Shame: The Values of Mediterranean Society. Chicago: University of Chicago Press.

ALLAND, A. (1967) Evolution and Human Behavior. Garden City, NY: Natural History Press.

AMIR, M. (1971) Patterns in Forcible Rape. Chicago: University of Chicago Press.

ARENSBERG, C. (1937) The Irish Countryman: An Anthropological Study. New York: Macmillan.

BALL-ROKEACH, S. (1973) "Values and violence: a test of the subculture of violence thesis." American Sociological Review 30: 736-744.

BANCROFT, G. (1866) History of the United States. Boston: Little, Brown.

BARTHES, R. (1968) Elements of Semiology. New York: Hill and Wang.

BLACK-MICHAUD, J. (1975) Cohesive Force: Feud in the Mediterranean and the Middle East. Oxford: Basil Blackwell.

BLOCH, M. (1961) Feudal Society (L. A. Manyon, trans.). Chicago: University of Chicago Press.

BLUMENTHAL, H. R., R. HAHN, F. ANDREWS and K. HEAD (1972) Justifying Violence: Attitudes of American Men. Ann Arbor: Survey Research Center, Institute for Social Research, University of Michigan.

BRYSON, F. R. (1935) The Point of Honor in 16th Century Italy. New York: Columbia University Press.

CAMPBELL, D. T. (1975) "On the conflicts between biological and social evolution and between psychology and moral tradition." American Psychologist 12: 1103-1125.

CAMPBELL, J. K. (1964) "The kindred in a Greek mountain community," pp. 73-96 in J. Pitt-Rivers (ed.) Honour, Family and Patronage: A Study of Institutions and Moral Values in a Greek Mountain Community. Oxford: Clarendon.

CLOWARD, R. and OHLIN, L. (1960) Delinquency and Opportunity: A Theory of Delinquent Gangs. New York: Free Press.

COHEN, A. K. (1955) Delinquent Boys. New York: Free Press.

COON, C. (1954) The Story of Man: From the First Human to Primitive Culture and Beyond. New York: Alfred A. Knopf.

CURTIS, L. (1975) Race and Culture. Lexington, MA: D. C. Heath.

DeSAUSSURE, F. (1968) Cours de linguistique générale. Paris: Payot.

DOBZHANSKY, T. (1962) Mankind Evolving. New Haven, CT: Yale University Press.

——— (1964) "Cultural direction of human evolution," pp. 93-98 in S. Garn (ed.) Culture and the Direction of Human Evolution. Detroit: Wayne State University Press.

DOZIER, E. P. (1966) Mountain Arbiters: The Changing Life of a Philippine Hill People. Tuscon: University of Arizona Press.

DURHAM, M. E. (1909) High Albania. London: Edward Arnold.

ECO, U. (1976) A Theory of Semiotics. Bloomington: Indiana University Press.

EGLIN, P. (1976) "A methodological critique of ethnosemantics based on ethnomethodology." Semiotica 17: 339-369.

ETKIN, W. (1954) "Social behavior and the evolution of man's mental faculties." American Naturlist 88: 129-142.

EMERSON, A. E. (1958) "The evolution of behavior in social insects," pp. 311-335 in Roe and Simpson (eds.) Behavior and Evolution. New Haven, CT: Yale University Press.

FERRACUTI, F., R. LAZZARI and M. WOLFGANG (1970) Violence in Sardinia. Rome: Bulzoni.

——— (1973) Psychological Testing of the Subculture of Violence. Rome: Bulzoni.

FRASHIERI, K. (1964) A History of Albania. Cambridge: Cambridge University Press.

GARN, S. (1964) Culture and the Direction of Human Evolution. Detroit: Wayne State University Press.

GASTIL, R. D. (1971) "Homicide and a regional culture of violence." American Sociological Review 36: 412-426.

GINZBURG, L. (1955) On Jewish Law and Lore. Philadelphia: Jewish Publication Society of America.

GOEBEL, J. (1976) Felony and Misdemeanor: A Study in the History of Criminal Law. Pennsylvania: University of Pennsylvania Press.

HACKNEY, S. (1977) "Southern violence," pp. 505-527 in H. D. Graham and T. R. Gurr (eds.) Violence in America. Beverly Hills, CA: Sage.

HALLOWELL, I. A. (1950) "Personality structure and the evolution of man." American Anthropologist 52: 159-174.

HASLUCK, M. M. (1954) The Unwritten Law of Albania. Cambridge: Cambridge University Press.

HARDY, M. J. (1963) Blood Feuds and the Payment of Blood Money in the Middle East. Leiden: E. J. Brill.

HENRY, J. (1959) "Culture, personality and evolution." American Anthropologist 61: 221.226.

HESS, H. (1970) Mafia and Mafiosi: The Structure of Power (E. Osers, trans.). Lexington, MA: D. C. Heath.

HOBSBAWN, E. J. (1959) Primitive Rebels: Studies in Archaic Forms of Social Movement in the 19th and 20th Centuries. New York: W. W. Norton.

HOROWITZ, I. C. and G. SCHWARTZ (1974) "Honor, normative ambiguity and gang violence." American Sociological Review 39: 238-251.

IANNI, F. (1972) A Family Business: Kinship and Social Control in Organized Crime. New York: Russell Sage.

IVES, G. (1970) A History of Penal Methods. Montclair, NJ: Patterson-Smith.

JERISON, H. J. (1964) "Interpreting the evolution of the brain," pp. 45-74 in S. Garn (ed.) Culture and the Direction of Human Evolution. Detroit: Wayne State University Press.

KELLOGG, W. N. (1968) "Communication and language in the home-raised chimpanzee." Science 162: 423-427.

KWAN, K. and T. SHIBUTANI (1965) Ethnic Stratification: A Comparative Approach. New York: Macmillan.

LOCKE, J. (1975) [1610] Essay Concerning Human Understanding. Oxford: Clarendon.

LORENZ, K. (1966) On Aggression. New York: Bantam.

MALINOWSKI, B. (1926) Crime and Custom in a Savage Society. London: Routledge & Kegan Paul.

——— (1944) A Scientific Theory of Culture. Chapel Hill: University of North Carolina Press.

MASTERS, R. D. (1976) "Genes, language and evolution." Semiotica 12: 295-319.

MULVIHILL, D. J. and M. M. TUMIN (1969) Crimes of Violence, vols. 11, 12, 13. Staff Report to the National Commission on the Causes and Prevention of Violence. Washington, DC: U.S. Government Printing Office.

NEWMAN, G. R. (1978) The Punishment Response. Philadelphia: Lippincott.

——— (1979) Understanding Violence. Philadelphia: Lippincott.

——— (1976) Comparative Deviance: Perception and Law in Six Cultures. New York: Elsevier.

NEWMAN, G. R. and C. HAFT (1977) "Violent subcultures and gang delinquency." (unpublished)

NORMANDEAU, A. (1968) "Patterns and Trends in Robbery." Ph.D. Dissertation, University of Pennsylvania. (unpublished)

PERISTIANY, J. G. (1965) Honour and Shame: The Values of Mediterranean Society. Chicago: University of Chiago Press.

PETERS, E. L. (1951). "The Sociology of the Bedouin of Cyrenaica." Ph.D. Dissertation, Oxford University.

——— (1967) "Some structural aspects of the feud among the camel herding Bedouin of Cyrenaica." Africa 37: 261-282.

PETTIGREW, T. F. and R. B. SPIER (1971) "The ecological structure of Negro homicide." American Journal of Sociology 67: 621-629.

PIGLIARU, A. (1970) Il Banditismo in Sardegna: La Vendetta Barbaricia. Milano: Guiffre.

PITTMAN, D. J. and W. HANDY (1964) "Patterns in criminal aggravated assault." Journal of Criminal Law, Criminology and Police Science 55: 462-470.

PITT-RIVERS, J. (1966) "Honour and social status," in J. G. Peristiany, Honour and Shame: The Values of Mediterranean Society. Chicago: University of Chicago Press.

RICHARDSON, R. (1943) Texas, the Lone Star State. Englewood Cliffs, NJ: Prentice-Hall.

SAPIR, E. (1949) Language. New York: Harcourt Brace Jovanovich.

SCHERER, K. R., R. P. ABELES and F. C. FISCHER (1975) Human Aggression and Conflict. Englewood Cliffs, NJ: Prentice-Hall.

SEAGLE, W. (1941) The Quest for Law. New York: Alfred A. Knofp.

SONNICHSEN, C. L. (1962) The Story of the Great Feuds of Texas. New York: Devin-Adair.

SONNICHSEN, C. L. (1957) Ten Texas Feuds. Albuquerque: University of New Mexico Press.

SPUHLER, J. N. (1959) The Evolution of Man's Capacity for Culture. Detroit: Wayne State University Press.

STARK, R. and J. McENVOY (1970) "Middle class violence." Psychology Today 4: 52-60.

TAYLOR, I., P. WALTON and J. YOUNG (1973) The New Criminology: For a Social Theory on Deviance. New York: Harper & Row.

U.S. Department of Justice, Federal Bureau of Statistics (1977) Uniform Crime Reports. Washington, DC: U.S. Govenrment Printing Office.

U.S. Department of Justice, Law Enforcement Assistance Administration (1974) Criminal Victimization in the United States. Washington, DC: U.S. Government Printing Office.

WALLACE, A.F.C. (1961) Culture and Personality. New York: Random House.

WALLACE-HADRILL (1962) The Long Haired Kings and Other Studies in Frankish History. London: Methuen.

WASHBURN, S. L. and V. AVIS (1948) "Evolution and human behavior," pp. 421-436 in Roe and Simpson (eds.) Evolution and Behavior. New Haven, CT: Yale University Press.

WEIDENREICH, F. (1951) "Morphology of solo man." Anthropology Papers, American Museum of Natural History 43: 205-290.

WHORF, B. (1956) Language, Thought and Reality: Selected Writings. Cambridge: Technology Press/MIT.

WOLFGANG, M. E. (1958) Patterns in Criminal Homicide. Philadelphia: University of Pennsylvania Press.

WOLFGANG, M. E. and F. FERRACUTI (1967) The Subculture of Violence. London: Tavistock.

FORMAL AND INFORMAL SOCIAL CONTROL IN CROSS-CULTURAL PERSPECTIVE

JEROME KRASE
EDWARD SAGARIN

Although in all societies informal (nonlegal) unofficial mechanisms play a great part in the reaction of people to those who violate the norms, the major attention of researchers, particularly those focusing on modern and western societies, has been on formal and official social control. Little information is available on the role and efficacy of informal methods for the control, discouragement, suppression, and punishment of those involved in patterns of deviant behavior. By contrast, anthropological studies of primitive and traditional societies are by definition studies of informal social control, due to the frequent absence of legal-rational entities, or their existence in a form indistinguishable from the elders, the kin group, or the community.

FORMAL AND INFORMAL: DICHOTOMIES AND IDEAL TYPES

For the purposes of this essay, the oft-cited distinction

of Toennies (1963) between Gesellschaft and Gemeinschaft will be used. The Gesellschaft is the ideal-typical formal group, often called an association-type society. It is an organic whole, a society based on relations or roles, in which persons are not involved with one another as whole beings but rather in their specific capacities in which they are related to one another. Gemeinschaft is a community-type society in which the functional integration is based on shared values and affectional ties. The family, village, peer, ethnic, or religious group can easily be seen as the Gemeinschaft which exercises informal control over behavior offensive to group values. This informal control is often seen by outsiders as "irrational" (for example, the pronatal mores of food-starved developing countries, or the demonstrations of Islamic women against equal rights for their sex).

The ascendancy of the Gesellscaft society and formal groups can be viewed in historical perspective as not having led to the elimination of Gemeinschaft and informal social organization, but instead to the restructuring of multileveled societies in which social activities are influenced and controlled by a continuum of norms ranging from purely informal to purely formal. Especially in ethnically diverse countries and in developing countries, tensions between these two types of sanctions can be expected.

Kurt Wolff (1964:650) points out that "in all social interaction, insofar as the person limits or conditions the actions of others or has his actions limited and conditioned by others, by social groups, communities, or societies of which he may or may not be a member," such mechanisms are social in character and hence constitute social control. The mechanisms may involve symbols, manipulation, internalization, socialization, sanctions, and other forms; it is sanctions that interest us here. A distinction between formal and informal sanctions in social control was made by Roucek (1978:11), who saw the informal exemplified "in the function of folkways and mores" and the formal "by the explicit establishment of procedures and the delegation of specific bodies to enforce them (laws, decrees, regulations, codes)."

In modern society, the ultimate authority in the formal system is the political state, with its monopoly of legitimate power of coercion, and operating via legal-rational agencies such as police, courts, penal institutions, legislatures, and administrative and executive bureaucracies. In contrast, the ultimate authority in informal control is less easily identified and is vested in a wide variety of traditional and/or primary groups of a religious, kinship, peer, occupational, and other character. Adding to the diversity of informal social control systems are the extreme variations in the temporal duration and "legitimacy" or "right" of social entities to exercise their influence or control, and the "right" of individuals or groups to reject the pressures of the controllers.

As with other theoretical definitions, the formal-informal dichotomy is a heuristic device which, in the real world, is not easily separable. They too often operate simultaneously in support of conflicting relationships, with important informal systems in such formal structures as the police, the armed forces, the courts, and legislative bodies. The existence and efficacy of informal networks in administrative and industrial bureaucracies has been noted by Blau (1963) and Gouldner (1954), respectively, and was earlier recognized by Weber (1947:137).

Between an informal system, in which the group functions without specificity of charges, adjudication of guilt, and authorization to inflict punishment conferred upon it by the state, and the formal system, in which there is legislation, arrest, adjudication, and punishment by personnel specifically authorized for these tasks, there are many halfway stops. These are exemplified by such diverse measures as diversionary programs in America for youths, comrade courts or people's courts in many European countries, and formal sanctions taken by nongovernmental bodies — legally permitted but not empowered to do so — such as the Roman Catholic and Orthodox Jewish courts.

INFORMAL:
THE RELATIVELY UNSTUDIED SANCTIONS

Sumner (1906) made what was perhaps the most thorough attempt to amass detail on social control, as it applies both to everyday behavior and to the most important conduct affecting, or believed to affect, the welfare of the society. However, Sumner's emphasis was on the variety of approved and disapproved types of conduct, with only incidental mention of the reaction by the government, religious orders, kinfolk, or others to the violation of such conduct.

The formal mechanisms of control have been given the greater amount of attention by social scientists, particularly in their studies of western societies. The formal are usually more visible, more quantifiable, and more easily validated than are informal and unofficial sanctions. In many ways, "informal social control" is a residual category; that is, it encompasses all social control that is not formal.

In contrast, much less is available on the role and efficacy of informal methods of controlling deviant activities. Exceptions to this rule of inattention are the anthropological studies; but their descriptive nature, accumulated as ethnographic detail, does not easily lend itself to cross-cultural comparisons.

There are several interrelated reasons for the emphasis placed on the study of formal mechanisms of control. As societies technologically advance, greater proportions of human activities become the concern and domain of formal social agencies which are politically empowered to assume the tasks of once traditional control entities. For example, Cohen (1969) notes the growth of government control over sexual behavior in a sample of 60 countries as both an end in itself and a means of political control (but in many developed countries, there has probably been a reversal of this trend during the past decade, if not longer). It may appear to some that only deviant behavior which falls between the cracks of formal institutional purview are susceptible to informal social control; but informal mechanisms for the control of almost all forms of deviance, including that subject to legal-formal sanctions, continue to be important in all modern societies.

The emphasis placed by social scientists on standardized and quantitative methods of analysis and evaluation has led to a concentration on the formal at the expense of informal mechanisms. When one looks for rates or other indicators of deviant behavior, it becomes necessary to deal with organizations that record incidence or frequency, and this is usually a formal agency of social control. These agencies do not record all types of deviance, only those with which they have been specifically empowered to deal. Cross-culturally, it is not as difficult to make meaningful comparisons among police, courts, prisons, and official punishments as it is to compare attitudes that manifest themselves in ostracism or ridicule.

Studies of informal social control of deviance are by nature time-consuming. They require intensive understanding of cultural and subcultural variations as well as linguistic differences and nuances. Furthermore, the salience of findings from qualitative research is suspect because of the wide range of informal methods of social control resulting from the greater impact of situational, ethnic, religious, class, age, and other potential subcultural variables.

Those who do comparative studies of deviant behavior can face the task in two different ways. The researcher can emphasize the variation from one society to another, ranging from approval and encouragement to strong disapproval and negative sanctions (and including indifference and tolerance without approval), for a given type of behavior. In another perspective, the researcher can look at behavior disapproved in two or more societies, or preferably in almost all, and note the diversity of the social sanctions imposed on the transgressor.

Actually, there are relatively few types of behavior universally defined as deviant, although modern societies seem to be moving in the direction of accepting the concept that some activities are *mala in se* (evil in themselves). However, not only do official punishments differ, but the unofficial or informal sanctions differ, as do the definitions that interpret the behavior as falling within the purview of deviance. It would appear, then, that the study of informal methods employed to control specific behaviors and informal social control agents, rather than the differential disapproval of specific modes of conduct, might lead to some useful generalizations.

A common pitfall in doing cross-cultural research on deviance is found in a prior selection by the investigator of what constitutes deviance. If deviance is a quality not of intrinsic evil but of the reaction of hostility, outrage, or some other negative manifestation by the audience, then it must be related to the particular societies that make such negative evaluations and show such reactions. This does not deny that some acts are evil in and of themselves, but that they often are not seen as evil within the society. Furthermore, it may be precarious when one leans on the anthropological evidence because it is sometimes based on reports of travelers, missionaries, explorers, and warriors, or on informants who may have misunderstood or mispresented. Arens (1979) has recently claimed that, although "everybody knows" that there were cannibals among primitives, there is no evidence of institutionally and socially approved cannibalism that can stand up under scientific scrutiny.

SEXUALITY:
THE WEST AND THE EAST

The potential pitfall in prior selection of deviant activities for cross-cultural analysis is seen in the area of sexual deviance. In American society, it is generally agreed that homosexuality, prostitution, and adultery are looked upon with sufficient disfavor by a large enough part of the population to qualify as deviance. To a segment of the population even *discussion* of sex is outrageous, and the dissemination of information on birth control is disapproved. Yet, in other societies, mistresses, heterosexual concubinage, and polygamy (or more accurately polygyny) meet little disapproval and in fact are often approved. In the Orient — particularly in those segments of the population not reached by Christianity — sexual activity does not have an essential quality of "sin," but rather of play or recreation, when it is not specifically employed for procreation. There is little social control over adult consensual sexual conduct, so long as it does not negatively affect other social responsibilities.

Many behaviors that westerners would regard as deviant are not subject to moral judgments in Japan. The Japanese are not socialized to feel guilt for the performance of normal bodily functions, including sexual activity. This perception of sex, combined with the need for achievement and the rigors of family responsibility which are deeply ingrained in the Japanese culture (see DeVos, 1973), has led to the view of sexual gratification as being natural in the Japanese context. Especially for males, it is viewed as ego-boosting and a reward for achievement (in itself not sharply different from the attitudes found in the west, except that the latter are circumscribed by prohibitions and an aura of sin). Historically, however, the family, with its conjugal couple, was not defined as the appropriate place for sexual recreation. Other family responsibilities, such as having a clean and orderly household and attending to the proper upbringing of the children, were paramount, and frequent sexual activity between husband and wife was frowned upon if seen as interfering with more important household duties. Sexual activity outside of marriage was hence considered not only acceptable but "expectable" behavior.

What western nations define as "adultery," with the attendant, primarily informal sanctions, has no direct equivalent in the Japanese culture. Extramarital relations are deviant only to the extent that they present a danger to the family or the communal unit. Romantic attachments present the greatest danger, as they threaten commitment to one's spouse. Although the frequency of adultery among men, far greater than among women, may not be unlike that in American society (Kinsey et al., 1948, 1953), in Japan this seems to be met with less of a facade of outrage and with a greater degree of openness and institutionalization. Thus, a common and acceptable form of extramarital sex for the male is through the patronage of prostitutes or through the acquisition of a mistress. But the situation becomes deviant, in the sense of arousing anger, when too much time or family resource is spent in the pursuit of recreational sex. Gossip and rumors concerning expensive or time-consuming recreation circulate easily and almost inevitably reach family centers. Relatives, friends, and neighbors then are able to shame the deviant back into appropriate appetites. To the Japanese, being talked about is a powerful sanction to a far greater extent than in the west.

The role of women in the informal social control network is woven into the fabric of society. Females are socialized to be publicly subservient to males, but are also expected to be assertive, and indeed aggressive, when it comes to family responsibilities — the latter including the control of their husbands. Men are socialized to depend on females for ego gratification and therefore for approval and for a public indication of success. Men expect to be shown deference, particularly in the presence of others. But given the openness of Japanese communal society, the woman has ample opportunity to "bring her husband to ground" in the view of onlookers. This informal power of women to shame their husbands easily and publicly is also evidenced in Hindu caste society, but it is not alien to the western world, as it is found in Mediterranean villages.

Japan has a long history of prostitution as a respected profession. The Geisha life and high-priced consorts have carried with them a high degree of social prestige, directly related to the cultural value placed on achievement and to the high consciousness of status. Prostitution, except at the lowest levels of the occupation, has no negative connotations. The female prostitute was seen as an independent woman who was evaluated by success in her field of endeavor, and inasmuch as she did not constitute a threat to the family, she was not subject to informal social pressures. Some modern prostitutes are less socially acceptable because they have taken on a western aspect of "toughness" and have moved out on the streets for solicitation of customers.

Some have argued that changes in the modern Japanese family, paralleling in many ways changes taking place elsewhere in the world, have made recreational sex between spouses more acceptable — and, with feminism, more demanded by increasingly liberated wives. This may have depressed the market for prostitutes, leading achievement-oriented prostitutes to seek more vigorously the pursuit of "sleazy" commercial sex. There is less need for ego gratification through the companionship and sex with doting females who are paid for a display of their affection as new spouse roles emerge.

Intricate and often contradictory attitudes mark the sexual scene in Japan. Teenagers are not socialized to view sex per se as immoral, but to take note at all times of how their conduct will affect their family and community responsibilities. Middle-class families, with aspirations of upward mobility, are likely to exercise strict control over the sexual activities of their offspring, but with greater stress on the control of females. For young people to engage in sex is not itself a sign of delinquency, but it may lead to other problems, including poor work in school. The drive for success is uppermost, be it in school, at work, or in marriage.

Homosexuality has had a long history of tolerance in Japan, and has been subject almost exclusively to informal control. Except for public solicitation, homosexual activity between consenting adults is not against the law in Japan, although it is stigmatized in all but a few circles.

When one adds to the sexual scene a depiction of alcohol and other drug use in Japan, what emerges is a society deeply involved with informal social control. Attitudes about the use of alochol are generally positive, and the Japanese express tolerance toward the use of drugs, but without approval. Similar views toward alcohol, recreational sex, and other pleasure-producing conduct are found in Korean society (Kim, 1973).

THE CHINESE SCENE

Chinese and Japanese societies share many cultural values. However, due to history and to their divergent geographies, the countries have developed striking political, economic, and technological differences. Nevertheless, some similarities can be found in the informal social control mechanisms and in the abstract view toward deviant behavior.

Like Japan, China was catapulted into the modern era directly from feudalism. Left behind, largely undisturbed, were the communal ways of life and traditional attitudes. The moral precepts of Confucianism continue to operate in informal relations, which stress filial piety and the central importance of the extended family in social life.

A. A. Wilson and his associates (1977) contend that in the People's Republic, the state became the ultimate extension of kin (as was Shintoism in Japan). In effect, the state became the "moral entrepreneur" of Chinese society. It injects its ideological substance into social rules and effectively employs various mechanisms for sanctioning appropriate and inappropriate behavior. The employment of these methods by the state would generally mark a shift from formal to informal, but what the Chinese apparently did was to make formal use of informal sanctions.

Many western observers of Chinese society have described the phenomenon of what they call "thought control" in Communist China. Other than in the fantasy world of George Orwell, which bears so many striking and frightening resemblances to a world which is only a few years away from 1984, literal thought control is impossible. However, all societies have attempted to exercise strong influence over what people think. The emphasis in China on thoughts, rather than on actions, derives from an age-old view that subjective and objective experiences are not dichotomous but are opposite ends of an ontological continuum (Munro, 1977). Knowledge of this ancient pragmatism in Chinese philosophy may illuminate current attitudes about deviant behavior. Because action derives from thought and is a continuation of it, people are not punished for their deviance — they are "reeducated."

This shift from punishment to education necessarily brings into play a system of informal social control. In a society with so strong a family influence, it would be expected that such control would be exercised by kin, but the state as extension of kin makes it possible to replace the family and nonetheless retain the informal nature of the sanctions. Traditionally, the family takes a restitutive as a possible alternative to a legal-punitive attitude toward deviant members, and the state both buttresses and replaces the family in that task.

The Chinese family also exercises its greatest social influence by seeking to prevent deviance through socialization (as is the case in western societies) and through close supervision of behavior in communal settings (not present in most of the western world). Later, the state becomes more directly involved in these functions via officially organized communal residential and work-place groups. These groups act in lieu of the extended family, or as a sort of official extended family. When a member is viewed as straying, he is brought back into the fold by verbal or other social persuasion. Action that would be construed as punitive rather than educative, corrective, or rehabilitative is rarely taken by such groups, except during periods of "cleansing'' such as took place during the cultural revolution, and such periods are indubitably set in motion by central authorities.

The Chinese state utilizes family, neighborhood, and clan as well as work extension groups to guide individuals into ideologically acceptable behavior. Greenblatt (1977) notes that in China the social control system is extremely "elastic." Almost overnight, definitions of what constitutes deviance can change. The legislative legitimation and codification of criminal law did not begin until many years after the Communist ascendancy, and has not at this time been completed. The elasticity of normative prescriptions and proscriptions makes it imperative that the state exercise absolute control of the mass media, but the latter are tied to official small-scale and quasi-informal groups which meet regularly in communal settings to practice "struggle, criticism and self-criticism" centered on instructions from central authorities.

In China, more than in most other nations, it is difficult to speak of formal and informal mechanisms of social control as separate entities. They are fused and often indistinguishable. However, the teachings of proper behavior, through formal and informal methods, run parallel courses. The oral tradition made wide use of parables, utilized today by central authorities in the production of books, newspapers, film, theater, and even dance. In these parables, those who betray the revolution come to the same ingnominious end as those who betray their families and shirk family responsibilities.

Even in formal positions, the Chinese see themselves as an integral part of some informal social group. Therefore, the threat of removal of group support becomes a devastatingly powerful informal mechanism. Local neighborhood, work, or other groups meet on a regular basis and serve routine functions of control through "study and life examination," that might bear some resemblance to consciousness-raising as it thrived for a time in the United States, except that in China the line of conduct to be achieved is laid down from above. The groups range in size from three to about 30 members, who engage in face-to-face peer group interaction. They articulate their problems and trace these back to "errant thoughts." When deviants are discovered by the group (or created, for that matter), they are shown the errors of their ways and guided back to normality. The maximum penalties imposed through the small group are labeling and shunning. The withholding of the social support of the group can constitute severe punishment.

The power of informal small-group sanctions is illustrated by Greenblatt (1977:92), who quotes from an interview with a "right-leaning" deviant:

> No one would smile at me. No matter where I went, comrades would stop their conversations. Their laughter would cease, and they would step aside until I passed. When I went to the cafeteria, everyone turned away from me. When comrades in my small group received tickets to the movies, I wasn't given any. If I went to a movie on my own, I stood in the back of the theater to watch because I didn't want to be seen or to be made even more unhappy knowing that people would only move away if I sat down. I didn't have a friend in the world. At night, I would stay in my room and cry. I couldn't even stand to let the sun into my room during the day. I would draw the curtains so that no one would see me. It went on like this for months.

It would appear that, despite strong government influence in the informal group setting, such groups nevertheless have a vitality and independence of their own. Bennett (1977) shows that the informal organization of cadres and activists in small groups exhibits differences, with higher-level cadres more fearful and concerned with observation of their behavior because more is expected of them by central authorities and the "masses." Therefore, they try to develop strong attachments and friendships within their groups which can protect them when necessary from formal authorities and provide relief from tension.

In short, Chinese society offers an excellent example of the utilization by formal control agents of informal mechanisms of control. There is evidently little conflict between the two systems; and if informal control is still widely used, it is not because formal systems have broken down, but because they (the formal) can be more effective with the tools and even the facade of the informal.

THE SOVIET UNION AND
THE PROBLEM OF ALCOHOLISM

In a discussion of the problem of alcoholism in the Soviet Union, Connor (1972) demonstrates how informal social organizations can promote alcohol abuse, with a resultant clash between the norms of small groups and of a centralized political authority.

That Russia is a traditional drinking culture and that the abuse of alcohol is widespread in the Soviet Union is readily admitted. There is a wide gap between the attitudes of modern urbanized and collectivized peasants and the demands of formal bureaucratic agencies. Whereas the government and the Communist Party may view drinking as excessive and see its potential for social harm, this attitude is not widely shared among the people. A drinker is a "real man," and refusal to drink is often regarded as insulting, peculiar, or just stupid in foregoing one of life's pleasures (Connor, 1972:40). Children are socialized to admire drinking in their families, while at the same time they are exposed to a constant deluge of propaganda on the evil effects of drinking. For the male particularly, participation in heavy drinking bouts comes to be accepted and expected, and when he is of age to enter such activities, he goes through what might be termed "drinking rites of passage." A first experience at becoming intoxicated is the achievement of manhood, the epitome of masculinity and of solidarity with fellow workers. Connor (1972:104) notes that young workers are expected by their older comrades to "wash down" their first paycheck.

Informal tolerance of drunkenness is also prevalent in the lower echelons of formal control agencies. Connor (1972:44) cited a local factory manager who commented on a worker's excessive drinking which led to the disruption of his family life: "Well, so a man drinks. It's his money he spends, nobody else's. He beats his wife? Well, she's his wife!"

The concern of Soviet authorities with heavy drinking is not the result of a Puritanical attitude toward drinking. Authorities see alcohol abuse much the same way as Americans see drug abuse: as a cause of secondary deviance. Although the small number of cars makes drunken driving less of a problem than in the United States, drinking is held responsible for juvenile delinquency, vandalism, loss of work, family breakdown, and problems of health.

As in other postrevolutionary countries, Russia has coopted informal work organizations to handle alcoholism and other deviance. Although centrally directed, the operations are essentially communal, using particularly the power of shame and humiliation to bring members back into line. Newspapers report stories of workers breaking down before their comrades, bursting into tears, swearing never again to become intoxicated, and becoming good production workers and living exemplary lives. Such stories are repeated frequently.

Like the People's Republic of China, the Soviet Union is almost totally controlled by the formal power structure. Both societies offer less leeway toward individual deviation from the norms and less tolerance for deviant behavior than do the western countries, and both utilize the pervasive power of informal groups and traditional norms to combat those who would subvert national goals.

THE DEVELOPING COUNTRIES

Although some distance always exists between formal and informal systems of social control, it is in the developing countries that this distance is potentially the greatest. In the highly developed nations, informal controls are frequently hidden, because the formal and informal structures are apparently congruent with each other. The high rate of social change in developing countries creates new conflict, particularly in the competition between the generally traditional systems of control and the newly instituted ones. The codification of official norms into law and the crystallization of formal social control systems occur more rapidly than the emergence of any national normative consensus.

Although the particular practices and ideas about deviance in developing nations vary considerably, some generalizations can be made. There is generally a small degree if not a complete absence of self-consciousness among primitive people. There is collective rather than individual responsibility for actions. Therefore, according to Seibel (1972), the sanctioning process is directed toward the reintegration rather than the banishment or alienation of the deviant.

Restitution and indemnification are frequently used to expiate a wrong among primitive peoples and in less developed countries, whereas in the developed nations of the world violations of the norms are not rectified by such means. Howell (1954:25) noted in his study of the Nuer, a well developed African tribe, that adultery is absolved by the payment of six head of cattle and homicide by the payment of 40 head of cattle, each to the aggrieved group.

Gibbs (1963) provides another description of informal court systems in Africa. In the Kpelle Moot, groups, not individuals, are represented. For example, a group member accused of taking a goat from another will be defended by his own kinsmen against retaliation, but only if the goat was not taken in violation of his own group's norms. Stealing may be appropriate or inappropriate and is reacted to accordingly.

The form of punishment when transgressors are subjected to informal control varies considerably in primitive societies. The Ashanti, a highly centralized African tribe, were noted for deriding and ridiculing those who did not conform. Members subject to such shaming were sometimes driven to suicide. Corporal punishment has been inflicted by religious groups, such as in Islamic countries, and perpetrators of adultery (particularly women) have been stoned.

In rapidly urbanizing nations, the family and clan tend to lose their power over the individual, and the society begins to depend less upon informal sanctions to uphold standards of behavior deemed necessary in the society. Large collections of people who have migrated from the countryside are assembled in developing cities. They lack the necessary intergroup social ties and hence cannot depend upon informal mechanisms for the resolution of disputes. The new anonymity brings about freedom from the careful and watchful eye of family, tribal religious leaders, and peers, with a resultant increase in many forms of socially disapproved behavior.

In developing countries, according to Clinard and Abbott (1973), crimes of property are on the rise, and this is seen as an indicator of economic growth and development. There is increased public concern in the cities about crime, and increased reporting of illegal activities to formal authorities. This reliance on the formal may be less a result of trust in government as of a feeling of helplessness in chaotic situations. There seems to be an increase in violence in the developing nations, and some of this may be an indicator of an informal system of control emerging to replace the once powerful and now largely defunct indemnification, restitution, and retributive systems.

The distinction between rural and urban deviance is particularly striking in underdeveloped areas of the world. "Close personal relationships, rigidity of customs and convention prevent any disapproved practice from flourishing in the villages and rural areas," wrote Clinard and Abbott (1973:62-63). In the cities people are often relieved of the pressure of the strict village codes and adopt the practices and customs that flourish as marginal activity in urban centers. Illicit sexual behavior is hence more prevalent, but also less subject to severe negative sanctions. African prostitutes, for example, do not see themselves as pariahs, according to Dubois (1967), and pimps and other intermediaries are not as necessary a part of the prostitution scene as they are in Europe and America.

In Africa, the breakdown of strict village codes related to sexuality develops with great rapidity because of the large percentage of migrants to the cities who are unmarried or who travel without their wives in search of work. Their presence in large cities increases the demand for nonmarital sex, even though it is frowned upon in the villages from whence they came, and many of whose values they retain. The contrast between village and urban attitudes toward adultery is noted in remarks by men in Kampala, who speak of having "dismissed" their wives when they returned to the villages and found that they had been unfaithful, although the same men engaged in extramarital sex when they had been in the cities.

An investigation of crime in developing African cities sheds light on informal control of deviant behavior. Growing children are frequently influenced by the mass media and are used by adults for illegal activity. Dependence on the family and on schools is weakened with the rapid urbanization. With the collapse of traditional informal networks for controlling deviant behavior, the society leans heavily on formal agents of control. However, the newly urbanized population is unready to accept the legitimacy of police and courts. Residues of the tribal mores are evident, particularly the small concern for "outsiders" which serves to legitimate the victimization of persons from other groups. As the composition of developing cities ensures that most people are strangers to each other, the realm of "acceptable" criminal behavior widens. Even within a tribal or ethnic groups, the eclipse of community and the urban-rural distinction reduces the power of family or other informal institutions to exercise effective control over deviant behavior.

In contrast to the general breakdown of informal control systems in African cities, the informal control of children remains effective, particularly in Zambian villages. As seen by Clifford (1967), intermediate and extended family members deal with "bad" children: "Cursing, fighting, stealing, laziness, insolence, running away, lies, causing damage, and illicit sex" are prohibited by strict surveillance and control.

Nevertheless, traditional systems can survive the journey to the city, particularly if enough members of a tribe arrange to live together. Migrants often try to maintain village or tribal enclaves in urban areas, but informal systems of control eventually break down because traditional inhibitions are weakened by the heterogeneous social environment and the erosion of the power of the community. It is said that less criminality is found in the behavior of individuals with a strong family and tribal bond, but it is possible that the community shuns the transgressor as much as the alienated individual turns to crime. Low-crime areas appear to be those with strong family and tribal systems. As a generalization, African traditions of informal social control are derived from and rooted in the village. Urban migrants with restricted contact with outsiders are most likely to maintain traditional ties and uphold the traditional moral codes, but again the temporal sequence is unclear.

THE LATIN CULTURE
AND HOMOSEXUALITY

Informal systems of social control present many potential influences on the incidence and character of deviant behavior. They share with formal systems the power to define deviance, teach what are the appropriate and inappropriate behaviors and attitudes, and use their influence to promote or repress them. Informal systems also have the power to reduce or increase the incidence of deviant behavior by controlling the opportunities and situations for the expression of negatively sanctioned conduct. The example used to illustrate this will be the Latin (and specifically the Mexican) attitude toward homosexuality, as described by Carrier (1976).

As in many other societies, male homosexuality is portrayed by the Mexican mass media as a sickness and its practitioners as shameful creatures. Although one might expect an attitude of compassion in a country with so strong a Catholic influence, such compassion is seldom encountered, and in its place there is ridicule, hostile humor, and other expressions of condemnation in the mass media and in everyday interaction. This contempt is not accompanied by formal, legal sanctions; in fact, there are no legal prohibitions against homosexual acts between consenting adults in private.

Nonetheless, there is an interplay between the formal and the informal as governmental authorities, probably in response to mass pressure, attempt to keep homosexuality out of the view of the public. People are harassed often arrested when they attempt to congregate in bars, clubs, and other areas.

As in other Latin cultural systems, males are expected to exhibit machismo qualities of virility and strength in both appearance and activities. The Mexican male is socialized to seek sexual outlets, but only as the dominant partner in all relationships. With strong ties between parents and children, the unmarried of both sexes and regardless of age are expected to live with their families, to show deference to parents, and submit to parental supervision. For those males seeking homosexual outlets, such arrangements create especially stressful situations, for they are under the watchful eye of parents, siblings, extended family members, and neighborhood acquaintances.

The strong informal sanctions against homosexuality apply primarily, if not sometimes exclusively, to those males with effeminate mannerisms and who permit themselves to be subordinate to their partners. For dominant males, some homosexual contacts and experiences meet with little social disapproval, although they are not overtly approved, either. The dominant ones have not relinquished their maleness, and they often define only the partner (or insertee) as homosexual or with a slang synonym of highly pejorative character.

In the Latin family, parents encourage their sons to show their masculinity, to find heterosexual partners, and to marry. The discovery of homosexuality as a continuing and ongoing rather than an episodic process, as a preference rather than for *faute de mieux*, brings shame not only upon the individual but upon the family, and there develops a tacit if not open understanding that there shall be pretense, concealment, and an effort to save reputations.

In this situation, sons continue to act "macho" and spend considerable time and energy in intricate covering activities. The cover will include such tactics as the expression of intense interest in females, particularly passersby, with whom there is little likelihood that one will become involved.

While the macho concept is often thought of as a lower-class phenomenon, it is probably widespread throughout Latin societies. In the middle class, strict family life and careful supervision reduce the possibility for the development of a homosexual subculture. Young men showing signs of effeminacy are carefully scrutinized by parents, who place upon them many restrictions, including curfews. In this situation, young men of homosexual predilections may develop extremely strong masculine fronts; these are the men likely to have the most extensive network of contacts, while they also harbor the greatest fear of exposure. If their activities or even their interests should become known, they would be subject to the sanctions of informal groups, sanctions ordinarily reserved for the effeminate. This may well be because they are not defined as heterosexuals by preference who have chosen a male partner for lack of a female or as an expression of the subjugation of the other; rather, they are linked with the effeminates and the insertees.

As in other systems of informal sanctions, the mechanism for their expression and the severity that they assume are not well defined. Mexican fathers are said to be more hostile to sons veering toward homosexuality than are the mothers, but banishment from the home, or voluntary departure from it, is unusual.

Thus, there develops a great pressure on boys to be masculine, and, as in many other cultures, those who cannot make it retreat and adjust (or maladjust). A common form of scolding directed at a very young boy might be, "Act like a man, don't act like a *maricon*" (or *puto* or *joto*, all three being pejorative terms for the male who submits his body for sexual use by a man). Young boys are urged by older brothers, fathers, and male friends to have sex with prostitutes and with the "bad girls" of the neighborhood. As in other societies which have developed an encouraging attitude toward sex for young males while discouraging female sexuality for "good girls," there is an imbalance between demand and supply. In this situation, effeminate boys, pre- and postpubescent, become alternative targets for those boys seeking to demonstrate their masculiniity and at the same time obtain sexual outlet. Some of these early contacts are likely to be relatives, friends of the family, and neighbors — the very people who are charged with enforcing the informal code that expresses hostility toward homosexuality. Thus does the deviant — the object of social ignominy — become both product and victim of the informal system of control.

GENERALIZATIONS AND DIRECTIONS

Informal social control is a pervasive characteristic of human societies. People individually and collectively express their approval and disapproval, they encourage and discourage, they reward and punish. Such mechanisms exist in the family, where it is part of the socialization process, starting almost immediately after birth. It is found among peers and neighbors, in schools, at work, and in prisons.

With the rise of sophisticated societies having recognized and legitimated political structures, bureaucratic divisions of labor, rational-legal systems for governing, personnel who alone are authorized to affix government-sponsored punishments, and usually written codes that specify that which is wrong and decree in advance the negative sanctions to be imposed on transgressors, the formal largely tends to replace the once informal. If the formal system were able to be carried out with objectivity and impartiality — punishments imposed alike on the powerful and the powerless — the displacement of the informal might have been a great step forward toward a more just society. This would have been the case because informal sanctions are based on no system of trial, no adjudication of guilt or innocence, no sense of fair play. Rumor falsely based replaces the charge as well as the cloak of presumed innocence in which all defendants are said to be robed.

The ascendancy of the formal, however, follows no such ideal pathway. Power and privilege become paramount for individuals, families, social classes, and ethnic and racial groups. Disillusionment sets in. There is too much law, it is charged. In the words of Kadish (1967), there develops a crisis of over-criminalization. A historic debate, particularly in the western world, rages. Patrick Devlin (1965) staunchly defends the concept that the law is the symbolic codification of the moral precepts of a society and should retain that role. H.L.A. Hart (1962) counters that law has as its goal the protection of the state and individuals, and that freedom itself demands that law be excluded from areas where activities and preferences do not constitute a threat to personal or public safety. In the United States, the demand for decriminalization has been heard; Schur (1965) emphasized that it is a socially desirable step for "crimes without victims," Geis (1979) for conduct "not the law's business," and Duster (1970) warning against "the legislation of morality."

Nevertheless, some countervailing forces are seen in the modern world. The overthrow of the Shah of Iran and the struggle of Islamic forces to institute a theocracy was accomplished by a call for the formalization of sanctions (and extremely strong ones) against types of behavior formerly ignored in law or punished only rarely by the state. This is not to be interpreted as suggesting that the former state had been less punitive, but that the punition had been more actively directed against political enemies than nonpolitical deviants.

Although the German concentration camps under the Nazis were notorious for their imprisonment and murder of Jews, gypsies, and Communists, less known is that there was a round-up and imprisonment in those camps of homosexuals, with specially colored triangles of their own to identify the category into which the prisoner fell.

Historically, with the rise of urbanism and the decline of the extended family (both worldwide phenomena), it would appear that there has been a movement from the informal to the formal, but that, under the influence of strong libertarian and antitotalitarian pressure, there has been a reversal of this trend.

Thus, in the interests of protecting children (a libertarian concept), the Swedish government has outlawed corporal punishment inflicted on children by their own parents. When severe, punishment of this type is outlawed in many countries, where it is defined as child abuse, assault, or under other rubrics. The Swedish edict appears to go far beyond this. What occurs here is a reverse trend: namely, government action to reinstitute formal sanctions at a period of history and in a nation where the opposite courses have been pursued. All this is motivated by the same libertarian ideology that has informed the decriminalization movement. But whereas the child was once subjected to informal sanctions, now the parents are subjected to formal ones for invoking the informal.

In the United States, the move toward decriminalization of many activities is making headway. Only a few people have addressed the question of what occurs after an activity, once subjected to both formal and informal sanctions, is eliminated from the purview of the law. Skolnick and Dombrink (1979) have noted that all such conduct does not become institutionalized. Among many alternatives, one can redefine some problems as being medical (as drug addiction), or continue to subject them to informal disapproval and discouragement through education (as many would suggest for prostitution), or embrace the complete acceptance of the formerly criminal as an alternate lifestyle for those so choosing (as many gay rights partisans are advocating for their cause).

Still another development has occurred in the rebirth of informal and unofficial vigilante movements in many parts of the world. Such forces, constituting almost a shadow government and often with the aid and complicity of official government personnel, have been powerful in Italy (particularly Sicily) and in the United States (more in the south than elsewhere). A deep sense of frustration at the inability of the police to diminish crime and to satisfy victims and their friends and relatives with speedy arrests, and with the courts to obtain speedy trials, guilty verdicts, and to mete out severe punishments, has led to a resurgence of attitudes favorable to those who would "take the law into their own hands." The informal here replaces the formal because of the alleged failure of the latter.

In the cross-cultural examples that we have cited, there can be seen greater similarity in the modern world than dissimilarity. The attitudes of the Latins, and specifically the Mexicans, toward homosexuality do not deviate strongly from those found elsewhere, including the United States. The permissive world of the Japanese in things sexual has analogies with the double standard toward sex found almost worldwide; Geisha girls notwithstanding, the Japanese streetwalkers are not treated appreciably differently from prostitutes in the west. Ethnographic detail may have overemphasized the exotic, the element of culture shock that faced missionaries, travelers, and anthropologists, whereas distinctions in the modern world from one culture to another may be diminishing.

We would suggest that cross-cultural comparisons nevertheless offer several difficulties, stemming primarily from the following factors:

1. The dichotomy between informal and formal mechanisms of social control is artificial. The informal and formal exist on graduated continua, and they often merge into each other.

2. Social scientists generally place an emphasis on what is being done in a society to prevent deviance, but little emphasis has been placed on the manner in which informal control (and formal as well, but perhaps to a lesser extent) acts both to promote and to inhibit deviant expression.

3. There is a wide variation in cultural and subcultural definitions of what constitutes deviant behavior, and, relatedly, there may be a "lack of fit" between the official and the unofficial norms, both prescriptive and proscriptive.

4. There is a virtually unlimited range of social entities that can and do exercise informal control over deviance.

5. Finally, there is equally unlimited diversity in the methods for exercising such control.

REFERENCES

ARENS, W. (1979) The Man-Eating Myth: Anthropology and Anthropophagy. New York: Oxford University Press.

BENNETT, G. (1977) "China's mass campaigns and social control," pp. 121-139 in A. A. Wilson et al. (eds.) Deviance and Social Control in China. New York: Praeger.

BLAU, P. M. (1963) Dynamics of Bureaucracy. Chicago: University of Chicago Press.

CARRIER, J. M. (1976) "Family attitudes and Mexican male homosexuality." Urban Life 5: 359-375.

CLIFFORD, W. (1967) "Juvenile delinquency in Zambia." United Nations Report No. SOA/SD/C5.3 (April 30).

CLINARD, M. B. and D. J. ABBOTT (1973) Crime in Developing Countries: A Comparative Perspective. New York: John Wiley.

COHEN, Y. (1969) "Ends and means in political control: state organizations and punishment of adultery, incest and violation of celibacy." American Anthropologist 71: 658-687.

CONNOR, W. D. (1972) Deviance in Soviet Society: Crime, Delinquency and Alcoholism. New York: Columbia University Press.

DEVLIN, P. (1965) The Enforcement of Morals. New York: Oxford University Press.

DeVOS, G. A. (1973) Socialization for Achievement: Essays on the Cultural Psychology of the Japanese. Berkeley: University of California Press.

DUBOIS, V. D. (1967) "Prostitution in the Ivory Coast." Fieldstaff Reports, West African Series, Ivory Coast 10: 2.

DUSTER, T. (1970) The Legislation of Morality: Law, Drugs, and Moral Judgment. New York: Free Press.

GEIS, G. (1979) Not the Law's Business. New York: Schocken.

GIBBS, J. P., JR. (1963) "The Kpelle Moot: a therapeutic model for the informal settlement of disputes." Africa 33: 1-11.

GOULDNER, A. W. (1954) Patterns of Industrial Democracy. New York: Free Press.

GREENBLATT, S. L. (1977) "Campaigns and the manufacture of deviance in Chinese society," pp. 82-120 in A. A. Wilson et al. (eds.) Deviance and Social Control in China. New York: Praeger.

HART, H.L.A. (1963) Law, Liberty, and Morality. Stanford, CA: Stanford University Press.

HOWELL, P. P. (1954) A Manual of Nuer Law. London: Oxford University Press.

KADISH, S. (1967) "The crisis of overcriminalization." The Annals of the American Academy of Political and Social Science 374: 157-170.

KIM, S. D. (1973) "The night clubs of Seoul, Korea." Urban Life 2: 314-330.

KINSEY, A. C., W. B. POMEROY and C. E. MARTIN (1948) Sexual Behavior in the Human Male. Philadelphia: Saunders.

——— and P. H. GEBHARD (1953) Sexual Behavior in the Human Female. Philadelphia: Saunders.

MUNRO, D. J. (1977) "Belief control: the psychological and ethical foundations," pp. 14-36 in A. A. Wilson et al. (eds.) Deviance and Social Control in China. New York: Praeger.

ROUCEK, J. S. (1978) Social Control in the 1980's. Westport, CT: Greenwood Press.

SCHUR, E. M. (1965) Crimes Without Victims. Englewood Cliffs, NJ: Prentice-Hall.

SEIBEL, H. D. (1972) "Social deviance in comparative perspective," pp. 251-281 in R. A. Scott and J. D. Douglas (eds.) Theoretical Perspectives in Deviance. New York: Basic Books.

SKOLNICK, J. H. and J. DOMBRINK (1979) "The legalization of deviance," pp. 73-88 in E. Sagarin (ed.) Criminology: New Concerns. Essays in Honor of Hans W. Mattick. Beverly Hills, CA: Sage.

SUMNER, W. G. (1906) Folkways. Boston: Ginn.

TOENNIES, F. (1963) Community and Society. New York: Harper & Row.

WEBER, M. (1947) The Theory of Economic and Social Organization. New York: Oxford University Press.

WILSON, A. A., S. L. GREENBLATT and R. W. WILSON [eds.] (1977) Deviance and Social Control in China. New York: Praeger.

WOLFF, K. H. (1964) "Social control," pp. 650-652 in J. Gould and W. L. Kolb (eds.) A Dictionary of the Social Sciences. New York: Free Press.

THE SINGLE-STANDARD DEVIANT

S. GIORA SHOHAM

In this chapter I shall try to highlight some correlates of social deviance which are related to my recent personality theory (Shoham, 1979), the gist of which follows.

The main core vectors of my continuum were denoted as participation and separation. By participation I mean the identification of ego with a person or persons, an object, or a symbolic construct outside himself, and his striving to lose his separate identity by fusion with this other object or symbol. Indeed, love is one of the manifestations of ego's quest of particiaption. Separation, of course, is the opposite vector. I have used these opposing vectors of unification-fusion and separation-isolation as the main axis of my theory in conjunction with three major developmental phases. The first is the process of birth. The second is the crystallization of an individual ego by the molding of the "ego boundary." The third phase of separation is a corollary of socialization when one reaches one's "ego identity" (Erikson, 1956). The strain to overcome the separating and dividing pressures never leaves the individual. The striving to partake in a pantheistic whole is ever present and it takes many forms: if one avenue toward its realization is blocked, it surges out from another channel. Actual participation is unattainable by definition. The objective impossibility of participation is augmented by the countering separating vectors, both instinctual and interactive. At any given moment in our lives there would be a disjuncture, a gap between our desires for participation and our subjectively defined distance from our participatory aims. I have denoted this gap the Tantalus Ratio, which is the relationship between the longed-for participatory goal and the distance from it as perceived by ego (Shoham, 1979). These core vectors are related to the fixation of the separant and participant personality types. These in turn are related to the crystallization at later orality of a separate self out of the pantheistic mass of totality and early orality. This is in the ontological baseline by which the self is defined by the nonself; that is, the object. The coagulation of the self marks the cut-off point for the most basic developmental dichotomy: from birth and early orality to the phase where the ego boundary is formed around the emerging individual *seperatum* and from later orality onward. In the first phase, any fixation that might happen, and imprint thereby, some character trait on the developing personality is not registered by a separate self which is capable of discerning between the objects which are the source of the fixation-causing trauma and the self as its recipient. The experiencing entity is a nondifferentiated pantheistic totality. On the other hand, if the traumatizing fixation happens at the later oral phase after the objects have expelled the self from their togetherness by a depriving interaction with it, the self may well be in a position to attribute the cause of pain and deprivation to its proper source — the objects. I have proposed, therefore, a personality typology which is anchored on this developmental dichotomy of pre- and post-differentiation of the self (Shoham, 1979). The molding process is the nature and severity of fixation which determines, in turn, the placement of a given individual on the personality type continuum. However, the types themselves are fixated by developmental chronology: the *par-*

ticipant at predifferentiated early orality and the *separant* after the formation of the separant self. The participant core personality vector operates, however, with varying degrees of potency on both these personality types; but the quest for congruity manifests itself differently with each polar personality type. The participant aims to achieve congruity by defacing and annihilating himself, melting back, as it were, into the object, achieving thereby the pantheistic togetherness and nondifferentiation of early orality.

The *separant* type aims to achieve congruity by overpowering or "swallowing" the object. I have denoted the congruity aims of the self-effacing *participant* as *exclusion*, whereas the object-devouring separant wishes to achieve congruity by *inclusion*; that is, incorporating the object in his outreaching self.

We postulate a self that contains along a continuum both the components of interactive object relationship and the nonobjective being, which longs for participant omnipresence. This, of course, relates to our separant and participant core personality vectors, the dynamic interplay of which is being structured into corresponding polarities within the self.[1] I postulate, therefore, a duality of man's adaptation to his environment. Only when his inner self reaches a certain *modus vivendi* with the other interactive component of the self can a human being function properly vis-à-vis the normative system of society. This is based on my contention that our inner self is mostly structured around the "participant" core vector which strives to unify with the object and melt into it, whereas the interactive self is largely structured on the "separant" core personality vector which aims to swallow the object and incorporate it into itself. The successful synchronicity between these two vectors makes for a viable *modus vivendi* between the individual, his objective surroundings, and his human and normative environment. This, however, is a dialectic which tries to synthesize two totally divergent modes of perception, orientation, and cognitive directions. The cognition of the self is inwardly directed and megalomanic because it is coagulated from the pantheistic mass of early orality when the ego reigned supreme without any contrasting objects. On the other hand, the object, other people, and the normative system are the contrary, contrasting, and then oppressing "not self" which ever seems to menace and deprive ego of its birthright of choice and uniqueness.

My thesis in this chapter is that deviance valuewise could be predisposed by an individual adopting in an exaggerated manner one stance on the inner-interactive continuum of the self and not the one which is linked to the dialectical synthesis between these two components of the self. One extreme example which we would term as the participant single-standard deviant would be Kleist's Michael Kolhaas who projected on society his inner sense of justice and expected the normative system to comply with this inner image. The normative system of society was naturally reluctant to comply with these expectations, with tragic results for Kolhaas. This is in line with the age-old reproach of mothers to their rebellious sons: "if you bang your head against the wall your head is going to get hurt because the wall will not give in."

What is important to note here is that the extreme interactive-oriented type would not be stigmatized as a deviant by the power elite and the normative system because this seems to be the mode of the conforming majority of individuals in any society which would absorb any mandate coming from the power elite and applaud every new rule, fad, or fashion so long as it is backed by the people in power and by the normative structure. Revolutions shifting the normative system into diametrically opposite directions also carry with them the complying conformist majority. All those goose-stepping Nazis becoming goose-stepping ardent supsporters of the DDR: the mobs shouting in unison the name of Khomeini were the same mobs who used to shout with the same gusto the name of the Shah. In Israel, after Prime Minister Begin's party came into power, there suddenly was an avalanche of declarations of previous membership of the Irgun Zvai Leumi which totaled something like ten times the known real membership of this organization.

As stigmatization constitutes a very powerful component of social deviance, the type who is skewed to the interactive self is over conforming, would rarely be stigmatized, and hence would rarely be declared as deviant. Consequently, our single-standard deviant would mostly be of the inner-directed self who projects his notion as to how his surroundings should look and behave onto a reluctant normative system. I will recapitulate the model of social deviance I postulated elsewhere (Shoham, 1976).

Self Concept + value deviation + deviant behavior + social stigma + cognitions of transcedence $\longrightarrow$ social deviance.

This Chapter relates exclusively to the value deviation component of this model, yet it should be regarded within the wider context of the model. No single component can be fruitfully related to social deviance in itself. It should be integrated within the wider multivariate concept of the groups of factors which are linked in various contexts with social deviance. I shall, therefore, try to describe some tenets of the single-standard deviant in the wider context of social control and its inevitable clash with the normative system of society. If we take the bourgeois system of values without delving into the tricky definition of what is a bourgeois, we can argue that one of the basic qualities of a middle class and its equivalents in other societies is their double or multiple standards.

Types like Sinclair Lewis' Babbitt, the English middle class as described by a great number of writers from Dickens to Kingsley Amis, and the *bourgeois gentihomme* who is probably the archetype of the European middle and upper class display their multiple standards not only as their main characteristic but their main means of survival. Without developing a keen sense of the double intent, double-talk and double meanings, no bourgeois could carry on his precariously balanced relationship with his employers, colleagues, and wife. Double moral standards as far as sex is concerned enabled the Victorian gentleman to keep his outwardly righteous and austere puritan facade because there were something like 10,000 whores in Victorian London to cater for his lurid whims. He could feel himself very charitable and generous toward some sporadic isolated David Copperfields to white-wash his conscience and strengthen his selective perception toward child labor and a working day of 16 hours. As part of the rituals of social occasions, parties, meetings, cocktails, teas and gatherings around a chamber music group, or an Italian opera singer as well as in endless salons, cafe society, or, in the Israeli institution of Friday nights after-TV gossip circles, one should make the right noises, structure one's ideas, tone of voice, and the "right" demeanor around the multiple standards of a given group. Meetings of stockholders; managerial decision-making sessions; university senate gatherings; and, of course, executive boards of political parties, governments, and the assemblies of legislators usually have the morals and the aims of a Cro-Magnon cave dweller who sets out with his club to hunt for food or for a female. Yet all this is cached by ritual etiquette, custom, mores, and the conviction that language should be used to disguise one's intentions. This outwardly blasé, polite, and uninterested appearance hides the real covetous intentions of the bourgeois, law abiding, party member, executive, manager, and bureaucrat. We claim that the deviant either cannot or would not adjust himself to this double and multiple standard either because he does not understand the system or because his rebelliousness is more important to him than complying with the multiple standards of the normative system of society.

I envisage the continuum of the object-oriented individual versus the self-oriented one, which I prefer to denote as the separant and the participant. The extreme participant would be very much aware of the objects, other people, and the normative system of society. His successful or unsuccessful efforts to manipulate his surroundings would indeed be geared toward optimizing his position vis-à-vis the group and its normative system. This necessitates different standards when they relate to themselves and other standards when they relate to other people. Indeed, the gist of the defense mechanisms as expounded by Freud and the whole psychoanalytic movement is that they enable the individual to exist in value-based conflicts only, because he places himself on a different attitudinal and value level than his surrounding others. Projection, displacement, reaction formation, the camel syndrome (seeing derogatory attributes in others while ignoring the very same traits in oneself) are only a few of these defense mechanisms which make possible the normative viability of men in society. This brings to the fore the basic notion that adjustment to the normative system of society (that is, being nondeviant), actually necessitates a multiple standard orientation. Adjustment is preached not only by mothers, school teachers, and executives, but also (and sometimes mainly) by psychiatrists. Mothers warn their children, "Don't make trouble. If you do you will get hurt," meaning that they should comply with rules, otherwise they will have to pay for their noncompliance. The teacher poses the same threat by grading his students and the ominous possibility of throwing them out of school. The boss might point out quite bluntly that if "you don't do that or this and behave according to accepted modes of behavior in the firm, you will simply be fired at the end of the month." As for the psychiatrist, the odds are even greater — either behave as everyone else or go to a madhouse. This is the gist of psychiatry as a tool of social control, not only in Soviet Russia, where it is used like many other modes of coercion there with Byzantine bluntness, but also in the west, and especially in the United States. The institutions for the mentally ill, the psychiatrists and clinical psychologists and other lay analysts, whatever their creed, dogma, method, and system, preach and operate on the basic assumption that one has to adjust to a given normative system which is contradictory, oppressing, depressing, and levels down the uniqueness and creative conspicuousness of the individual, otherwise he will be subjected to all kinds of treatment, stigma, and other strenuous tools of social control. The whole antipsychiatrist trend from Szasz to Laing realized this, but then they cut the branch on which they sat. Any nonpsychiatric type of treatment is geared to a certain type of behavior change and adjustment to a given set of norms, including anarchy, the normlessness of which is a dogma. Consequently, even the antipsychiatrists pressure their patients to adjust to a given system of normativeness. What the antipsychiatrists want is a non-treatment or a nonadjustment adjustment, which is not only a contradiction in terms, but any attempt to implement its goals by their professed means inevitably leads to failure. The roaring failures of Laing and Cooper in their attempts to translate their theoretical premises into treatment projects are too self-evident to need further comment.

We could again take the example of psychoanalysis itself which sprang out of the notions of propriety prevailing among the Viennese bourgeousie with more than a touch of Jewish morality manifested in the figure of its founder. Psychoanalysis was no doubt a rebellious movement against the hypocrisy of the *fin-de-siècle* European bourgeousie for whom sex did not exist except in the whorehouses and in the "dirty" minds of adolescents. With the advent of psychoanalysis, permissiveness indeed became more and more the rule — but up to a point. This point in itself became a tool of exploitation which led again to the double standards epitomized so clearly in the case of the seducer in *Candy*. There the old lecher tells the young girl that she only thinks that he is having sex with her, but what he was actually having with her was much more sublime and glorious, which he had to teach her to perceive. Here again we reach new vistas with the self-fulfillment craze and the "turning on" which become the dogma and the regimens of treatment personnel and their priests. What should be pointed out is that the whole structure and the normative fiber of the bourgeoisie, so succinctly expressed by the myriads of novelists and playwrights, and more theoretically by Max Nordeau in his classic work on the "accepted lies of society," is based on the ability to comply with a multiple standard normative system in which one or more standards contradict the others. The bourgeois also embeds himself into a cocoon of a make-believe security and balloons of self-assertion which are as viable as the first pin-prick piercing them by a bully or a maniac. Consequently, in order to reach a modus vivendi with this contradictory and conflictual normative system, one has to be indoctrinated into methods of duplicity which the socializing agencies are reluctant to do. The school teacher will not teach the children that truth is not the best policy, that loyalty brings one to discard one's own interests for the interests of others, and that manners are only very sleek tools to achieve one's aims in a more efficient way than brute force. The reason for this is that the teacher himself is either a middle-class bourgeois or aspires to be one. His own double standards do not allow him to divulge the honest and sad truth that honesty and loyalty are not the best policies to achieve one's aim in a competitive society. The teacher leaves the children to learn this the hard way. Yet he teaches them one set of facts and values and covertly or implicitly intends that they see through his duplicity and grow up by themselves. It is a matter of conjecture what would happen if teachers would tell their pupils the truth from the very first grade at school.

Parents rarely tell their children the facts of life from a very early age. More often than not they give them the usual "wait till you grow up and find out for yourselves." The implication here is that both parents and socializing agencies are caught in the inevitable vicious cycle of the multiple standards, and they are either unable or unwilling to cut the Gordian knot and point out to the young of the species what and where are the conflictual standards in the normative structure of society.

The failure of penal treatment may also be linked to our present premise because the treatment personnel have to convey to the criminals that their only way to survive is to adjust to contradictory "rules of the game." The treatment man is unable to preach this adjustment to the multiple standards of society because he would admit thereby the duplicity of the system he works for and belongs to. This in a sense is the basis of the double and triple binds that penal treatment personnel all over the world find themselves in when confronted with their charges. The criminals, on the other hand, are ideologically committed, most of them by coercion and a few by choice, to a single-standard ideology and way of life because social stigma would not allow a prisoner or an ex-con to be reintegrated in "law abiding society." This, again, is more proof both to the treatment man and to the criminal of the inevitable duplicity and hypocrisy of the "law abiding society" so that the rift is deepened and widened between the two. The crux of the message sent to us by Jean Genet when he described his compulsive single-standard crime and deviance in contrast to the "treasures of duplicity" of "your world" is that the bourgeois society stigmatized him and cast him from its midst because he would not adjust to its multiple standards. Indeed, Genet might be clinically portrayed as the perfect psychopath, but for our purposes he is also an archetypal single-standard deviant. Another portrayal of the single-standard deviant is the classic image of Prewitt in *From Here to Eternity*, who projected onto the world his own rigid single standard expecting the world to comply to it — of course, it did not — and will not.

The parameters by which the participant and separant personality types are defined are presented in Table 9.1

The "stimulus seeking" of the separant and the "stimulus aversion" of the participant may be related to the ingenious experiments of Petrie (1967; Petrie et al., 1960). She found that introverts tended to increase subjectively the size of the stimuli (augmenters) whereas extroverts decreased it (reducers). This, of course, is related to the "stimulus hunger" of the extrovert-reducers and the "stimulus aversion" of the introvert augmenters. She also reestablished that augmenters (participants) were more tolerant of sensory deprivation and naturally less tolerant of pain. I am well aware that I am substituting Eysenck's introvert and extrovert with participant and separant, but I am concerned here with only two character traits — activity and excitability — of the five which comprise Eysenck's types. These two apply to my typology, whereas the others may not. Therefore, it is more appropriate to use my terminology instead of Eysenck's which may cover more conceptual ground than I need (Eysenck, 1967).

The research findings surveyed provide an empirical anchor to the activist — quietist or the "interactive" dimension of this typology. I will proceed now to link some pertinent findings to the ontological dimension which is the "object-inclusion" of the separant and the "self-exclusion" of the participant. As mentioned earlier, the separant aims at "devouring" the object and incorporating it into himself, whereas the participant wishes to exclude or isolate himself and melt back into the object or the nonobjective preawareness. Colquhoun and Corcoran (1964) have demonstrated that introverts are better task performers in

TABLE 9.1   Personality Types, Dimensions, and Traits

Separant	Participant
Interactive Dimension	
Activist	*Quietist*
"Stimulus hunger"	"Stimulus aversion"
High vulnerability to sensory deprivation	Low vulnerability to sensory deprivation
Low sensitivity to pain	High sensitivity to pain
High sensory threshold	Low sensory threshold
Reducer	Augmenter
Ontological Dimension	
Object-Inclusion	*Self-Exclusion*
Group performer	Isolate performer
"Field dependence"	"Field independence"
Intolerant of objective ambiguity	Tolerant of objective ambiguity
Intolerant to ideational ambiguity	Tolerant of ideational ambiguity
Normative Dimension	
Outwardly Aggressive	*Inner Castigation*
"Extrapunitive"	"Inropunitive"
Sanction orientation	Moral orientation
High risk taker	Low risk taker
"Other-directed"	"Inner-directed"
Conformist	Nonconformist

isolation, whereas extroverts perform better in groups. Furneaux (in Eysenck, 1967), stated,

> It is entirely consistent with the known characteristics of the extrovert to assert that he has a strong and continuing set to attend to stimuli associated with the activities of other people, and that the situations which lead him to enter states of high drive are predominantly interpersonal in character.

This better performance of the extrovert in group situations has been related to his stimulus hunger. However, the higher motivation and drive in an interpersonal situation reported by Furneaux shows the dependence of the extrovert-separant on the togetherness of the group. He functions better not vis-à-vis the others but *amidst* the others, within them and through them. The others serve thus as the necessary medium for the better performance of the separant because those others are vital catalysts and as such are necessary components of his personality structure. Of even greater significance to our present premise are the findings which may allow us to link the separant (extrovert) to a higher "field independent." These two concepts, as well as Witkin et al.'s (1962) later studies on "psychological differentiation," relate to the object, setting, and environmental perception while performing a task. The "field dependent" displays a low psychological differentiation because he is dependent in his performance on cues stemming from the overall gestalt and the background set of the situation. In other words, performance here is dependent on the configuration of the surrounding objects. On the other hand, the "field independent" and the one who displays higher psychological differentiation relies on his own cognitive cues and not on the outward gestalt of the objects.

It should be pointed out that Cohen and Silverman (1962) found that the field dependent, who, like our separant, is object dependent, was more vulnerable to sensory deprivation, which again is a major characteristic of the separant (extrovert). As might have been expected, the separant's "hunger" for stimuli made him less vulnerable to pain and more field- (that is, object) dependent.

I shall add here another trait for which I have not as yet found empirical evidence: I hypothesize that the separant is intolerant of object ambiguity. He would grasp things, others, and situations which are clearly defined with boundaries. On the other hand, the participant would be tolerant of ambiguities relating to objects, but he requires clear-cut abstractions. The objective haziness serves his quietist and mystical inclinations, but he is intolerant of any ideational ambiguities which may blur his concern with unity and the ultimate reality beyond objective appearances.

The third normative dimension of our typology deals with the self-object relationships. We may recall that the participant type who has been fixated at nondifferentiated early orality tends to be a depressive "bad me" surrounded by a good object, whereas the separant "good me" is the outwardly aggressive "good me" surrounded by a depriving object. Consequently, the participant would be "intropunitive," the guilt-ridden self-blamer, whereas the separant would tend to be an "extrapunitive" blamer of others. I shall proceed to enumerate some traits which I hypothesize as related to the present dimension, although no empirical evidence has been found in support of this hypothesis.

I hold that the participant tending to blame himself and consequently more ready to legitimize norms would be "morally oriented"; that is, he is internally controlled by the deeply internalized norms so that external repressive sanctions are unnecessary to secure compliance. This hypothesis is based on Rommetveit's theory on the internalization of social norms (see Thibaut and Kelly, 1959) and it differs from such expositions as Rotter's internal versus external loci of normative control. Rotter (Rotter et al., 1962) imputes to his "internal controller" a belief in his ability to manipulate the external world as well as to change the political system by involvement in social affairs. This characterizes not our participant but the diametrically opposite separant type. The latter would tend to be "sanction oriented" (Thibaut and Kelly, 1959). Being outwardly aggressive, he would not tend to legitimize norms but would comply with them for fear of sanction only. Consequently, the separant would be a higher risk-taker than the participant, as the separant tends to manipulate objects and operate through others; he tends to be "other directed" as described by Riesman (1950). The "other directed" has his normative antennae ever attuned to others and their approval. Consequently, he tends to be a conformist, in the sense of Crowne and Marlowe's (1960) approval motivation and need for affiliation. It should be stressed that all the character traits we have mentioned above, both the hypothetical ones and those which have been empirically verified, are by no means an exhaustive list but a mere illustration of measurable parameters to tie our theoretical dimensions and typologies to empirical anchors. Also, they may be useful indicators for the adequacy of my personality core vectors as the underlying sources for the various behavioral patterns and traits.

I hypothesize that the chances of a person becoming a single-standard deviant are greater if he moves more to the participant pole of the personality continuum. He would thus tend to disregard the value system of his surroundings and cherish more his own convictions. Consequently, the chances of a conflict would be greater. On the other hand, the separant would be aware of the exigencies of his surroundings and try and reach a *modus vivendi* with them. I am providing thus a scaffolding for the initial identification of deviance which should be tied up to other typologies of deviance in order to enable a fair prediction. I realize the difficulty of translating this study into operational, measurable variables, but I assume my exposition to be of value to the macroanalysis of deviance, taking into account the whole personality of the prospective deviant.

NOTES

1. I have denoted the participant ontological core of self by the Hebrew word *Ani*. Its etymological meaning is "I," but in Kabbalist doctrine, *Ani* and *Ain* (nothingness), having the same Hebrew letters but in a different order, are interchangeable and synonymous. Consequently, the *Ani*, the "I" longing for participant nonbeing, is the Tantalic objectless component of the self. My interactive object-related component of the self will be denoted by the Hebrew word *Atzmi*, which may be translated into English as "myself." Its root, however, is *etzem*, object in Hebrew, and is therefore most appropriate in denoting my object-related interactive self.

REFERENCES

COHEN, S. and A. J. SILVERMAN (1963) Body and Field Perceptual Dimensions and Altered Sensory Environment. Durham, NC: Duke University Press.

COLQUHOUN, W. P. and D.W.J. CORCORAN (1964) "The effects of time of day and social isolation on the relationship between temperament and performance." British Journal of Social and Clinical Psychology 3: 226-231.

CROWNE, D. P. and D. A. MARLOWE (1960) "New scale of social desirability independent of spychopathology." Journal of Consulting Psychology 24: 349-354.

ERIKSON, E. (1956) "The problem of identity." Journal of American Psychiatric Assocaition 4.

EYSENCK, H. J. (1967) The Biological Basis of Personality. Springfield, IL: Charles C Thomas.

PETRIE, A. (1967) Individuality in Pain and Suffering: The Reducer and Augmenter. Chicago: University of Chicago Press.

PETRIE, A., W. COLLINS and P. SOLOMON (1960) "The tolerance for pain and for sensory deprivations." American Journal of Psychiatry 123: 80-90.

RIESMAN, D. (1950) The Lonely Crowd. New Haven, CT: Yale University Press.

ROTTER, J. B., M. SEEMAN, and S. LIVERANT (1962) "Internal v. external control of reinforcements: a major variable in behavior theory," in N. F. Washburne (ed.) Decisions, Values, and Groups, Vol. 2. London: Pergamon.

SHOHAM, S. G. (1976) Social Deviance. New York: Gardner Press.

——— (1979) The Myth of Tantalus. Queensland, Australia: Queensland University Press.

THIBAUT, J. W. and H. H. KELLY (1959) The Social Psychology of Groups. New York: John Wiley.

WITKIN, H. A., R. B. DYK, F. H. FATERSON, D. R. GOODENOUGH and S. A. KARP (1962) Psychological Differentiation. New York: John Wiley.

ECONOMIC CRIMES FROM A COMPARATIVE PERSPECTIVE

MARIA ŁOŚ

This chapter presents a comparative analysis of the economic crime in "capitalist" and "communist" countries. It focuses on crimes which are related to the "criminal" nature of the particular economic system, and on those which are directly or indirectly determined by the rules of organization of the particular economy. The analysis is concerned with comparing the relationships between various crimes and the economic organization of societies, and not with comparing specific forms of behavior, since the same types of economic behavior assume basically different ideological meaning in "capitalist" and "communist" countries.

FOUR GENERAL CATEGORIES

Any attempt at a comprehensive review of the existing definitions of economic crimes is bound to be lengthy, and, most likely, rather boring. Therefore, a brief presentation of my understanding of the concept of economic crime will not make any specific references to the existing literature. I distinguish four different types of phenomena which can be described as particularly important forms of economic crimes.

The first kind of economic crime is related to the very nature of an economic system which is seen as criminal in light of some external criteria, often alien to the legal system in force. The three further types see crime more conventionally through the binding legal norms.

Thus, *the second kind of economic crime* points to those violations of the law which can be seen as directly or indirectly determined by the nature of the economic system. I would call these crimes "restrictive" economic crimes,[1] as they result from the existing economic pressures which narrow down the possibilities of real choice and can be predicted in light of our knowledge of a given economic system. The two remaining types of economic crimes refer to the behavior which violates the rules of the given economic system and is usually directed against nonindividual property.

The third kind of economic crime is not necessarily determined by the economic system; it is distinguished by its direct orientation toward economic gain. The nature and occurrence of such activity may depend on a variety of factors of psychological, cultural, social, economic, and political nature. This kind of crime is generally committed by the self-seeking individuals or groups. It may be called "anarchic," in the sense that it does not constitute an outcome of the overwhelming pressure of economic forces, but is largely undertaken as a result of a more or less free choice and initiative.

The final kind of economic crime can be defined as "resistance" crimes. These are criminal abuses of the economic system or crimes against nonindividual property which are motivated by, and which express, a resolute disapproval of the rules of that system.

Naturally, such a typology has shortcomings, but so do all others. It should also be noted that different kinds of economic crime may overlap and some activities may be too versatile to be assigned to just one of the above-described categories. Yet, the proposed typology, with its emphasis on the dominant nature of the economic structure, is useful for the purpose of comparison between different socioeconomic systems. The main objective of the present study is precisely to discuss and compare the basic features of economic crime in the developed capitalist countries and in the centralized communist ones. The comparison will be basically between the western multiparty democracy on the one hand and the Soviet Union and Eastern European countries on the other. I intend to pursue it by focusing on the *first two* categories of economic crime, because of their crucial importance for any attempt to grasp the nature of the *relationship between different sociopolitical systems and economic crimes produced by them.*

This task is bound to be basically of a qualitative nature, since the available statistics and other quantitative data are scarce, unsystematic, and grossly unreliable. Moreover, they are clearly unsuitable for comparisons to be made between economic systems which are fundamentally different. The chapter is not written from the Marxist perspective, in the sense that it does not use the exaggerated and oversimplified caricature of the capitalist economy often treated as a dogma by the Marxist writers. Nor does it accept the idealized vision of the communist society still seen by many Marxists as a realistic and desired option. If the idealized utopia of communist society is used for the sake of comparison between communism and capitalism, one would similarly have to use a utopian model of capitalism (for instance, an attractive utopia presented by Nozick, 1974). If the comparison is to be carried out between two existing types of socioeconomic systems, it certainly cannot rely on a theoretical perspective which is geared to a total critique (as well as a practical destruction) of one of those systems and an unqualified glorification (and practical realization) of the other.

Yet, it should be emphasized to the credit of western Marxist scholars that many important aspects and forms of economic criminality have been recently brought to light and have been studied as a part of the complex economic organization of the capitalist society. Insofar as Marxism recommends studying social phenomena in the context of the broader structure of economic interests, its importance cannot be underestimated.

My basic objection, however, would be that it does not provide any useful conceptual guidance for the studies of the present communist countries. Even in the case of the capitalist countries it leads to very peculiar and distorted results whenever a researcher decides to rely solely on the implications of the writings of Marx. A more relaxed and unorthodox attitude toward Marxist heritage, coupled with the concern for social reality rather than ideological dogmas, have led many sociologists to most revealing and valuable findings. Certainly economic crimes in capitalist societies constitute one of those areas where such an approach has proved to be both productive and promising.

CRIMINAL ECONOMIC SYSTEMS

Capitalist Countries

When speaking about the criminal economic systems I use the word "criminal" in an unconventional way to signify something which is not only permitted but even protected by the legal system.

The best-known example of such an approach is the Marxist critique of the basic institutions and relationships of capitalist economy, the private ownership of the means of production, the ruthless profit orientation of the ruling class, and the inevitable exploitation of the working class. Naturally, an orthodox Marxist interpretation cannot see these phenomena in terms of criminal violation of the law because they constitute the actual core of the capitalist economic relationships and the law is subordinated to them, being obliged at the same time to secure their perpetuation. Nevertheless, many radical criminologists criticize the traditional concern with conventional crimes, pointing to the human costs and disastrous social effects of capitalist exploitation, discrimination, and labor alienation. At the same time, they are usually aware of the fact that criminalization of these practices would never be possible under the existing circumstances where the legislative processes, as well as the whole domain of law enforcement, are subordinated to the ruling economic interests and where such legal changes would threaten the very basis of the system.

In this connection, some attempts have been made to explain the spurious nature of various laws which look like real concessions on the part of the business elite, but which are, in fact, to its advantage or are at least equipped with various safeguards which make enforcement practically impossible. Moreover, an important ideological function of such laws has been stressed which consists of pacifying radical moods and reemphasizing democracy.

> These laws [which recognized trade unions] were used as part of an overall strategy for preempting the radical potential of an increasingly powerful trade union movement — they suggested that America was really a democracy since everyone, rich and poor alike, was subject to legal constraint. But when the danger was neutralized, when the unions were coopted, the laws could be safely ignored.... .

> The occasional implementation of laws that attack the rich seemingly gives content to the claim that the state is neutral and controlled by the people [Pearce, 1976: 100, 104-105].

Although there is much truth is this, it is too one sided an analysis to be fully convincing. There exist many regulations which are clearly contrary to the financial interests of the dominant economic class. It would be difficult to argue that they were always crucial to the survival of that class and have been enacted under the threat of revolution. Consequently, the power structure in the democratic western societies cannot be fully identified with the economic class structure.

> Laws which provide minimum wages, specify certain conditions for safety and cleanliness, restrict misleading advertising and profitable mergers, are not of merely peripheral concern to this class, even though they are, in general, weakly worded and poorly enforced. One can mention, as many do, that laws like this are concessions made, even written by, the ruling class to ward off really fundamental changes, but one is, in this case, admitting that there are variables at work which seriously challenge the power of the dominant class, at least potentially. Such a

thesis is not conceded by many Marxist theorists [Snider, 1978:144-145].

Communist Countries

Sociologists, publishing in communist countries and grossly restricted by censorship and political control, do not offer any far-reaching critiques of the economic organization of the centralized communist society. Some of the critical Marxist commentators in the west describe these countries as basically the same as the capitalist ones, with their characteristic profit orientation and exploitation of the worker. Yet, to anyone who has some experience of living in both, the differences between the two most probably would be much more basic and striking than apparent similarities.

The state ownership of the means of production in the communist countries bears, of course, some similarity to both state and private ownership of the industries in capitalist countries insofar as it is necessary for the worker to sell his labor for a salary. Yet, the one-party state monopoly over the means of production, as well as over the totality of the political and social processes, implies the full ideological unity of the political and economic interests and, therefore, the sheer impossibility of any legislation interfering with the centralized, plan-oriented organization of the industry. Even more significant, it excludes the existence of any trade unions which would represent the interest of the employees rather than employers (that is, the state). Furthermore, the monopoly of the one-party state over the mass media excludes the possibility of any countercontrol or pressure by the nonparty majority.

Since complete information about the structure of the state budget is never available to the citizens in these countries, it is difficult to give an accurate picture of the allocation of industrial profits. No doubt, any surplus contributes to a considerable degree to the wealth of the political elite, but, above all, it is being ploughed into the ideological machinery, which includes defense, internal security, state and party bureaucracy, and propaganda. Even if precise data are not available, it may be safely assumed that the distribution of the industrial and trade profits in the capitalist countries is structured in a substantially different way. They are certainly appropriated to a larger degree by the private "bosses" of the economy, but it must also be emphasized that the trade unions secure a much higher level for workers' wages. Moreover, the tax revenues are spent to a greater extent for social welfare, public investments, and facilities. These, in turn, are at least partially controlled by bodies such as the parties in opposition, the mass media (which are not censored by any central political agency), competing experts, free public associations, as well as voters at large whose support the party in office wants to secure. All these factors are nonexistent and, indeed, banned in the communist countries.

What is even more significant in this context is that *many economic activities which would be considered criminal under capitalist laws constitute the very core of the communist economy*. Examples of such activities include the expropriation of property without compensation, the forced collectivization of farms, the systematic discrimination and persecution of the small-scale private producers, the economic monopoly and price fixing, and the requirement of "voluntary" (that is, unpaid) work to fulfill the state's economic plan. On the other hand, *most of the economic activities characteristic of the western capitalist countries are criminalized in the communist countries*. They include any private initiative to set up more large-scale businesses, attempts at competition in business, international contacts by the private businessmen, flexible changes 'of economic targets, and strikes and other means of collective negotiations. The existence of such basic differences between these economic systems and between the laws which regulate their functioning implies that possible "external" critiques of each system must resort to the laws of the other system or to more general, human rights (see, for example, Schwendinger and Schwendinger, 1975) or else to rules of "natural" justice.

In conclusion, any direct comparison of "economic" crimes in the capitalist and communist countries is practically impossible, because *the same types of economic behavior assume basically different ideological meanings in each system*.

Therefore, the comparison undertaken in the following pages attempts to grasp forms of activity specific to each of the discussed types of societies, which may be meaningfully related to the proposed general categories of economic crimes mentioned at the outset. Of particular importance is the second category, which is clearly crucial to any comparative analysis, since it refers to those crimes which are determined by the very nature of the respective economic system.

"RESTRICTIVE" ECONOMIC CRIMES[2]

Capitalist Countries

Poverty traps and "scrounging" on the welfare. The capitalist society, with its fundamentally nonegalitarian premises, must inevitably produce poverty if we consider that poverty is a relative notion and refers to the situation of those worst off. In particular, the capitalist system does not possess sufficient mechanisms to eliminate unemployment-, health-, and age-related poverty. The social and cultural visibility of large personal wealth, as well as of the relative affluence of the majority of the population, makes the suffering of the poor more acute and their stigmatization more drastic. The segregation of the poor and the moral criteria of many welfare policies contribute highly to the accumulation of deprivation. The earnings-related social insurance schemes are, of course, biased against those in low-paying employment who are least likely to have any savings when they lose their jobs because of their age, disability, or other reasons. The trade unions take care of those at work, but have little time for those who fall out of the labor force into the claimants category.

The deterioration of one's material situation and the growing dependence on welfare institutions are generally perceived as a loss of respectability and personal failure. There may therefore exist some correlation between this accumulated pressure of poverty and certain deviations. However, there is insufficient contemporary evidence to show that they include actual criminal actions, unless some other factors associated with group poverty (such as ethnic discrimination) occur simultaneously. Yet, in the affluence-oriented society, the poor are perceived as a threat to order and in the absence of other, proved targets for criticisms, they are often accused of *robbing the taxpayers of their hard-earned money* by relying too eargerly on welfare schemes. Although the amounts fraudulently received seem to be very small,[3] the conflict between the unemployed and the employed produces considerable tension which leads to further worsening of the situation of the former and pushes them to the social margin where they are more likely to become involved with the police and law-breaking. Moreover, it is worth emphasizing that public hostility and suspicion against the unemployed intensifies during the times of growing unemployment,

> at the very time when it is most difficult for them to find a job, a paradox which is usually attributed to the fact that the same period has seen a fall in the standard of living of the population as a whole [Deacon, 1978:126].[4]

Recent rediscovery by radical writers of the Marxist concept of "relative surplus population" brings some interesting insights into the ways in which the *unemployed are repressed and controlled*. Their marginal status obviously reduces their stake in the maintenance of the system and poses a threat to it, yet their powerlessness and economic dispensability renders them increasingly susceptible to the mechanisms of official control (see Spitzer, 1975). The growth of prison populations during the period of recession and increased unemployment suggests that "[a]n expanding criminal justice system is the only way late capitalism can 'integrate' the surplus population into the overall economic and political system" (Quinney, 1978:132).

Employee theft, fiddling, pilfering, and dealing. This kind of behavior may have some political meaning and it may reflect workers' social consciousness in at least two ways. The first is the awareness of the class conflict and workers' exploitation, which is shaped to a large degree by the trade unions' ideology. This leads mainly to employee theft where the employer is victimized.

[I]n nations with a tradition of union management conflict, such as the United States, employee crime against the corporation may be more common because of an attitude that the corporation provides benefits to workers only because of threat and coercion rather than out of sincere concern for their welfare. This feeling may create a climate of resentment and a desire to get back at the company in whatever way possible. Disgruntled workers often rationalize theft by saying that they are underpaid or abused by their employer [Conklin, 1977:67].

A second possibility arises when the employer offers (perhaps in order to survive in a competitive business world) very low wages to his employees, but hopes that they would find ways to make some additional money at the expense of the firms' customers. Mars (1974) argues on the basis of his observations on pilferage in the docks that

> pilferage in the actor's definition of his position is perceived as a legitimate means of redressing an exploitive contractual situation. Considered in this light, pilferage can then be appreciated as having possible implications for working class consciousness. It is perhaps a device which, in part at least, expresses alienation in an alternative manner to more open industrial and political action. This may well be one reason why managements have been reluctant to take action to eradicate it [Mars, 1974:226].

Another example is provided by Ditton (1977) in his detailed description of the bread salesman's fiddling of his trusting British customers:

> [W]hilst learning the job, the recruit is gradually made aware of the fact that "mistakes" (responsibility for which he has already agreed to) and thus "shortages" are inevitable. Once low pay and long hours have become a reality for him, he is considered to be morally and technically ready for a demonstration that both problems may be solved by overcharging customers. For most men, the relief of finding a solution dilutes any remaining moral qualms [Ditton, 1977:17].

Despite the low wages, employees' bond to the firm is strengthened, and the firm gains additionally as the salesmen return a part of the fiddled income to cover the inevitable shortages. The salesmen become businesslike in their efforts to maintain sufficient income levels and resent any mention of changes. Fiddling is not in opposition to the core business values of the capitalist economy; rather, those values ''have sedimented at the blue collar level as a subtle, wry, reflection of the sentiments from which they were initially derived'' (Ditton, 1977:176). Moreover, the common involvement of the employees in fiddling and pilferage fosters a spirit of individualism which may effectively prevent unionization of the workforce. In some situations, the management may try to discourage unionization by making anyone who tries to initiate it a visible scapegoat and by branding him a pilferer (Mars and Mitchell, 1977).

It seems that the exploitative and alienating conditions of employment may create some sort of *opposition and sabotage* as soon as they are perceived as such and the employer is seen as a class enemy; or they may evoke *adjustment and adoption of the fiddling ideology* where some solidarity with the employer and a more ''egalitarian'' survival attitude is manifested (''everybody is cheating,'' ''everybody wants to live,'' and the like). The first is more likely when the firm (or corporation) is rich and impersonal and the trade unions are both radical and vindictive. The described attitude may be genuine or it may simply help to neutralize the criminal nature of the commonly practiced behavior. The second kind of response is more likely to occur in the case of a more mediocre employer and more personal relationships within the firm, where there is no strong union influence. Needless to say, the scope and forms of such ''part-time crimes'' also depend to a large degree on the technical aspects of the organization of work, the opportunities for theft, the contacts with the clients, and so forth.[5]

It may, however, lead to some distorted views of reality, if pilferage, fiddling, and dealing are seen only in terms of more or less conscious political strategies or the supplementing of low wages. These attitudes are quite widespread, and, apparently, they satisfy the diverse social needs of the people involved. When work is boring, the tasks' structure rigid, and the whole economic system alien, this hidden framework of illegal relationships may provide some fun, strengthen personal bonds, and foster an illusion of control over at least some aspects of the economic processes. When reading Henry's description of the rituals and emotions which accompany the creation of hidden trade networks, one cannot resist feeling that these are games people play in the hope for some excitement, meaningful involvement and importance. Apparently, in these petty dealings and tradings, people are not always motivated by the desire of profit. Many of the goods are "passed" to friends or relatives without any gain. What counts is rather some *exchange of favors, good status in the network, competition with others, involvement in a meaningful community activity*, and so on.

> If we look at the actual, as opposed to the theoretical or declared, pricing policy in a trading network, we find that it is determined less by market values than by the closeness of the relationship between trading partners [Henry, 1978:91].

According to the results obtained by Henry, the hidden trading networks are based on the principles of reciprocity and community sharing, which would be termed "irrational" by economists. Nevertheless, the people belonging to them explain their actions in terms of rational, market-exchange principles. This may be caused by the fact that in the money-based industrial societies *the market system is the dominant mode of exchange*, and a possibility or, indeed, *need for other types of exchange, is largely underestimated*.

> [P]ilfering, fiddling and dealing, taken together, are forms of personalized reciprocal exchange or, at the very least, mark the point at which items from market or redistributive economies are dematerialized and the transactions personalized [Henry, 1978:112-13].

Black market. Black market activities exist in all countries although their scope and nature may significantly differ. In the western capitalist countries they revolve chiefly around goods which are condemned by the state as vices. The most extensive of all seem at the moment to be black marketeering in narcotics.

More varied black market activities emerge, of course, during wartime, or in times of postwar shortages and rationed supplies of various goods (see Clinard, 1952), but they usually disappear with the changing conditions.

The hidden trading and dealing analyzed in the preceding section of this chapter seem to be different from the real black market activities because the former involve cheap goods sold or "passed" at prices lower than market prices, while black market prices are always well above the official ones.

The black markets depend on the general market laws, but because of their precarious status they are bound to involve substantial amounts of corruption. The most widely researched is the corruption displayed by the police. As usual, the most spectacular evidence has been provided by American researchers, but there are good reasons to think that the practice is much more widespread. For example, British Scotland Yard men, still internationally known for their respectability, when subjected to similar pressures and temptations are likely to lose their rectitude (see Cox et al., 1977).

It may be mentioned in passing that there is a clear tendency on behalf of the organized liberal lobbies to press for the elimination of as many prohibitions as possible because of the limits to the free choice they impose and the corruption they inevitably involve. (It may concern probitions in such areas as "soft" drugs, prostitution, pornography, and so forth). Yet, the likelihood of legalization of the "hard" drugs is rather remote, as in modern countries whose organization is subordinated to the requirements of a highly demanding technology as anything which may weaken people's self-discipline and disturb their contact with reality must be perceived as at least potentially destructive and considerably risky. This point may be relevant when contrasted with the situation in communist countries, as will be described below.

Corporate crimes. Capitalist corporations have a profit-oriented nature, yet the contemporary capitalist laws make illegal any "surplus" profits obtained by obstructing the efficiency of competition in the given area. It produces a difficult *contradiction between the paramount economic value of individual profit and the expected commitment to democracy.* It would be unrealistic to assume that large corporations would voluntarily avoid exploiting advantages gained from their sheer size as well as initial market success.

There are many ways in which such economically rational but illegal goals can be achieved. Various studies on corporate crime (especially in the United States) point to common instances of price-fixing; the taking over of smaller firms; reducing competitors' sales; pressurizing or bribing dealers not to stock a competitors' product; pressing the banks to charge their competitor higher rates of interest or to deny them credit; stealing industrial secrets; deceptive selling; and reducing competition in foreign markets through payoffs to foreign agents or government officials in order to secure sales, to change import restrictions, or to receive favorable tax treatment (see, for example, Conklin, 1977).

Sometimes illegal techniques are used to simply overcome rigid and outdated regulations which restrain any initiative and, in effect, any legitimate effort to achieve economic objectives in the changing reality.

> One factor which affects the market structure of an industry is government regulation. Regulations may be conducive to bribery, kick-backs, and payoffs. For instance, the Knapp Commission Report of Police Corruption in New York City found that police regulation of the construction industry was a "serious corruption hazard." Bribes were necessary to get anything done in the "maze of City ordinances and regulations." Paying bribes were less expensive than obeying the law [Conklin, 1977:54].

Another important feature built into the nature of business transactions in the capitalist system is personal trust. The only alternative to it would be a costly overbureaucratization of the economy, which is clearly contrary to the vested economic interest. Yet, trust may also be directly conducive to certain business crimes. In the modern economy trust is often skillfully reinforced by the use of the computer because of the common assumption that "anything which comes out of a computer must be correct" (Conklin, 1977:57).

Individual incentives to employees to participate in potentially illegal practices are determined by the whole system of division of tasks and rewards within the corporation, which often depends on the willingness to go along with whatever schemes of increasing profit the corporation adopts.

An obvious opportunity for large-scale abuses of "business ethics" exists in the case of the leading international corporations. They do not feel restrained by the national laws, and the international economic regulations are not sufficiently precise and binding to prevent them from making "too much" profit. In this respect, especially visible are large American-based monopolies which attempt to control not only foreign markets, but also foreign sources of raw materials. *Their strategies cannot be explained in isolation from the international politics as they both influence it and depend on it.*

> Since the First World War, they have been involved in the administration and direction of American foreign policy. Their confidence in the competitive advantage held by American business, their need of new markets, and the importance of raw materials that were either naturally available abroad, or could be more cheaply produced in "undeveloped" countries, explain this involvement [Pearce, 1976:101].

The exploitation of the unregulated international market, so as to violate domestic laws with impunity, is also manifested in the widespread use of mainly Swiss banks in order to evade tax payments, to reinvest funds controlled by organized crime, and to make illegal campaign contributions (see Conklin, 1977:56).

The corporate executives' inevitable involvement in the foreign policy of their own governments, as well as in the corporations' direct deals and negotiations with foreign governments, open broad possibilities of corruption. Several international scandals and the investigations which followed them have revealed that *bribery is a standard procedure in the world of international trade* (Jacoby et al., 1977).

The almost endless stream of corporate testimony seems to indicate that payoffs and bribes are (a) the only way of doing business overseas, (b) have been going on for years, and (c) are functional for the business involved" [Clark and Hollinger, 1977:147].

Political corruption. The interests of the economic elite and political elite do not always fully coincide. There are, however, many ways in which they may make their coexistence mutually acceptable and profitable. Some of these ways would be inevitably illegal, although the degree of such inevitability and the extent to which the illegality is introduced to this relationship depends on the political tradition of the country, election rules and procedures, the existence of the tradition of organized crime, and so forth. The best examples of the corruption of top politicians, as well as law enforcement agencies, are usually taken from the impressive record of organized crime in the United States. Yet, other western countries have usually some achievements in this area as well.

The large-scale Mafia-type organized crime which aims at the "nullification" of government (Cressey, 1969) is in fact not typical for most capitalist countries; therefore, I shall exclude it from the present analysis. The opposite of ruthless violence and terror is a soft, subtle corruption and mutual "understanding" between the economic elite and politicians. A Canadian researcher points out:

The political elite are also important, for they have theoretically at least, the power to allow business to block enforcement of these laws, or to get them enforced. ...The need not to antagonize the powerful economic elite is a strong countervailing pressure, for many reasons. Money is one. Political figures in the main two federal parties depend on corporate funds for campaigns. In addition, many have the same outlook as businessmen, because they were in business, will be again when they leave politics, or because they are from the same social class and have strong social and family ties with businessmen. ...General non-enforcement of the economic laws also gives them a weapon to use on those occasions where the interests of the economic and the political elite conflict [Snider, 1978:160-161].

The enforcement or nonenforcement of the laws governing the behavior of corporations is clearly a political issue; however, it is often argued that it is not the politicians but the law enforcement agencies who are directly responsible for it. It may be interesting, therefore, to look first at the reasons why so few cases are ever brought to their attention. One of the causes certainly is the vague wording of these regulations which builds a bias into the legislation. Obviously, lack of clarity discourages litigation and makes it difficult to obtain conviction. This can hardly be seen as accidental[6] and unrelated to the dominant interests of the business elite and to their power to determine the way in which relevant laws are written, which make it most difficult to challenge most practices of the giant firms (see Snider, 1978). Moreover, it is an area where it is not at all clear who is the actual offender, who should be penalized, and what is the prevailing "philosophy" of punishment. There is a great difference between the legal perception of the "conventional" and "corporate" criminal (Solomon, 1977:649; Schrager and Short, 1978):

In narcotics laws, everyone who sells, has possession or even has equipment is liable, whereas in corporate laws, sometimes the immediate perpetrator himself is not liable, only his anonymous employer, the corporation [Snider, 1978:159].

Of course, when it is not made quite clear who is the responsible offender, sanctions too have to show some ambiguity and they usually boil down to fines which are absorbed by innocent parties such as stockholders, consumers, and taxpayers (see Dershowitz, 1961). The notion of "victim" is equally loose and little effort seems to be made to clarify it. The public is not always aware of the extent and effects of the corporate crime, but in light of Conklin's review of various sociological surveys it may be accepted that "the public is not so much permissive toward business crime as it is resigned to it" (Conklin, 1977:

109; see also Geis, 1978:286). Smaller firms would not report against larger companies because of their dependent relationship with them and because they might have been forced to violate the law themselves in order to survive. It has also been discovered in industrial espionage cases that victim corporations do not file charges because of the fear of the possible disclosure of trade secrets during the course of a criminal trial (Nelson and Wolfe, 1977).

In addition to the mechanisms which secure the reluctance of the victims to report against corporations, one has to note the existence of the administrative bodies which screen the cases before they eventually reach the courts (for example, the American Federal Trade Commission or the Canadian Restrictive Trade Practices Commission). There is some evidence that many cases were discontinued or settled in the process without ever being sent to the courts. "The heavy reliance on administrative enforcement reflects the power of legitimate organizations to affect legal definitions governing their actions" (Schrager and Short, 1978:411). Even if a further legal action is taken, it is usually a civil one. Criminal action is reserved for the most notorious or persistent cases. But in these cases, too, the wealth, influence, and, especially, the ability to hire the most skillful lawyers and experts give the dominant companies a clear advantage over the newer or smaller firms. In more extreme cases the use of bribes and intimidation may additionally strengthen the position of the major companies. And, in case of failure, they are more likely to be able to inhibit or control the publicity being given to the case by the mass media.

> The media are owned by many of the same people who own corporations. Moreover, they all depend on businesses for advertising revenue. ...Stories on conventional crime are given out by the police: upperworld offenses are more likely to be hidden or to require a lot of hard work to get details. The danger of libel suits is also much greater [Snider, 1978:160].

Some contemporary criminologists would also argue that criminology itself has in a way been corrupted by the dominant economic interest. First, it has chosen to portray the "white collar criminal" in a much more restrained way than the conventional criminal; second, it has contributed to the image of the "white collar" crime as a basically victimless crime or, at least, a bloodless one (which overlooks the numerous victims of industrial accidents; unsafe vehicles; exposure to toxic agents, radiation, pollution, food or drug-poisoning; and so on); and, third, it has reinforced a false assumption that the public is not concerned with these kinds of offenses because it is not able to grasp their nature.

In fact, it has been mainly the merit of some journalists, self-appointed experts, and outspoken consumer "rights" defenders that the practical consequences and the real victims of the "corporate" crimes have become less obscure. These activists have stimulated the mobilization of public opinion and a rapid development of the consumer movement, as well as the awakening of some criminologists.

In sum, whether we define the described situation as corrupted or as simply biased, there is ample, even if unsystematic, evidence that *the structural position of the corporate elite empowers it to achieve a privileged status not only in the domestic and international markets, but also in the area of law enforcement.*

Communist Countries

"Parasitism" and alienation. In the capitalist countries it is believed that many social problems result directly from unemployment and economic deprivation of some groups. The situation is more complicated when, in those countries which have abolished a capitalist system, it is officially assumed that there is and can be no unemployment and poverty. Certainly, a planned economy allows the state to adjust the number of jobs according to the current demand, but it can be done only up to a point. Both the financial costs involved in the creation of jobs and the humane costs connected with shifting the manpower to those areas with new job opportunities pose difficult problems. Moreover, grossly inadequate wages and depressing working conditions, especially in unskilled labor, do not always provide

employees sufficient incentives to stay in jobs or to look for them. Some people lose their jobs because of their poltiical views or activities, and they cannot find alternative employment, as the jobs are virtually monopolized by the state (who dismissed them in the first place).

As a result, there exists a relatively large group of people who are in fact unemployed. The fact that their existence is ideologically unacceptable in a production-oriented society has contributed to the mergence in most communist countries of the "anti-parasite" laws, which make it *a criminal offense to stay out of both the employment and schooling system*. The typical punishment is forced labor. However, there are no available data about the enforcement of these laws and the extent of the actual criminalization of "parasites." Some countries, like Poland, for example, have resisted attempts at the introduction of an anti-parasite law and the use of forced labor as a distinctive kind of penal sanction. However, none of those countries has been able to establish anything similar to the unemployment benefits in the western countries. Not only do the unemployed forfeit financial support, they also lose their rights to the free health services, reduced-price medicines, and, usually, the use of nurseries or kindergartens for their children (the fees may be too high for them anyway).

Poverty is another forbidden word in the communist countries, and, as a consequence, there is no supplementary benefits system which would be based on a right to the basic maintenance for a family in case of acute want. There are some forms of poverty relief, but they are more reminiscent of the nineteenth-century charities than of any modern welfare system. It is forbidden to conduct any research on poverty or unemployment in the communist countries, but the available results of criminological inquiries show that *juvenile delinquency is strongly connected with the economic and cultural deprivation* at home (in particular, a number of research materials published in Poland in *Archiwum Kryminologiczne*, edited by Stanislaw Batawia and supplied with brief English summaries; see also Kolakowska-Przelomiec, 1975).

Alienation is a vague word, and it seems that in contemporary communist countries it may be substituted by a more common description, *alcoholism* (although, of course, the range of consequences of the alienation is much broader). Alcoholism is recognized in the communist countries as an acute and growing social problem, but any direct studies on its social causes and actual extent are generally discouraged. The accepted explanataion is a cultural one, and it is relatively easy to conduct research on the "drinking culture," which includes studies on the occasions for drinking, habits connected with drinking, and kinds of alcohol consumed.

> One must admit that in Western Europe, while they drink more than we, they drink wisely, devil take then! They drink most often on a full stomach and mainly less strong or mixed drinks. ...But to fight with traditions is difficult, and eradicating them demands much time [*Literaturnaia Gazeta*, May 13, 1970:13, quoted in Connor, 1972:42].

A typical conclusion from such studies is that a prime cause of drunkenness is "early socialization of young men into the view that 'to be a real man' one must drink. Such socialization, deviant in terms of the regime's expectations, takes place mainly in primary group settings" (Connor, 1972:51). As far as ethnological explanation of alcoholism is concerned, it is largely reduced to the theory of learned behavior. According to Connor, Soviet specialists view alcoholism as a pathological habit which one develops by drinking, especially when one increases the intake of alcohol over time (Connor, 1972:54).

It is, however, clear that cultural explanation is just a smokescreen which allows one to talk about the problem without going too far in the search for the causes. It seems that — to some extent at least — *the real roots of the problem are of an economic and political nature* and are connected with the general feeling of complete lack of influence on the part of both white- and blue-collar workers, disorganized and unsafe working conditions, low wages, deficiencies of the consumer market, and overcrowded housing. The widespread drinking at the work place indicates clearly the lack of involvement and respect for the work tasks; the common practice of payday drinking bouts by factory workers suggests that perhaps the level of wages is insulting to the workers and insufficient to care for the family needs (the available data substantiate such an interpretation); the share of alcohol in the family grocery budget makes one think that perhaps the availability of alcohol is disproportionately easier than that of food, soft drinks, and so on. (For instance, in Poland in 1972, 22.6 percent of the money spent on food was spent on alcohol; Swiecicki, 1977:166.)[7]

Finally, the pattern of drinking in order to get drunk suggests that it is escapistic behavior rather than an enjoyable leisure activity. It has been estimated recently in a Polish publication that 800,000 people get drunk each day; the total Polish population is about 34.5 million, but heavy drinking is typical for men of the 21-39 age group (see Falewicz, 1976:352). According to another source, in the early 1960s the average Polish man aged 18-59 was drinking monthly 11.5 litres (more than 2.5 gallons) of vodka (Batawia, 1973:2).

Of course alcoholism is not a crime. Yet a *compulsory treatment* is recommended by the law, and the sentence to rehabilitation through forced labor is not uncommon in several countries. Other forms of penalizing chronic drinkers can also be found. For instance, the 1972 decree of the Central Committee of the CPSU and the Council of Ministers of the USSR prohibited free treatment of medical problems related to, or caused by, heavy drinking; it also directed that alcoholic patients be denied sick leave (Treml, 1975:172).

It has been confirmed by the results of many studies that the *majority of the recorded crimes against the person* (for example, in Poland 80 percent, *robbery* 67 percent, *murder and homicide* 53 percent, *rape* 56 percent) were committed by people who *were under the influence of alcohol*. As far as general crime statistics are concerned, a quarter of the suspects were alleged to be drunk during the perpetration of the crime. According to the results of a study of 100 young recidivists, 83 percent of them were heavy drinkers (all quoted from Szelhaus, 1975). In this sense, *alienation and alcoholism caused by the lack of opportunities, senselessness of the surrounding reality, economic deprivation, and centralized political pressure are conducive to* widespread criminal violations of law and to the vast prison populations in these countries. The well-publicized correlation between crime and alcohol is politically convenient, as it narrows down the search for causes of crime by directing attention to personal disorders and the deplorable tradition of the "drinking culture."

Finally, one should not overlook an additional economic aspect of the question of alcoholism in the communist countries. It is simply an enormously profitable business, as the prices of alcohol do not have to bear any relation to the costs of production which are, in fact, minimal. This assumption of *the prominent role of alcohol in the global revenue* structure is confirmed by the results of analyses undertaken by Treml:

> In the last 10-15 years turnover taxes collected on sales of alcoholic beverages in retail trade and in dining and drinking establishments comprised some 10-12 percent of all state revenues and more than one-third of all taxes paid by the population. ... [T]axes on alcohol in the last 15 years have just about covered, and in the last few years even exceeded, Soviet defense spending. The financial benefits derived by the state from alcohol are not restricted to tax receipts. Indirect evidence suggests that the production of alcohol beverages is highly profitable, and so is trade and distribution of these products [Treml, 1975:163-164].

Crimes against nationalized property. A problem which greatly concerns the authorities in communist countries is the *common lack of respect for nationalized property.* It manifests itself above all at the work places where theft is not only widespread, but is seen as fully legitimated under circumstances which are generally perceived as illegitimate and unjust. Chalidze describes bitterly the early origins of this attitude:

> To obtain funds, both the Social Revolutionaries and the Bolsheviks were active in organizing armed robberies, which were euphemistically known as "expropriations." ... [During the Revolution, the Bolsheviks] declared that in the future all property of any magnitude would be held in common, and they

incited the proletariat to pillage. In the name of the State they plundered the churches and took over the private possessions. In the course of time the proletariat came to realize that communal ownership meant simply that property, instead of belonging to an individual, now belonged to a superproprietor, the State; but initially they believed that they were seizing property in order to make it their own, although it was to be held in common and not individually. . . .

With all its propaganda, the new regime did not succeed in persuading people to protect state property as their own; they continued to regard it as someone else's and treated it accordingly. This seems to be true today of the entire population; everyone steals a bit here and there [Chalidze, 1977:21-22, 28].

In addition to the common feelings of hostility against "them," for whom one works, there are also some other factors at work. The wasteful organization of work and the *mindless subordinaton to the central plan discourages genuine involvement in the productive tasks* and stimulates individualistic orientation which facilitates pilferage and cheating of the employer. Inadequate wages make moonlighting a necessity, but there are no legal ways to acquire the parts, materials, or tools to carry out the side work (as the "means of production" they cannot be owned or purchased privately). Therefore, "a typical feature of Soviet life is that people often steal socialist property not for personal use but as a means of carrying on their lawful occupations" (Chalidze, 1977:195).

The penalties for the theft of nationalized property were very harsh under Stalin, but after his death a much more liberal policy was introduced into the Soviet Union and Eastern European countries. In most of these countries, the Workers' Courts were established to deal with the problem by educational rather than penal means. They have not proved to be effective, but there are no new ideas on how to cope with the problems. In some countries the Workers' Courts have been so unpopular that most of them gradually ceased to exist (as, for example, in Poland). This has been caused to some extent by the high proportion of white-collar staff among judges while almost all defendants were blue-collar workers (see Łoś, 1978:811-814).

According to the existing statistics, the greatest losses (both in stolen goods and defrauded money) are usually sustained by the state and cooperative commerce. Other extremely vulnerable areas are the construction and food industries: both dealing with goods and materials which are often unavailable in the open market and attractive for the black market operators. *Even though petty theft is routine and found practically everywhere, certainly much greater losses are caused by the wasteful organization of the economy*: political rather than economic management of the processes of production, general disorganization and lack of coordination among various segments of industry, oversized bureaucracy, and inflexible planning.

Moreover, quite significant losses are effected by organized cliques of those who do not steal just for themselves or for occasional dealing, but who organize it on a much larger and more profitable scale. Very big affairs are probably relatively rare because of the fear of punishment, which may be extremely harsh (even the death penalty, not uncommon in the 1960s), fear of informers, limited opportunities to spend large amounts of money, and so forth. But the pattern in both large and small cliques is similar and is mainly determined by the specific features of the communist economy and the fact of suppression of private initiative.

The common characteristics of this economy — lack of incentives, waste, and ineffectiveness of organization of production — open opportunities for the *introduction of illegal incentives and increased productivity, the fruits of which are illegally appropriated*. For example, Majchrzak (1965) describes in detail activities of the criminal groups in the leather tanning industry in Poland. One of the typical patterns consists in introducing to a tannery large amounts of illegally bought raw skins together with the legal ones and, at the end of the processing, withdrawing them for black market sale. The participants of the ''gang'' are selected according to their positions in the factory, and they are only required to avoid mixing up the two lots of skins and do some double recording.

Cooperation of selected truck drivers, convoyers, guards,

and other employees is also crucial for carrying out the tasks. If the goods are to be distributed through the state stores (instead of the black market) some of their employees also must be included in the scheme. To achieve a satisfactory level of protection and security, it is usually necessary to buy the collaboration of internal and external control inspectors, as well as of the director of the enterprise. The workers work harder with no extra pay, but they may get some satisfaction from working in an unusually well organized enterprise with staff who care about the results and do everything to facilitate the production processes, to avoid any unnecessary stoppages, and to achieve high-quality products. Such a technique for the *creation of a parallel illegal enterprise within a legal one* has been utilized in many other branches of production; for example, in the meat and food processing industry. Modified versions of such a procedure can be introduced successfully in most state enterprises. According to Chalidze (1977:169-170), "unregistered production within a state enterprise" is a common form of offense in the Soviet Union, and "those who are brought to book for such activities are generally also charged with stealing socialist property and abusing their official position.

It has been widely documented that securing the cooperation of the people who occupy strategic positions is, as a rule, very easy, whether by use of bribes (in the case of controllers), special payments for extra jobs (for example, drivers), or shares in the profits (directors, bookkeepers, foreman, and others). Of course, in the events of trouble, various forms of blackmailing or even physical terror may be employed.

The operators of such criminal cliques usually have splendid political reputations, skillfully use current ideological slogans, and have convenient connections with influential people. They may easily deal with the eventual critics, either on political grounds or by charging them with defamation (Majchrzak, 1965; Daszkiewicz, 1971).

It is worth emphasizing that the existence of the double structure and double recording of the ongoing productive processes is *possible only because of the typical occurrence in communist enterprises of complicated patterns of spurious activities* which easily accommodate further expansion of fiction. In the organization of a communist economy the only officially relevant and clearly formalized dimension of management is a hierarchical one; the only relevant types of activities are planning and reporting back on the fulfillment of the plan. These activities preoccupy much of the energy of any enterprise, although they are irrelevant from the point of view of effectiveness of its real production. In order to carry on productive tasks and effective cooperation with other enterprises, very different types of relationships have to develop — namely, the horizontal networks of contacts, agreements, and exchanges. They are bound to be largely informal and to employ skillful means of evading the impractical and inconvenient implications of the centralized, hierarchical command. Chalidze observes that in the Soviet Union

> the production goals of the Plan for an enterprise often cannot be fulfilled on schedule without violating the detailed prescriptions of the Plan for payroll, etc., or committing some other illegal act such as bribery to procure needed supplies [Chalidze, 1977:172].

Similarly, the directors of the Polish enterprises interviewed by Kurczewski and Frieske (1977) stressed the importance of the following factors in maintaining the operative horizontal cooperation: use of personal contacts and relationships, reciprocity of services and exchange of goods, settling matters over a social drink, gifts, and so forth.

> A director may easily lose his reputation if he does not conform to norms of conduct such as prohibition against disclosing the internal affairs of the world of managers to first level supervisory units or to a ministry, or the obligation to fulfill commitments one has accepted [Kurczewski and Frieske, 1977:501].

This horizontal solidarity among the managers as well as among lower staff responsible for similar tasks in the cooperating units or enterprises counteracts the coercive fiction of the plan and punitiveness of the vertical control. The following quotation from Kurczewski and Frieske's research report sheds additional light on the significance of those informal and, strictly speaking, illegal, developments:

> [T]he directors told us that the first level supervisory agencies often enforce rules that these agencies themselves see as irrational. This increases the conflict in the directors' professional role. It is a thousand times worse to be hampered by a rule that the supervisors do not believe in than by one they will defend. If the opinions of the directors are correct, then the first level supervisory agencies exercise control, impose sanctions, and make rules primarily in order to avoid criticism from the Central Planning Agencies and, even, criminal prosecution [Kurczewski and Frieske, 1977: 1977:494].

Under such circumstances, *illegal efforts to deceive or neutralize control agencies are seen by insiders as justified and necessary* for the survival of an enterprise and fulfillment of productive tasks. They create a solidarity of joint effort to do business despite all the rigid bureaucratic obstacles, yet "[t]his climate of relations among managers may also undercut respect for the law by the employees and may legitimate criminal conduct in their eyes" (Kurczewski and Frieske, 1977:503). *The workers, who are aware of this everyday law-breaking by the management, are less likely to detect those situations when the system of illegalities becomes subordinated to the individual rather than collective interests.* In any case, the widespread methods of "stalling" the official administrative procedures, although vital in preventing the complete collapse of the centralized economy, lead nevertheless to wasteful escalation of private resourcefulness which inflicts large financial losses upon the economy as a whole. The key difference between superficially similar developments in the capitalist and communist countries is that while in the former they assume basically features of the "hidden economy" (Henry, 1978), in the latter they certainly constitute a fully developed system of the "counter economy" (Smith, 1976).

Immense losses are also caused by incompetent or dishonest export agents (Naumowicz, 1970:9). Jobs in foreign trade often tend to be distributed according to the political rather than rational (professional) criteria. They are considered not only politically sensitive, but also very attractive. Therefore, they are often given to the incompetent, but politically worthy, people in reward for their merits or as a consolation when they have been deprived of other, more desirable offices. Naturally, information about this kind of economic wastefulness is fully suppressed, and it is spread mostly through informal channels. This tendency is even more pronounced in case of information about the instances of gigantic wastefulness of resources and of people's efforts caused by ideological (mis)management of the economy which is founded on fictitious premises and ruled by secret decisions and policies.

Black market. Black markets flourish where there is prohibition or scarcity of goods. Both these phenomena are common in the communist countries as the inevitable side effects of the centralized state economy.

The communist econony, based on the principle of state ownership of the means of production, has been gradually forced to accommodate some margin of private economic enterprise. It has been realized that the rigid system of long-term planning and hierarchically centralized management is not able to respond to the changing demands in the consumer market and to the individualized expectation in the area of some personalized services. After 1956,[8] both the Soviet Union and the Eastern European countries relaxed to some extent their ban on private craft and small enterprise, but it continues to be a crime to engage in prohibited types of trade or industry. Naturally, the extent to which private initiative has been actually legalized varies very much from country to country and from one "ideological wave" to another.

The dependence of the illegal producers on the black market for the supply of tools and raw materials as well as for sales of their products is quite understandable. More strikings is the fact that the legally established private enterprises have to rely on them as well. The ideologically determined regulations of the market make it practically impossible for private persons to buy machines, materials, or other items necessary for carrying on production. A private producer may obtained authorization to purchase limited amounts of the required articles, but if he wants to make a profit and to be able to pay taxes, he has to produce and sell more than he is permitted and, often, more than he is prepared to reveal to the revenue office. Therefore, he is forced to pay black market prices (or bribes) for the materials essential to his production if his business is to make any sense economically. Moreover, the officially allotted supplies may be of such low quality that the profit-oriented producer may be better off paying black market prices for more suitable materials.

> Most people would doubtless prefer to buy their necessary sup-
> plies honestly, but the State makes this impossible. For instance,
> one cannot buy leather to make shoes, upholster chairs, or bind
> books. So when a man is charged with making shoes illegally, he
> is usually also charged with stealing leather from the State — an
> excellent example of how, by prohibiting a harmless activity, the
> State incites people to commit more serious offenses [Chalidze,
> 1977:166].

In some cases, tools, new materials, construction materials, or chemical substances (for example, fertilizers) can be purchased legally only in the "hard currency" stores. Then, however, the producer has to buy hard currency from the black market dealers (there is no legal exchange), or engage in even more risky criminal operations which involve smuggling and contraband. *There is no way by which the legitimate private business in the communist countries could be freed of criminal stigma and of the necessity to cooperate with the criminal underworld* unless the basic principles of economic organization were rethought.

According to Chalidze, " 'speculation' defined as 'the purchase and resale of goods or other articles for gain' is more severely punished in the Soviet Union than any other form of private enterprise" (Chalidze, 1977:174). Nevertheless, "speculation" is a common phenomenon in the communist countries, where many essential goods are in short supply because of the deficiencies of state planning and distribution, as well as regulations which ban various goods from the consumers' market. Chalidze quotes a typical example of "functional" speculation: "When, as often happens, goods are available in Moscow but not elsewhere, speculators who buy them in Moscow and resell them in the provinces are countering geographical discrimination" (Chalidze, 1977:176).

These practices are so common that people no longer notice the illegality of the transaction when they routinely buy meat, eggs, vegetables, foreign cloth and records, carpets, and toilet paper from the door-to-door or corner salesmen, from "under the counter" in the state stores, from their own clients, customers, or patients, from some unidentified middlemen, and so on. (To the political functionality of these and similar arrangements points M. Dobbs, 1977.) Practically everyone is in need of something which he cannot obtain legally, but quite frequently he himself has access to the goods or services which are scarce in the market. That is why, apart from the typical money transactions, there emerge *numerous networks of complicated exchanges of goods, services, or even information*. Survival of both the citizens and economic organizations (illegal, private, as well as state-owned) depends strongly on these mutual services. For instance, the enterprises routinely acquire goods in excess in order to trade them later with other enterprises for other goods which are temporarily unavailable.

For example, the chief of the Supply Division of a particular plant might telephone his counterpart at another plant who he knows, and asks him, "Ivan Petrovich, you wouldn't happen to have such-and-such a shaped metal, say, ten tons of it?" Ivan Petrovich: "Of course Evsev Abramovich, we can find it for you. But what you can give me in exchange? You wouldn't have, say, ball bearings of such-and-such a diameter?"... And in this manner very long chains of barter arise [Katsenelinboigen, 1977:73, quoted in Henry, 1978:115].

A generally taken-for-granted assumption that one's needs cannot be satisfied by ordinary, legal means leads to omnipresent corruption and the emergence of an intricate web of illegal or semi-legal bonds among people.

Social corruption.

Internal corruption grows out of the very nature of the communist economics — chronic shortage of consumer goods, their poor quality, the interminable delays in obtaining service and repairs, a centralized planning system that decides what people should wear or consume, whether they like the product or not [Jacoby et al., 1977:38].

Intrinsic shortcomings of the centralized state economy and administration lead to the development of a variety of black markets and to a peculiar economic underworld. They also lead to the thorough corruption of the bureaucracy at all levels. These developments are complicated even more by the preponderance of political criteria in the system of promotions and privileges, as well as the distribution of some restricted goods (for example, apartments, telephones, and fur caps), welfare services (nurseries, reduced price holidays, better hospitals, and the like), or other opportunities (entrance to university, passports to travel abroad, and so on). Therefore, "[w]hat the elite get legally through their special stores and system of privileges, ordinary people are forced to seek illegally in the country's countereconomy" (Jacoby et al., 1977:39).

Some ways around these political and bureaucratic barriers may be opened if one is able to find suitable "connections" to reach informally the responsible clerk or official or else, if one finds the appropriate way, to hand him a bribe or arrange a mutually acceptable exchange of services (favors). Very often a "go-between" is used who can discuss more freely with both parties their conditions set by the other party; the chain is broadened and often turns into a long network of mutual favors. If, for instance, a telephone official insists on having an imported coffee set, the telephone applicant tries to find somebody with a "contact" in the shop which might have received imported China. A friend may promise help because his girlfriend knows a girl in such a shop. Therefore a small gift for the kind friend and flowers for girlfriend are in order. The salesgirl may in fact be able to "put aside" one of the sets which never reach the shelves of the store. But she would expect in return a place in the nursery for her child. The search for an appropriate person continues. In the end, all claims are miraculously satisfied, and the telephone clerk receives an attractive coffee set which he could not buy directly from the shop. Instead of an impersonal and prosaic transaction in a state store, a whole new network has developed and a number of people have managed to satisfy their particular needs. It does not follow, however, that these arrangements have made those people more satisfied than they would be otherwise. *The overall social costs of "mutual-favor-networks" are enormous*: witness the loss of time, humiliating experiences, inevitability of using one's own friends as middlemen in dubious transactions and negotiations, and demoralization of employees who constantly abuse their offices to respond to the pressures and to settle their own problems. Besides, the network mechanisms work to the advantage of those better off and well connected who have stronger bargaining power, as well as of those who have fewer moral scruples.

It is interesting, however, that such complex networks of corruption serve clearly as a stabilizing factor, for any change would disturb dangerously the existing, tested, and familiar arrangements and could bring to light common involvement in law violations. One may maintain that it gives to the system some sort of peculiar legitimacy, as Podgórecki argues in his analysis of the "tertiary social control":

> If behind the given legal system (which is rejected by the population at large as unjust, undemocratic, etc.) there operates a complicated infrastructure of mutually interdependent interests then this legal system may become accepted, not on the basis of its own merits, but because it creates a convenient cover-system for the flourishing phenomenon of "dirty togetherness". Then each institution, factory and organization serves...as a formal network which gives a stable frame of reference for an enormous amount of mutual semi-private services, reciprocal arrangements [Podgórecki, 1979:203].

The occurrence of such arrangements may not always be triggered by a spontaneous and grass-roots self-defense of the people who want to survive. Some of their forms may be manipulated and stimulated by the official power centers to counterbalance "private" cliques and to control profits flowing from corruption and fiddling:

> The bureaucratized administrative apparatus especially in the case of state-owned economy becomes so routinized, inelastic, decentralized, and powerless that the central organs may see no other way to keep this apparatus functioning than by saturating it with their own ramified "mafia" [Podgórecki, 1979:200].

These widespread forms of social corruption should not overshadow the political corruption and bribery in international trade. There are, of course, no reliable data on the corruption of the party elite in the communist countries. Certainly, incentives to corruption related to the political elections, present in western democracies, are absent under the one-party communist regime. The votes of people have no meaning in the communist political system.

As far as corruption in the area of international trade and business is concerned, there is no reason why it should be significantly different than in the case of the capitalist countries. Not surprisingly, however, the evidence is so scarce and unreliable that it is impossible to discuss it seriously. Jacoby et al. quote several international scandals and cases of serious corruptions and extortion in which communist officials were involved. Yet, their general conclusion, although rather plausible, is not sufficiently backed up by hard data and should be treated rather as a hypothesis than a fully corroborated statement:

> Because internal corruption is endemic to the communist system, it ineluctably conditions a privileged elite to the habits of corruption in their external relations with other communist officials in the Eastern block countries and with the Western and Japanese businessmen who negotiate with the state enterprises [Jacoby, et al., 1977:40-41].

State crimes against consumers. In the communist countries, the state has a monopoly over the prices, which, of course, is not in itself a crime, according to the communist laws. However, the communist economy, which is not directed by the market laws and which proscribes competition, has not yet achieved an economically meaningful formula for determining prices.

Prices of the consumer goods and food go up continuously, as in fact they do in the west. Yet, many complicated and often illegal tactics are used by the state to avoid open price increases and achieve the same effects in more hidden ways. A common trick consists, of course, in repacking and renaming the same products whenever prices of certain goods are to be raised. Another widespread practice consists of the introduction of new, supposedly better and more expensive products, which would give some range of choice to the consumers for a brief period of time before the older, cheaper articles are withdrawn. Another often-used tactic is the introduction of the new stores with higher-quality goods sold at "market prices," which are much higher than the standard ones. It is a perfectly safe practices, since no one has a right to ask what is the economic meaning of the "market prices" in the nonmarket economy. The prices in these special stores are very high indeed, but for many scarce goods and food articles it may be the only — although not very egalitarian — chance to obtain them. There exist also many hard currency stores where otherwise unobtainable foreign and domestic goods are offered (they may range from food, cloth, and cosmetics to coal, agricultural machines, tools, chemicals, cars, apartments, and houses).

The quality of the articles on sale may also be manipulated. For instances, the price of butter may remain unchanged, but it may contain a higher proportion of margarine; sausages may be pumped with water; ground meat may contain ever more bread; and so forth.

These and many other similar practices are widely used in the communist countries. Naturally, some of them may occur also in the capitalist countries. Yet, in the latter there are at least three factors which attempt (with varied success) to curb them: courts, competition, and consumers' organizations. In the communist countries, first of all, one cannot expect any legal intervention in the policies and arrangements undertaken by the state; second, competition is illegal; and, finally, any spontaneous organizing against the state's policies is penalized (certainly, under the given circumstances, any consumers' movement would belong to this category).

Of course, some exemplary penalties may be administered against selected stores or producers in order to veil the real nature of the policy of deception practiced by the state. Yet, even if a particular state enterprise is found guilty of producing substandard products (or, for that matter, polluting the environment or maintaining unsafe or unhealthy working conditions), the penalties are purely symbolic; not only because the average fine is not high enough — as is usually the case in the capitalist countries — but, above all, because of the spurious nature of the punishment which involves payment of the state's money from one state purse to another. No one is really bothered by the whole operation. In the worst case, the workers' bonus payments would be stopped, but workers do not need to be perceived as a threat where strikes are banned.

CONCLUSIONS

In the previous section I attempted to describe several types of economic crimes as they appear in the capitalist and communist countries. In both cases, I was searching for types of law-breaking behavior which appear to be closely related to the very nature of the economic organization of society. In some cases, a described behavior seemed to be inevitable and causally linked to the nature of the particular economy. In other cases, the link was less direct, but it could still be argued that those crimes were facilitated or provoked by the dominant economic order.

I analyzed the whole range of behavior. I deliberately did not want to limit myself, for instance, to the analysis of the "crimes of the powerful" only in order to demonstrate my attitude toward them. In fact, I did not wish to make judgments on the presented types of crimes or their perpetrators. My main aim was to ascertain who, and to what extent, is "criminalized" —

pushed toward some form of criminal involvement, as a result of particular, communist or capitalist, organization of economy. I wanted also to see in which way this "criminalization" affects those involved and whether there are any political mechanisms which may counter or reduce certain crime-producing aspects of the economy.

I started with the assumption that there are probably some categories of people who are not participating actively in the economic processes and because of this might be treated with suspicion by the economic and political "establishment." And, indeed, in both types of societies, the unemployed are certainly discriminated against, controlled, and reduced to the "surplus labor pool" which grows or shrinks according to the changing labor market. The problem seems to be more sizable in the capitalist countries, while its treatment is probably more harsh in the communist countries. There are, however, some more essential differences. In the former case, the unemployed are perceived as threatening since they do not have a stake in the system and are probably the most dissatisfied group in society. Therefore, they are symbolically segregated, appeased with benefits as well as with some lipservice about the efforts to ameliorate the general job situation. Only when it does not work and they are becoming "dangerous" in the eyes of the "establishment" is the intervention of the criminal justice system seen as justified. This becomes more inevitable when the unemployed population contains a growing proportion of young and socially conscious people. What is important, however, is the fact that unemployment is seen in the capitalist society as a problem, because of the capitalist and state efforts to achieve legitimacy of the prevailing relationships of production and political "hegemony."

In communist societies, the authorities do not try to solicit support of the people in order to legitimize existing economic organization. The attitude toward "surplus population" is repressive because its existence negates an ideological dogma. Devising laws which define this population as criminal secures consistency of the ideology with reality. The unemployed are believed to be a direct product of the capitalist relationships of production; under communism one can find only criminals whose crime is defined as a "parasitic style of life."

Petty theft and fiddling seems to be common in both types of societies. It was suggested that in the capitalist countries it is mainly motivated by the feelings of injustice and of hostility toward employers; by necessity to supplement the low wages; and by attempts to create a more meaningful exchange economy and more intense involvement in everyday life than is offered by the prevailing economic structure. The same motives may be present in the communist countries. There are, however, other factors which are very conspicuous there, and rather insignificant in the capitalist economy.

Petty theft and fiddling in a nationalized economy of the communist countries is, to a significant extent, caused by the workers' realization that what is not stolen is going to be wasted anyway. The organization of production is ineffective and wasteful because of the primary concern of the political authorities with the ideological criteria of the organization of economy which are contrary to the rational requirements of production processes. Another factor which contributes to the common occurrence of employee theft is connected with the total lack of legitimacy of the political and economic system and its laws. Moreover, the ideological slogans about the workers' ownership of the means of production, entirely contradicted by the reality, provoke feelings of bitterness, cynicism, and disrespect for the state property.

In light of empirical evidence, one may argue that under communism the enormity of economic tasks entrusted to the state must lead to the constant growth of the state power and bureaucracy. Such a tendency is obviously contrary to the Marxist thesis about the inevitable progress toward the withering away of the state. In democratic capitalist countries, the relative independence of the dominant economic interests from the political ones keeps in check the totalitarian tendencies of the state. Such tendencies remain unrestrained when the economic interests are unified with political ones and subordinated to the single dominant ideology.

It has been argued, however, that relative independence of

the economy may have some weighty and difficult-to-curb consequences. It may contribute not only to social inequality and exploitation of the workers, but also to the inevitable inequality and discrimination within the world of business. Most corporate crimes are related to the ruthless pursuit of profit which is the core value of the capitalist economy. Corporate crimes are committed on behalf of the profit-seeking corporation, and the financial gains are automatically shared by those directly involved. Organized crime within the communist enterprise is basically different because lawful profits of the enterprise are normally not shared by its executives. The only solution to the profit-seeking habits of many executives in communist countries is the creation of parallel production which is profitable and which is not controlled by the state. Such private initiative counters and discredits the ideologically based state economy because of its effectiveness, elasticity, and genuine human involvement — the features notably absent in the state enterprise. Being illegal, the private countereconomy certainly brings significant financial losses to the state, but, above all, it reveals the weakness of the economic system which does not recognize the fact that the reality in communist society is more forceful and real than the Marxist ideology which is supposed to guide it.

Black market activities are flourishing in western countries. They certainly provide a market for stolen or smuggled goods, but, more importantly, they respond to some morally derived prohibitions. Such prohibitions may be related to the basic religious and ideological beliefs as well as to important political and economic interests. However, they do not constitute the indispensable components of the capitalist organization of economy. Mobilized public opinion may gradually erode the legitimacy of these prohibitions, and shifts in the political interests may facilitate the introduction of legal changes.

In communist countries, economic structure is very different. The dominant economic organization, with characteristic hierarchical relationships designed to transmit economic command, does not provide a sufficient base for carrying out production. The hierarchical relationships secure routinized circulation of the fictitious information (plans, reports) which is bound to lose touch with the real production. The production-related relationships, exchanges, and cooperation are not incorporated into the ideological structure of the economy; therefore, they have to develop spontaneously, in an unplanned and thus banned manner. They have to be outlawed since they evade the State Plan — the fundamental legal document according to which economc processes are to be organized. Yet, without these intricate illegal production relationships, the economy would exist only on paper. The inevitability of the development of an underworld economic market is furthermore strengthened by the contradiction between the social and economic necessity of the existence of a private economic sector and the ideological unfeasibility of providing a legal and economic base for its functioning.

Economic crimes in both types of society have some features in common, but they also differ significantly. These differences are caused by the different ideologies and economic realities of these countries. The capitalist ideology is discreet and hidden; it has acquired a high degree of consistency with the economic reality, which it has been able to mold effectively. Moreover, it has become more or less absorbed and legitimized by the people's beliefs and lifestyles. Economic crimes are shaped by dominant values and are conditioned by market forces and economic cycles.

The communist ideology is coercive and doctrinaire; it has influenced the formal structure of the economy, but has never been embodied in the real economic practice. Moreover, it has not been accepted by, or even absorbed into, social consciousness. Economic crimes are motivated, to a large extent, by a counterideology (capitalist?) which cannot be accommodated within the rigid structure of communist economy. Both economic crimes and the country's economic development depend totally on the existence of black markets and social corruption which are generated by the official economic structure.

Western radical intellectuals are eager to promote the communist cause and have no doubts that it would pass the test of practical consistency.

In rejecting the boundaries of normal scholarship and bourgeois paradigms, the existing order is critically examined and the socialist alternative proposed. Embodied within critique and proposal is a politics of working class struggle and socialist revolution [Quinney, 1977:164].

These words are inspiring, yet it may be argued that although Marxist critique of capitalist economy is profound and practical, it does not necessarily follow that the alternative economic organization would not victimize workers even more. After all, somebody has to lose in an inefficient economy based on the ideological negation of the practical demands of production.

NOTES

1. I explain fully the distinction between "restrictive" and "anarchic" criminal situations in Łoś (1973).

2. "Restrictive" economic crimes are defined here as criminal actions directly or indirectly determined by the particular economic organization.

3. For example, British estimates point to £3 millions worth of welfare benefits "scrounged" yearly as against total payments of £13,000 millions. Yet, the war against "scroungers" still makes a good election issue (see *The Guardians*, May 1, 1979:10).

4. Yet, according to some research, the condemnation seems to be especially strong among those most affluent, educated, and secure who may not be so strongly affected by the economic recession (Smigel, 1970:41). The pattern may, however, differ in various countries and in different periods of time.

5. Henry maintains that in practice all jobs contain some fiddling, stealing, and dealing opportunities; and, although he emphasizes that it is not exactly the area which would readily lend itself to research, he has been able to collect quite an impressive bibliography of studies on the subject (Henry, 1978:113-114, 175-183).

6. Although it has to be remembered that in this area illegal and legal types of activities are so closely related that it is certainly very difficult to frame laws which would be fully precise and adequate (for critical analysis of anticombine legislation see, for example, Goff and Reasons, 1978).

7. For example, in 1971 in Sweden there was one store selling alcohol to 27,000 inhabitants, while in Poland the proportion was 1 to 840 (Falewicz, 1976:351). This information becomes even more meaningful when one considers the well-known fact of the scarcity of food and of desired consumption articles in the latter country. The situation is not different in the Soviet Union, where also "the volume of alcohol production and the great number of trade outlets for its sale receive their share of the blame for the persistence of drunkenness and alcoholism" (Connor, 1972:52).

8. Even before that time "some private enterprise was permitted, such as sawing and cutting wood, washing windows and floors, polishing shoes, and making knicknacks out of wood, bone, stone, clay and straw" (Chalidze, 1977:161).

REFERENCES

BATAWIA, S. (1973) "Rozmiary zjawiska czestego naduzywania alkoholu przez rozne kategorie pijacych" (Extent of heavy drinking among different categories). Problemy Alkoholizmu 5.

CHALIDZE, V. (1977) Criminal Russia (P. S. Falla, trans.). Essays on Crime in the Soviet Union. New York: Random House.

CLARK, J. P. and R. HOLLINGER (1977) "On the feasibility of empirical studies of white collar crime," pp. 139-158 in R. F. Meier (ed.) Theory in Criminology, Contemporary Views. Beverly Hills, CA: Sage.

CLINARD, M. B. (1952) The Black Market. New York: Holt, Rinehart & Winston.

CONKLIN, J. E. (1977) Illegal But Not Criminal. Business Crime in America. Englewood Cliffs, NJ: Prentice-Hall.

CONNOR, W. D. (1972) Deviance in Soviet Society. New York and London: Columbia University Press.

COX, B., J. SHIRLEY and M. SHORT (1977) The Fall of Scotland Yard. Harmondsworth: Penguin.

CRESSEY, D. (1969) Theft of the Nation: The Structure and Operation of Organized Crime in America. New York: Harper & Row.

DASZKIEWICZ, K. (1971) Klimaty bezprawia (Realms of Lawlessness). Warszawa: Ksiazka i Wiedza.

DEACON, A. (1978) "The scrounging controversy: Public attitudes towards the unemployed in contemporary Britain." Social and Economic Administration 12 (Summer).

DERSHOWITZ, A. M. (1961) "Increasing community control over corporate crime: a problem in the law of sanction." Yale Law Journal 71: 289-306.

DITTON, J. (1977) Part-Time Crime. An Ethnography of Fiddling and Pilferage. London: Macmillan.

DOBBS, M. (1977) "Will a bit 'on the side' keep the Poles quiet?" The Sunday Times September 25: 8.

FALEWICZ, J. K. (1976) "Spoleczne uwarunkowania alkoholizmu w Polsce" (Social background of alocholism in Poland), pp. 347-370 in A. Podgorecki (ed.) Zagadnienia patologii spolecznej. Warszawa: Polskie Wydawnictwo Naukowe.

GEIS, G. (1978) "Deterring corporate crime," pp. 278-296 in M. D. Ermann and R. J. Ludman (eds.) Corporate and Governmental Deviance. New York: Oxford University Press.

GOFF, C. H. and C. E. REASONS (1978) Corporate Crime in Canada. A Critical Analysis of Anti-combine legislation. Scarborough. Ontario: Prentice-Hall.

The Guardian (1979) "Scroungers: the facts and the challenge." May 1: 10.

HENRY, S. (1978) The Hidden Economy. The Context and Control of Borderline Crime. Oxford, England: Martin Robertson.

JACOBY, N. H., P. NEHEMKIS and R. EELLS (1977) Bribery and Extortion in World Business. A Study of Corporate Political Payments Abroad. New York: Macmillan.

KATSENELINBOIGEN, A. (1977) "Coloured markets in the Soviet Union." Soviet Studies 29: 62-85.

KOLAKOWSKA-PRZELOMIEC, H. (1975) "Srodowisko rodzinne w swietle badan kryminologicznych" (Family background in the light of criminological research), pp. 159-184 in J. Jasinski (ed.) Zagadnienia przestepczosci w Polsce. Warszawa: Wydawnictwo Prawnicze.

KURCZEWSKI, J. and K. FRIESKE (1977) "Some problems in the legal regulation of the activities of economic institutions." Law and Society Review 11: 489-505.

ŁOŚ, M. (1978) "Access to civil justice system in Poland," pp. 785-815 in M. Cappelletti and G. Bryant (eds) Access to Justice, Vol. 1: A World Survey. Milan: Dott. A Giuffre Editore, Alphenaandenrijn: Sijthoff and Noordhoff.

——— (1979) "Restrictive and anarchic deviance," in A. Podgórecki and M. Łoś, Multidimensional Sociology. London: Routledge & Kegan Paul.

MAJCHRZAK, I. (1965) Pracownicze przestepstwo i jego sprawca (White Collar Crime and White Collar Criminal). Warszawa: Ksiazka i Wiedza.

MARS, G. (1974) "Dock pilferage," pp. 209-228 in P. Rock and M. McIntosh (eds.) Deviance and Social Control. London: Tavistock.

MARS, G. and P. MITCHELL (1977) "Catering: low pay, low unionism and payment by the fiddle." Low Pay Bulletin (August).

NAUMOWICZ, Z. (1970) "Niektore zagadnienia dotyczace przestepczosci gospodarczej" (Selected problems of economic crime), pp. 5-32 in Prawnicy, Socjologowie i psychologowie o przestepczosci i jej zwalczaniu. Warszawa: Prokuratura Generalna.

NELSON, S. D., and C. R. WOLFE, Jr (1977) "Tightening the white collar: the criminalization of trade secret theft." The American Criminal Law Review 14: 797-821.

NOZICK, R. (1974) Anarchy, State and Utopia. Oxford: Blackwell.

PEARCE, F. (1976) Crimes of the Powerful. Marxism, Crime and Deviance. London: Pluto Press.

PODGÓRECKI, A. (1979) "Tertiary social control," in A. Podgorecki and M. Łoś, Multidimensional Sociology. London: Routledge & Kegan Paul.

QUINNEY, R. (1978) Class, State and Crime. On the Theory and Practice of Criminal Justice. New York: Longman.

SCHWENDINGER, H. and J. SCHWENDINGER (1975) "Defenders of order or guardians of human rights?" pp. 113-146 in I. Taylor, P. Walton, and J. Young (eds.) Critical Criminology. London: Routledge & Kegan Paul.

SCHRAGER, L. S. and J. F. SHORT, JR. (1978) "Towards a sociology of organizational crime." Social Problems 25: 407-419.

SMIGEL, E. O. (1970) "Public attitudes towards 'chiselling' with reference to unemployment compensation," pp. 29-45 in E. O. Smigel and H. L. Ross (eds.) Crimes Against Bureaucracy. New York: Van Nostrand Reinhold.

SMITH, H. (1976) The Russians. New York: Ballantine.

SNIDER, D. L. (1978) "Corporate crime in Canada: a preliminary report." Canadian Journal of Criminology 20: 142-168.

SOLOMON, H. (1977) "The economist's perspective of economic crime." American Crinal Law Review 14: 641-649.

SPITZER, S. (1975) "Toward a Marxian theory of deviance." Social Problems 22: 638-651.

SWIECICKI, A. (1977) Alkohol. Zagadnienia polityki spolecznej (Alcohol. Problems of Social Policy). Warszawa: Spoleczny Komitet Przeciwalkoholowy.

SZELHAUS, S. (1975) "Znaczenie alkoholizmu i naduzywania alkoholu w genezie przestepczosci recydywistow." (The role of alcoholism in the criminal recidive). pp. 219-243 in J. Jasinski (ed.) Zagadnienia przestepczosci w Polsce. Warszawa: Wydawnictwo Prawnicze.

TREML, V. G. (1975) "Alcohol in the U.S.S.R: a fiscal dilemma." Soviet Studies 27: 161-177.

11

ORGANIZED CRIME
A Social and
Economic Perspective

FRANCIS A. J. IANNI
ELIZABETH REUSS-IANNI

A PROBLEM OF PERSPECTIVES

Robert Redfield once remarked that the surest sign of the emergence of a new sub-discipline or area of research interest in science was analogous to what he has found to be characteristic of the establishment of small folk societies: a social structure organized by a kinship system made up of clans which shared a common folklore and mythology about the origins and values of the group. By Redfield's definition, the study of organized crime has established itself as an area, if not yet a community, of research interest. Not only criminologists, but sociologists, anthropologists, historians, economists, political scientists, jurists, journalists, film makers, political figures, and even poets and cartoonists have joined with professionals in the criminal justice system to define, describe, analyze, and recommend solutions for this peculiarly American social phenomenon. As a result, the definition of organized crime is ideologically rather than empirically derived. And the ideological positions are as diverse as the variety of perspectives which criminal justice professionals, social scientists, and journalists bring to the study of organized crime.

The criminal justice system professional is a practitioner, a pragmatic professional who finds it impossible to divorce theories and hypotheses from his responsibility to deal with what actually exists. Lewis Feuer (1973:86) has described this approach as one of direct confrontation with problems: "There is a normal human biological pattern in the confrontation of problems; the problem provokes ideas, plans of action, which in the normal biological process find fulfillment in action."

The social scientist, on the other hand, is a scholar, a man of ideas without any direct responsibility for practical affairs, and, as the criminal justice professional frequently points out, usually lacks the firsthand "real world" knowledge which only actual experience can bring. Edward Shils (1972:3) has described the scholar's style as follows:

> There is in every society a minority of persons who, more than the ordinary run of their fellow men, are inquiring and desirous of being in frequent communion with symbols which are more general than the immediate concrete situations of everyday life and remote in their reference to both time and space.

Finally, there are journalists and others whose defined tasks are to provide public information. They see their role as the relentless pursuit of the empirical facts and the reporting of those facts with immediacy and, it is hoped, with impact. In this role one usually finds that drama, color, and "newsworthiness" are valued. Analytic statements, contravening cases, the development and testing of hypotheses, and the stringent assessment of validity and reliability are not concerns of the same order that they are for the scholar. This does not necessarily mean that their "facts" are any more or any less true than those which must await the scholar's need to "penetrate beyond the screen of immediate concrete experience" or the practitioner's insistance that he identify the true facts existentially in the real world. It simply means that ideology shapes our views of what is false and what is true in the social world, our moral and cognitive perceptions, and, inevitably, the programs we propose for organizing or changing that social world.

These contradictory and often competing ideologies have resulted in more than a confusing portrait of what organized crime is in American society; they have made any attempt to define organized crime in operational terms virtually impossible. As a consequence, organized crime becomes a convenient explanation for any number of activities and problems which we cannot otherwise explain or rationalize. Consensus on combating organized crime has been impossible to achieve because how one views organized crime naturally leads to ideological differences in deciding how it may be controlled. Ideology in this sense is more than a preferred style of viewing the world; it molds and shapes the seeking of evidence, the means of analyzing what one sees, and schemes for organizing and implementing change in society.

Criminologists have traditionally used the term "organized crime" to distinguish the professional from the amateur in crime. Organized crime is structured, in this definition, by a cooperative association of criminals. Sutherland and Cressey's classic *Principles of Criminology* (1955:229) for example, defines organized crime as follows:

> [An] association of a small group of criminals for the execution of a certain type of crime, together with the development of plans by which detection may be avoided, the development of a fund of money and connections by means of which immunity or relative immunity may be secured in case of detection.

Thus, any gang or group of criminals organized formally or informally to burgle, shoplift, steal automobiles, or pick pockets is part of organized crime.

Government commissions and agencies, however, have tended to use a different definition which focuses on the idea of a criminal conspiracy. The President's Commission on Law Enforcement and the Administration of Justice (1967:187) defines organized crime as:

a society that seeks to operate outside the control of the American people and their working government. It involves thousands of criminals working within structures as complex as those of any large corporation, subject to laws more rigidly enforced than those of legitimate governments. Its actions are conspiracies, carried out over many years and aimed at gaining control over whole fields of activity in order to amass huge profits.

Any illicit activity intended to gain control or amass profits fits this definition. What is distinctive about organized crime here is its seemingly bureaucratic and conspiratorial character. For the criminal justice professional a variety of activities are equally defined — drug peddling, gambling, loan sharking, and any number of otherwise unrelated enterprises both licit and illicit. What holds them together in this definition is the fact that they are controlled by organized criminals. Organized crime in this definition is whatever organized criminals do.

While these definitions differ to some extent, there is an important element common to both. In both cases, the definitions focus on the criminals themselves and differ mainly in terms of size and complexity of organization (relatively small local groups as contrasted to a national syndicate) and the nature of the crimes involved (crimes in which there is a perpetrator and a victim and crimes in which illegal goods and services are supplied to those willing to pay for them). This is not a matter of coincidence, but results from the nature of the concerns which the criminologist and the law enforcement official bring to the study of organized crime. Both focus on the criminal act and thus on the criminal actor.

There is also an economic perspective for defining organized crime which grows out of the nature of the acts we have come to include within the generic definition of organized crime. One of the fundamental characteristics of the activity called organized crime is that it supplies illicit goods and services — illicit sex, gambling, illegal narcotics and alcohol, and stolen goods — to voluntary consumers. At the same time, organized crime is increasingly viewed as using the monies gained from these illegal activities to finance other related crimes such as extortion, hijacking, fencing of stolen goods, loan sharking, and criminal monopolization of legitimate business. Here organized crime is seen by economic analysts as part of the American enterprise system — one end of a continuum which has legitimate business as the other pole.

Finally, a number of social scientists have pointed out that organized crime also operates as a ladder of social mobility in America. Social history documents the successive movement of a number of ethnic groups in and out of organized crime. Cut off from more socially approved routes out of poverty, powerlessness, and the ghetto, ethnic youngsters learn on the streets of those same ghettos that crime offers a quick if perilous way out. Ethnic succession in organized crime is here viewed as part of the American social process by which minority groups struggle for a place in society and, as new and more socially acceptable avenues of mobility open, move on into respectability.

How one defines organized crime is of more than passing academic interest, since strategies for its control develop from an understanding of how and why it is organized. The criminal-as-professional definition, for example, has produced the widespread, local-level criminal justice system "violation-response" approach which is little different from attempts to apprehend street criminals. The criminal conspiracy theory leads naturally to the federal-level campaign of "attrition" for systematic development of organized crime control: "Strategy and tactics," "intelligence functions," "interdiction," "search and destroy," and other concepts which grow out of the military-intelligence approach to combating conspiracies are proposed here. If, on the other hand, organized crime is examined as a function of the market economy of the United States, then a different approach emerges — one of intervening in the production distribution process, of reducing the spread between profits and expenses, and of providing competitive legitimate markets through decriminalization. If one sees organized crime as a social system, another strategy — one based on social amerlioration and reform to control organized crime — seems appropriate.

What differentiates these various definitions, and what structures the disparity between the ideologies, is the continuing

debate as to whether the Mafia and Cosa Nostra are
synonymous with organized crime. The new perspectives provided by social scientists through both the economic analysis
and the social systems approaches have been instrumental in
redirecting some attention away from purely criminal to social
and economic factors in the origins, structure, operations, and
persistence of organized crime. As a result, existence of an
American Mafia is not necessary to support these perspectives.
The existence of an American Mafia is, however, critical to the
"official" conspiracy theory to provide an organizing structure
for organized crime which explains its persistence and seems to
transcend changing defintions of what is illegal and what is not.

The organized crime which now thrives in American cities,
however, has deep roots in our social and economic history. The
gangs of the western frontier and the "robber barons" who
transformed that frontier into financial empires in the late nineteenth century are part of our heritage of organized criminal activity. Not until the twentieth century and the growth of the
modern city did the dilemma of organized crime as we know it
come about. Urban history documents how the growth of the
American city results in a complex but demonstrable relationship among minority status, politics, and organized crime.

The Irish were first to form street gangs with colorful names
like "The Bowery Boys" and "O'Connell's Guards." By the
beginning of this century, the Irish had come to dominate crime
and big-city politics through which they eventually won
themselves respectability in construction, trucking, public
utilities, and on the waterfront. The aftermath of World War I
brought the era of Prohibition and speculation in the money
markets and real estate, arenas for power and profit over which
Jewish and eventually Italian gangs fought for control. It was
this trend which spawned one of the major controversies in the
analysis of organized crime as an American phenomenon.

PERSPECTIVE:
A NATIONAL ETHNIC SYNDICATE

As early as the last decade of the nineteenth century, when 11 reputed *mafiosi* were lynched by a New Orleans mob after having been accused of assassinating the city's police chief, it was alleged that the Italians brought organized crime with them when they came to America. Eighty years after the New Oreleans lynchings, a Harris poll indicated that a majority of Americans — a decisive 78 to 17 percent of the sample Harris chose — believed that "there is a secret organization engaged in organized crime in this country which is called the Mafia." A number of governmental investigatory bodies have held similar views. In 1951 Senator Estes Kefauver's Senate Crime Committee concluded that "there is a nationwide crime syndicate known as the Mafia whose leaders are usually found in control of the most lucrative rackets in their cities." President Lyndon Johnson's 1965 Task Force on Organized Crime described organized crime in America as follows:

> There is a nationwide alliance of at least twenty-four, tightly knit Mafia "Families" which control organized crime in the United States.
>
> All of the members of these twenty-four "families" are Italians and Sicilians or of Italian or Sicilian descent.
>
> Each "family" has a hierarchical structure of positions which regulates power in that family.
>
> These "families" are linked together by "understandings, agreements, and obedience to a nine-member commission."
>
> Members of these "families" control: (a) all but a tiny part of illegal gambling in the United States; (b) virtually all of the loan-shark operations in the United States; (c) the importation of narcotics; and (d) most of Las Vegas as actual owners or behind-the-scene owners. In addition, they have infiltrated labor unions, made liaisons which give them power over state and federal legislators and other officials in the legislative, executive, and judicial branches at local, state, and federal levels of government, and have complete control of a number of legal business enterprises (said to be worth billions of dollars).

Within this national structure, the Task Force Report describes a hierarchical structure within each local family which is the same throughout the country. Hierarchical separation is rigidly enforced up and down the organization, and this compartmentalization ensures that members at one level are insulated from all except their immediate superiors and those members of the next lower level who report directly to them. The effect is that if a street-level operative is arrested, he cannot implicate those above him and usually only a small number of members at his own level. It is this insulation, reinforced by a rigid code of silence in the face of official questioning, which is said to make law enforcement efforts to penetrate and destroy local and national syndicates so difficult. This hierarchical organizational structure also serves to define the roles and the division of labor within each "family" and across the nation, since the role definitions are bureaucratic to the extent that they are the same in each family.

A different structure emerges if one views organized crime as a social system. If, as a number of American social scientists and most European scholars who have studied both Mafia in Sicily and organized crime in America maintain, organized crime families are not consciously constructed formal organizations, but rather traditional social systems, products of culture, and so responsive to cultural change that a different model of organization emerges. Far from being hierarchies or organizational positions which can be diagrammed and then changed by recasting the organizational chart, they would, in this definition, be patterns of relationships among individuals which have the strength of social bonds such as kinship and which can be changed only by drastic, frequently fatal, action.

While World War I brought a halt to Italian immigration, its aftermath brought both Prohibition and the gangland wars which made the twenties roar. Prior to 1920, organized crime had been mostly in the hands of Irish gangs, but with the passage of the Eighteenth Amendment which brought Prohibition and a lucrative and still undeveloped source of power and profit, Jewish gangs and eventually Italians began to struggle for control.

With the repeal of Prohibition, the Great Depression, and the onset of World War II, the history of organized crime in America becomes both less colorful and less certain. Much of what we know about this period, then, comes from two public sources. Government law enforcement agencies and federal, state, and local investigatory commissions produced a number of reports which sometimes made their way to the public as books describing the emergence of a powerful bureaucratic national syndicate of crime. These governmental investigatory projects differed from previous efforts in at least two significant ways. First, they enjoyed wide media coverage which, particularly in the case of television, brought their findings and points of view directly into the homes of the public. Their methods of obtaining information were also more immediate and dramatic than had been true in the past. The use of wire tapping, electronic bugs, and other eavesdropping devices produced what was described as "the actual voices of Cosa Nostra planning and reminiscing over their crimes." There were even appearances by reputed members of organized crime syndicates who seemed willing to tell all before the cameras. The popular press, fed by these same sources, reported on the development of what the late Saul Alinsky was to call "a quasi-public utility."

At about the same time, there was a growth of popular literature — biographies and even autobiographies of criminals, gang-busting war stories by policemen or prosecutors, novels based on the information supplied by government agencies and the press — and eventually films which made "Mafia", "Cosa Nostra," and the associated symbols of that mystique household terms in America. The result is that, like much of recent history, it will be some time before the various threads, currents, and countercurrents are sorted out and definitive histories can be examined.

The conspiracy theory which surrounds ethnic crime in America continues to be revitalized and reinterpreted to explain away many of these problems. However, the differential definitons of what is and what is not organized crime, the alternate histories of how and why it came to be or grew up in America, and contrasting notions of the relationship between organized crime and the political and economic structure of society will continue to confound solutions to these problems, until we begin to look at organized crime empirically rather than ideologically.

COMBINING PERSPECTIVES: THE ANALYSIS OF SOCIAL AND ECONOMIC COSTS

One of the major reasons why such a socioeconomic approach to the study of organized crime has not been attempted is that, as a result of the definitional confusion, there has not been an established arena of activity within which to examine both the social and the economic costs and benefits of organized crime. Virtually all of the law enforcement data, which have served as the basis for most organized crime research, consist of case-intelligence files on individuals or on "secret societies" such as the Purple Gang, the Mafia, or Cosa Nostra. As a result, the structure of organized crime which defines the patterns of relationships among individuals involved in shared economic activities such as the selling of narcotics or the theft of securities are not separable from the social grouping patterns which result from ethnicity or friendship. Consequently, we have a great deal of information on the lives, habits, origins, and business tactics of the producers and distributors, but little or no information on the economy of organized crime, on its customers, or on the power brokers who protect it. Thus, neither the social systems nor the economic analysis approaches have provided sufficient explanatory and predictive power to support adequate public policy development. Organized crime's role as a producer of social "bads" such as illegal behavior and violence must be considered in the light of its economic "goods" of providing jobs and alternate routes of social mobility. Thus, organized crime must be defined, examined, and analyzed as a functional and viable social and economic institution in American society not fully explained by its crimnal character. We further propose that the social and economic complexity of the problem or problems is such that planning and policy-making concerning organized crime control requires a convergence rather than a single-discipline approach to the definition and analysis of the problem and to policy planning.

In studying organized crime, sociologists have focused primarily on the interrelationship among crime, politics, and ethnicity, while economists have proceeded from the assumption that organized crime is an illicit enterprise; they have centered their assertions about organized crime in the language of cartels and criminal monopolies. Obviously, both perspectives are necessary for the examination of this question. A sociopolitical understanding of established criminal groups and how they relate to client-victims and to protectors in various governmental areas is essential to an analysis of the market forces and other factors which have led to particular criminal-industrial structures, patterns of business infiltration, and the analysis of the economics of these businesses. How such a convergence perspective on organized crime can approach the ideological biases which affect the availability of the data and the analyses which grow out of them is obvious in three important questions still unanswered in the study of organized crime: (1) What is the level and diversity of market activity in organized crime? (2) What are the social and economic effects of organized crime in the United States? (3) What are the social policy alternatives for the control of organized crime?

The Organized Crime Market Place

The problem of definition also confounds estimates of the level of economic activity in organized crime. When the secret conspiratorial society model is used, the profit and loss statements provided by governmental and press estimates present a picture of a corporate structure collecting income in some centralized office and having a payroll department not unlike any other industrial corporation, such as U.S. Steel, except that it is much larger.

How such estimates are arrived at was accurately described by Max Singer in *The Public Interest* when he reported that

> mythical numbers may be more mythical and have more vitality in the area of crime than in most areas. In the early 1950's the Kefauver Committee published a $20 billion estimate of the an-

nual quotations taken for gambling in the United States. The figure actually was picked from the hat. One staff member said "We had no real idea of the money spent. The California Crime Commission says $12 billion. Virgil Peterson of Chicago says $30 billion. We picked $20 billion as the balance of the two."

Generally, however, whatever sources are used, the income figures cited for criminal societies and for individual organized criminals are astronomically high and are based on guesses. Because most analysts have concentrated their attention on the profits to criminal societies and their members, they have also tended to ignore the considerable business expenses involved in organized crime. The most obvious is the cost of protection. While there are no estimates of totals involved here, some idea is furnished by the report of the Knapp Commission established in 1970 to investigate police corruption in New York City:

> Plainclothesmen, participating in what is known in police parlance as a "pad," collected regular biweekly or monthly payments amounting to as much as $3,500 from each of the gambling establishments in the area under their jurisdiction and divided it into equal shares. The monthly share per man (called the "nut") ranged from $300 and $400 in mid-town Manhattan to $1,500 in Harlem.

Actually, there is no way in which the level of economic activity in organized crime can be monitored with anywhere near the precision of the Bureau of the Census' *Census of Manufacturers*, since there is no way to gain access to comparable data on organized crime. What is possible, however, is the development of a clearer understanding of illegal markets from which indirect estimating methods can be used to give better estimates of the level, direction, and magnitude of change and some index of activities — legal and illegal — involved. What is necessary in order to proceed to such an understanding of illegal markets is a clearer model of the workings of some specific matrices of illegal enterprises which provide empirical data on the number and size of firms, how they are structured, and how they relate to each other in terms of cooperation and competition, investment capital requirements and rates of return, market demands and methods of marketing and distribution, and the risks which result from their legal as well as illegal character. If a number of such models can be constructed, and particularly if such models can be developed for areas where organized crime holds monopolistic power (drug traffic, for example) and where there is legal competition (gambling and loan sharking, for example), it should be possible to develop predictive models for estimating the level of activity and the growth potential of specific illegal market areas.

The Social and Economic "Costs" of Organized Crime

While there is confusion over the economic structure of organized crime, it is in the cost-benefit question that the social systems and economic definitions of organized crime are presently most in conflict. Social analysts have generally described a variety of effects resulting from organized crime which are socially dysfunctional — corruption, increased street crime, and noncompliance with lawfully prescribed norms by client-victims as well as the organized crime activists themselves. In this model, corruption is generally viewed as a side effect or result (rather than an integral part) of organized criminal activity. Similarly, such associated costs to society from organized crime as the relationship between street crime and addiction produces a view that these are secondary effects of the narcotics trade. At the same time, social analysts usually deal with the movement of organized crime activists into legitimate business enterprises as a means of social mobility. Robert Merton, for example, suggests that in American society criminals strive for the same goals of wealth, status, and security as other Americans, and that once they overcome the barriers to achievement of these goals their movement into legitimate enterprise is a response to the same middle-class values as held by other businessmen (Ianni and Reuss-Ianni, 1977).

Traditionally, organized criminal activities were centered in the "vices" — gambling, prostitution, the illegal sale of alcohol and drugs, and loan sharking. Here, the case could be and has been made by jurists as well as by organized crime activists themselves that we are viewing "victimless" crimes, admittedly illicit activities in which the opposed victim is actually a customer for the illegal goods and services which organized crime provides. Ever since the Kefauver Committee report, however, there has been increasing official concern over the penetration of legitimate business sectors by organized criminal groups. In some cases, such as garbage collection in New York City, the charge is that whole sectors of business enterprise are monopolistically controlled by organized crime. In others, such as entertainment, legalized gambling (particularly in Las Vegas), restaurant businesses and food retailing, and pornography, organized crime is said to play a major and growing role. To some extent, the movement into legitimate business areas can be described as an attempt to "launder" monies taken in by organized crime syndicates in illegal areas such as gambling or drug traffic. It is also maintained, however, particularly by those social scientists who subscribe to the ethnic succession theory of the movement in and out of organized crime by minority groups, that this represents a traditional pattern of social mobility in America. Whether one or both views is correct, a major concern is that organized crime groups moving into legitimate business enterprises take with them illegal means such as extortion, murder, corruption of public officials, blackmail, and income tax evasion and so subvert and take unfair competitive advantage of legitimate business persons. Certainly, some of the illegal means attributed to organized crime activity in legitimate business sectors such as corruption or income tax evasion are not new to legitimate business enterprise, but the concern for organized crime movement is a major one both in government and in business itself.

Economic analysts of organized crime, on the other hand, have tended to propose that, in its market operation at least, organized crime operates like any other economic enterprise. As a result, economists have ignored the social costs of organized crime as nonquantifiable and so uncalculable in such analysis. Further, such analysts have considered the monopolistic character of organized crime as its primary economic character. James Buchanan (1973), in a discussion of the economics of crime and punishment, for example, describes the social advantages that accrue from organized crime (specifically prostitution in this example) as follows:

Presumably this is an activity that is "bad" in some social sense, as witnessed by the most universal legal prohibitions. (Whether or not particular individuals consider this to be an ill-advised social judgment is neither here nor there.) For many potential buyers, the services of prostitutes are "goods" in the strict economic sense of this term; these buyers are willing to pay for these services in ordinary market transactions. From this it follows that monopoly organization is socially preferable to competitive organization precisely because of the restriction on total output that it fosters.

The conflict between the two models does more than confuse public and official audiences. It reduces the explanatory effectiveness of both approaches and so reduces their utility for public policy development. Consider, for example, the question of legalization as a means of reducing organized crime through the provision of legal competition in illegal markets now controlled by organized crime. For example, Thomas Schelling (1971), the economist who served as advisor to President Johnson's Task Force on Organized Crime, has argued that since the purpose of monopoly has always been to suppress rather than enlarge supply, the present customers of organized crime would prefer "to see the activities become more freely competitive...by being released from illegality...[as] will those who dislike corruption." Recent attempts at the reduction of organized crime monopoly in gambling through legalization, however, have produced a number of obvious social costs. There is evidence, for example, that legalized gambling may attract new customers to gambling rather than lure away the present customers of organized crime. Of greater social impact is the fact, for example, that only certain forms of gambling have been legalized, while others, such as the numbers or policy game, remain illegal. By the mid-1970s, over 70 percent of all arrests for gambling in the United States was of Blacks who are a small percentage of the population and of the gambling public but are the principal customers of the numbers games.

Public Policy and Organized Crime Control

Law enforcement as a process is both poorly understood and

ineffective unless it is perceived as part of the inclusive process of public decision-making and policy information. This becomes particularly pertinent in the understanding of organized crime, since we know that the law enforcement system and the government system themselves must be considered as part of the matrix within which organized crime grows and thrives. Ever since Lincoln Steffens charged in *The Sham of Our Cities* that "the spirit of graft and lawlessness is the American spirit" we have almost tacitly accepted the role of corruption in the politics of the American city. Now, in the aftermath of the Watergate scandals, we seem to have developed the uneasy feeling that patronage, illegal and unethical practices, and other abuses of power we once attributed to the aldermanic level of politics are part of our national political ethics as well. While corruption of power is not an exclusively American tradition, comparative political studies do reveal that, compared with Western European nations at least, bribery, extortion, the purchase of the vote, and kickbacks in the award of contracts are associated with urbanization in the United States.

We have also long known that the corrupt political structures of major American cities and organized crime have always enjoyed a relationship in which success in one is heavily dependent on the right connections in the other. Such relationships are crucial to the development and survival of organized crime. In the relationship which led to the original or "vice-centered" view of organized crime, the aspiring ethnic, blocked from legitimate access to power and wealth, was permitted to produce and provide those illicit goods and services which our morals publicly condemn but which our mores privately demand, but always with the understanding that they must pay tribute to the political establishment. The rackets have always paid heavily into the coffers of political machines. The successful gangster, like the successful politician, was seen as a model who demonstrated to the masses of his coethnics that it was possible to achieve rapid and dramatic success even while defying the police and other oppressors. Then, when political power eventually came to the group, at least partly as a result of the connections and payoffs surrounding these same illicit activities, access to legitimate opportunities became enlarged and social and political assimilation facilitated. Thus, if community support for organized crime is one reason why it persists, corruption in both government and business is at least of equal importance. Two factors — the slum dweller's alienation from the political process and the persistence of that peculiarly American attitude that so long as slum dwellers commit crimes against each other, crime in the ghetto is not an American problem — have kept law enforcement officials indifferent to the real problems of minority crime.

There is considerable evidence of police indifference and even collusion in organized crime activities, but this evidence should be tempered by the realization that the police are usually the only visible representatives of the power structure at the street level where graft and corruption are most obvious. Price gouging by merchants; profits from dilapidated buildings for absentee landlords; kickbacks to contractors and bribes to inspectors; and, the ever-increasing evidence of corruption in the judiciary, city hall, and federal government as well, are equally obvious to the people on the streets of the inner city. These are lessons to which the organized crime activist and the politician have always been schooled and they should not be lost on policy makers.

Today, the most frequently cited policy alternatives to the local-level violation response and the federal-level response of attrition through the identification, surveillance, and prosecution of known organized criminals are legalization as a means of destroying monopolistic control and community crime control through changing public attitudes which support organized crime activities. Neither approach has been considered seriously because the explanatory models which support them are insufficient to provide substantive data for decision- and policy-making. Thus, exponents of each of these control models have proceeded from criticism of current policy without any middle- or long-term social and economic perspective which provides a comprehensive alternative model to describe and explain organized crime as a basis for policy recommendations.

The problem of organized crime is demonstrably one in which the structure of the contingencies for which policy must be framed or planning devised cuts across social, economic, and criminal justice concerns. It is our conviction, therefore, that the perspective needed for presenting alternative solutions which are both realistic and convincing must be as comprehensive as the problem itself. This is why organized crime specialists constantly call for "an interdisciplinary approach" which in policy science terms means the convergence approach — as contrasted to the single-discipline specialist approach — which has characterized much of the recent work in problem definition and analysis for policy and planning in areas such as urban development, national defense, and conservation. What is called for, then, is a convergence approach which (1) leads to the development of a comprehensive theory of organized crime which includes social and economic as well as criminal justice perspectives in order to (2) frame alternatives to present criminal justice and public policy postures which fail to address the contingencies of organized crime which cut across the traditional areas of concern. Viewed in this way, organized crime emerges as a functional part of the American social system; and, while successive waves of immigrants and migrants have found it an available means of economic and social mobility, it persists and transcends the involvement of any particular group and even changing definitions of legality and illegality in social behavior, not as an ethnic conspiracy, but as a social problem like any other social ill. As a result, any emergent definition must fall within a defined social, political, and economic matrix which brings together (1) a client public that demands certain goods and services that are defined as illegal, (2) an organization (large or small) of individuals who produce or supply these goods and services, and (3) corrupt public officials who protect such individuals for their own profit or gain. It is this matrix which describes the social and economic reality of organized crime. Unless we look at the variety of economic and sociopolitical patterns which bring the three levels together, public policy will continue to result in control strategies which are inadequate because they deal with only the most obvious actors (the "criminals") in the process.

The variety of perspectives and responses to the problem of

organized crime is also conditioned by the roster of choices, situational or doctrinaire, in appropriate courses of problem solution. Basic convictions about change in human society seem to divide three ways: There are those who believe that change best occurs in slight and progressive increments, others see hope only in wholesale social upheavals, and still others feel that society's problems carry in them the seeds of their own solutions. Most attempts at comprehensive crime control fail because we fail to agree not only on what it is but are equally divided on how to go about correcting it. Organized crime control demands that we attack all three groups — the consuming public, the supplying criminals, and the protecting politicians or organized crime will always be with us.

REFERENCES

ALEXANDER, Y. [ed.] (1976) International Terrorism: National Regional and Global Perspectives. New York: Praeger.

BOYLE, K., T. HADDEN, and T. HILLYARD (1978) "The facts on internment in Northern Ireland," pp. 103-115 in R. Crelinston, D. Laberge-Altmegad, and D. Szabo (eds.), Terrorism and Criminal Justice. Lexington, MA: D. C. Heath.

BUCHANAN, J. M. (1973) "A defense of organized crime?" in S. Rottenberg, The Economics of Crime and Punishment. Washington, DC: American Enterprise Institute.

FEUER, L. (1973) "Ideology and no end." Encounter April.

IANNI, F.A.J. and E. REUSS-IANNI The Crime Society: Organized Crime and Corruption in America. New York: New American Library.

President's Commission on Law Enforcement and Administration of Justice (1967) The Challenge of Crime in a Free Society. Washington, DC: U.S. Government Printing Office.

SCHELLING, T. C. (1971) "What is the business of organized crime?" The American Scholar 40: 643-652.

SHILS, E. (1972) The Intellectuals and the Powers. Chicago: University of Chicago Press.

SUTHERLAND, E. H. and D. R. CRESSEY (1955) Principles of Criminology. New York: J. B. Lippincott.

12

POLITICAL CRIME AND TERRORISM
Toward an Understanding

DANIEL E. GEORGES-ABEYIE

INTRODUCTION

What is meant by the terms "political crime" and "terrorism"? What conditions and factors motivate men and women to engage in acts of criminal violence against official state authority? How extensive is terrorism? What actions and policies have nation-states embraced in their desperate struggle against terrorism? Is terrorism and guerilla warfare ever effective in challenging state authority or in the overthrow of the legitimate nation-state governmental and social control apparatus? These are the questions central to the focus of this chapter.

The study of political crime and terrorism is at best complicated, emotion-laden, and riddled by conjecture and uncertainty. Much of the confusion and complexity that surrounds the study of political crime and terrorism centers on a series of extremely complicated and often emotion-laden definitional issues. The first issue centers on the nature of the subject in question — what is political crime and when is it terrorism or terroristic?

WHAT IS POLITICAL CRIME AND
WHEN IS IT TERRORISM OR TERRORISTIC?

There is no simple or universally accepted definition of political crime, much less terrorism. For example, is political crime a crime that challenges state authority? That is, is it an act of civil disobedience such as a riot, a rebellion, an insurrection, treason, sedition, looting, or assassination? Must an act of political crime be an act of criminal violence or the threat of criminal violence? For the sake of simplicity and uniformity of approach, I will contend that political crime is simply any criminal act that challenges the collective administrative authority of the nation-state as well as the nation-state's legal and actual right and ability to legislate rules of behavior (that is, make laws) as well as to legally enforce those rules of behavior (laws). An act of criminal homicide, assault, or forcible rape would not be a political crime unless that act of violence was intended as a challenge to the political order; that is, was an attempt to challenge and/or change a political policy (or law) or the very government itself. Acts such as terrorism (which I will define), assassination, insurrection, revolution, rebellion, and commodity riot[1] would be acts of political violence and thus subsets of political crime. Numerous volumes have been written on each of these subsets of political crime; I will not attempt to discuss each of these subsets in turn, but rather will focus on that subset of political crime which journalists and academicians have labeled guerilla warfare and terrorism.

What is Terrorism and Guerilla Warfare?

Similar to the term "political crime," the terms terrorism, terroristic, and guerilla warfare have been used, misused, and abused by governments, the mass media, and academicians alike. They are terms so heavily laden with political and emotional significance that one who attempts a national, much less an international or comparative, study of terrorism and/or guerilla warfare is sorely tempted to throw up his hands in

disgust and defeat. The following are a few of the most frequently quoted or utilized definitons of terrorism and guerilla
warfare. A cursory review of this maelstrom of "definitional of-
ferings" alerts one to the many delicate and complex issues
which surround these concepts.

(1) Bassiouni (1975:25) notes that the Republic of South
Africa's Terrorism Act is so broadly constructed that it labels
almost any form of social conduct which the government might
disapprove of as "terrorism":

> forcible resistance to the government or administration, acts
> which cripple or prejudice industry, acts which cause general
> dislocation, disturbance or disorder, acts which promote by in-
> timidation any object, acts which hamper or deter any person
> from assisting in the maintenance of law and order, any act
> which embarrasses the administration of the state, will be con-
> strued as an act of terrorism. To cause, encourage or further
> feelings of hostility between blacks and whites and other in-
> habitants of South Africa is another form of terrorism. Of
> course that makes the whole government of South Africa guilty
> under its own law.

(2) Paul Wilkinson (1977:49), Senior Lecturer in Politics at
University College, Cardiff, United Kingdom, defines political
terrorism as

> coercive intimidation. It is the systematic use of murder and
> destruction, and the threat of murder and destruction in order to
> terrorize individuals, groups, communities or governments into
> conceding to the terrorists' political demands. It is one of the
> oldest techniques of phychological warfare.

(3) The National Advisory Committee on Criminal Justice
Standards and Goals, Report of the Task Force on Disorders
and Terrorism entitled *Disorders and Terrorism* (Byrne,
1976:3-6), takes cognizance of at least four basic categories or
definitions of terrorism:

> *Political terrorism*...defined as...violent, criminal behavior
> designed primarily to generate fear in the community, or a

substantial segment of it, for political purposes.

Nonpolitical terrorism [defined as]...terrorism designed to create and maintain a high degree of fear for coercive purposes, but the end is individual or collective gain rather than the achievement of a political objective.

Quasiterrorism...a description applied...to those activities that are similar in form and method to true terrorism but which nevertheless lack its essential ingredient [the political purpose].

Official and State Terrorism [the legal and] oppressive policies of a state.

(4) Haas and Georges (1979) citing a paper by Elwin, noted that the crux of the problem which surrounds the definition of terrorism was highlighted in the 1972 United Nations General Assembly, where the members could not even settle on a satisfactory "official" definition of terrorism:

The division in world opinion boiled down to a basic conflict of vested interests. The well established Western countries sought to define terrorism as any act performed by an individual or group of individuals designed to undermine the authority of a legitimate government or state. While the relatively new "underdeveloped" countries, on the other hand, many of which were forged through revolutionary guerilla activity, argue that *acts of terrorism* have their roots in economic and political conditions [Elwin, 1977:298].

Crelinsten (1978:5) and Paust (1975:432) concur with the Haas/Georges thesis that one's political identification with the desire to suppress personal liberties of individuals, or control and prohibit challenges to the established political order, will affect the definitional parameters of terrorism.

(5) Frederick Hacker (1976), a prominent psychiatrist, takes cognizance of three types of terrorism: terrorism by "crazies," terrorism by "criminals," and terrorism by "crusaders" (what one might consider true political terrorists). Hacker not only recognizes three bassic types of terrorists, but also posits the belief that these theoretically distinct types of terrorists have different motivations, different victims, different objectives (au-

diences), and are confronted by different reactions by their objects.

Hacker notes that "crazies" tend to be governed by psychopathological urges, while their victims are often selected at random or according to a delusional system keying on the powerful and prominent. One should also note that the victims of "crazies" are highly endangered for short periods of time (Hacker, 1976). "Criminals" have no true political motives. Their motivation is self-aggrandizement via economic profit; for the "criminal," terrorism is merely a business activity and victim selection purely instrumental. It can also be stated that the danger to the victim varies with two things: the victim's response to the terrorist incident and the response by social control authorities (Hacker, 1976). The "crusader," unlike the "crazy" or "criminal," is often an unselfish and sacrificial individual, some are highly trained, others poorly trained and disciplined, some operate in bands, others act as solitary individuals. The "crusader's" victim is selected for symbolic and/or publicity value and is highly endangered during the initial phase of the terrorist incident and then again when social control authorities respond to the incident.

In sum, there is no single widely or universally accepted definition of terrorism. However, most definitions of true terrorism — that is, political terrorism — take cognizance of at least two elements:

(1) an illegal act of [criminal] violence or threat of criminal violence for a
(2) political purpose, that is, an act or threatened act of criminal violence with the intent of changing a specific governmental policy if not the government itself.

At this time it behooves us to address the issue of whether or not terrorism and guerilla warfare are one and the same, as well as whether or not a terrorist is a guerilla and vice versa.

IS A TERRORIST A GUERILLA?
IS A GUERILLA A TERRORIST?

Haas and Georges (1979) posit the belief that another aspect of the definitional dilemma is the distinction very often drawn between the terrorist and the (urban) guerilla. They note that part of this confusion stems from the fact that both of these phenomena have been frequently combined in recent revolutionary and national liberation struggles (Wilkinson, 1977:55). Guerillas, like terrorists, are engaged in acts of criminal violence against the state with the intent of at least challenging and changing a government policy if not the government itself; both have embraced such violent and criminal tactics as burglary (not a violent act), bank robbery, kidnapping, and assassination (Halperin, 1976:18). However, one often-cited distinction (with which this author does not concur) is the belief that the terrorist opts not to distinguish between military/government/police targets and civilian targets, while guerillas limit their violence to the nation-state and its ancillary services — for example, the military and the police. Another distinction often drawn centers on the "arena" of conflict; that is terrorists operate in the urban setting, the guerilla in the rural setting.

> The essence of guerilla warfare lies in the fact that the guerilla can hide in the countryside and this, quite evidently, is impossible in the city [Laqueur, 1976].

This author warns that no "hard and fast" rule in regard to the "arena" of conflict should be drawn. "Terrorists" have been known to operate in the rural context (note preindependence Algeria's FLN and the early activity of Sendic's MLN); guerillas with a predominantly rural focus have been known to engage in urban terrorism — as for example, the Che/Fidel urban "golpas," the Angolan MPLA, FNLA, and UNITA; while other groups have either had urban strategies which evolved into rural strategies (earlier Maoist strategy) or have operated in both contexts, such as the IRA-Provisional Wing (and its member organizations), the PLO, and the Palestinian guerillas of the Rejectionist Front.

(3) The size of the "organization" has been used, in part, as a factor in distinguishing between a terrorist and a guerilla band (Halperin, 1976:18). We are told that the membership of terrorist groups had to be small (that is, limited) in number because of the logistics problems of carrying out "military" operations in the relatively crowded urban setting, the problem of moving, hiding, housing, and feeding terrorist cadre, while the rural guerilla has a much more hospitable environment for such operations.

In summary, there are very few, if any, hard and fast rules that may be utilized in drawing clear distinctions between terrorism and guerilla warfare (and thus terrorists and guerillas). Table 12.1 offers a succinct but comprehensive summary of those factors that have been used to draw the theoretical/analytical distinction between terrorism and guerilla warfare. I will, however, use the terms terrorist and guerilla and terrorism and guerilla warfare interchangeably within the body of this chapter, since both are forms of political crime (more specifically, political violence) that are of interest to us as students of political violence.

TABLE 12.1   Factors Differentiating Between Terrorists and Guerillas

Terrorist	*Guerilla*
1. Urban focus.	1. Rural focus is primary.
2. Object of attack includes the property and persons of civilians.	2. Object of attack usually includes the military, the police, or government officials.
3. Operates in small bands of terrorist cadre (usually 3-5 members or up to 20 members in a larger spatial unit).	3. The organization can grow quite large and eventually take the form of a conventional military force.

HOW PREVEALENT IS TERRORISM?
WHAT FORMS HAS IT TAKEN?

The terror and frequency of mass media coverage of terrorist incidents would lead the naive to the false conclusion that we live in a world under siege by ruthless, blood-thirsty men (and to a lesser extent women) "hell bent" on death and destruction. However, a perusal of available data reveals quite the opposite: The number of persons actually killed or wounded in terrorist incidents is relatively low, compared with deaths resulting from other violent causes. Haas and Georges (1979) note that in one study by Jenkins covering the years 1968-1974, there were 507 incidents of political terrorism in which 520 persons were killed and 830 persons wounded. Haas and Georges go on to state:

Another analyst conducted a study of 87 countries for the 1961-70 decade based on reports in the *New York Times*. He found that terrorist incidents occurred in 67 of the 87 countries, killing approximately 4,600 persons (Laqueur, 1978:269). In a recent study of human targeting by terrorists for the 1961-70 period, the analyst found that noncombatant political figures were the main targets of terrorists (49 percent of the human targets), while military or police personnel were the second most frequent target (11 percent), with "random victims" constituting only eight percent of the human targets (Evans and Murphy, 1978:341).

Some researchers have categorized their data of terrorist acts into international incidents and transnational incidents. [A terrorist incident is international when it involves a country other than the terrorist's home country, and transnational when a terrorist is an autonomous, non-state actor who temporarily assumes the goals of another group for the duration of the act (Crelinsten, 1978:10).] The CIA conducted a comprehensive study of international and transnational incidents committed during the period 1967-75 by utilizing a data bank called I.T.E.R.A.T.E. (International Terrorism: Attributes of Terrorist Events). They found that international incidents had not increased during that period but that terrorist acts of a transational nature had multiplied, as did the number of groups and countries in which they operated. They counted 1152 transnational incidents since 1967: 501 bombings; 146 hijackings; 137 kidnappings; 103 incendiary attacks; and 63 assassinations (Heren, 1978:32). Another study for the same time frame found 931 international and transnational incidents including: 123 kidnappings; 31 barricade and hostage episodes; 375 explosions; 95 armed assaults or ambushes; 137 hijackings; 59 incendiary attacks; 48 assassinations; and 45 other acts of political violence. All combined, international and transnational incidents killed 800 persons and injured 1700 (Laqueur, 1978:270) [Haas and Georges, 1979].

In brief terrorist incidents, although far from common, have been on the rise during the period 1965-1976. During the period between 1965 and late 1968, the number of terrorist incidents was below 50 annually. By the end of 1975, however, the average number per year had leveled off to 175 (Laqueur, 1978:270). I would, however, warn that these data should not be taken at face value. Authoritarian and totalitarian states often classify criminal acts as terroristic acts if it is to their advantage to do so, while at other times they suppress all information on the occurrence of domestic terrorism. One should also note that state terror (that is, terrorism) is probably as common if not more common than terrorism by individuals (see *Disorders and Terrorism* as well as the annual reports of Freedom House and Amnesty International).

What Motivates Persons to Engage in Terrorist Incidents?

It is a common claim that terrorist motivations are almost as diverse and numerous as there are terrorist individuals and groups. I would state, however, that it is possible to group political terrorists by means of ideological backgrounds, if we exclude the psychopathological motivations manifested by that group of "terrorists" which Frederick Hacker has labeled "crazies." Anthony Burton's (1975) excellent short book on Urban Terrorism entitled *Urban Terrorism: Theory, Practice and Response* includes such an attempt at cataloguing terrorists.

Burton notes that urban terrorists come from the following 10 ideological backgrounds:

(1) Black racist with a Fanonian background;
(2) new left student-based middle class nurtured on the writings of Marcuse, Fanon, and Bakhunin;
(3) Castroite terrorist with a Guevarain and Debrayian background;

(4) Trotskyist with Trotskyist and Guillenist backgrounds;
(5) right wing reactionist nurtured on national history and threatened majority group identity;
(6) anarchist with Bakhuninist backgronds;
(7) Moscow-oriented Communist nurtured on the writings of Marx and Lenin;
(8) nationalist groups (sectional chauvinist) who look to their history, culture, and language for motivation;
(9) composite and eclectic groups (generally "socialist," anti-U.S.) with an independent political line that embraces socialism, nationalism, the examples of other movements, and the writing of Marighela; and
(10) Maoist Peking-oriented splinter groups that embrace the teaching of Mao and Giap.

Let us take a closer look at the terrorist tendencies outlined above.

(1) The anarchist terrorists are an especially difficult group of terrorists to "catalogue" and analyze, in part because of the considerable "ideological" diversity manifested by those who bear the "Black Flag" of anarchism. Some anarchists ally with the ideology of August Blanqui[2] — an ideology which champions the small, elite, cadre organization, which in essence is both the military and the political wing of the anarchist party or syndical (that is, it is the combat party in its purest form). It is the combat-ready cadre which is both suspicious of the general populace as well as suspicious of the existing government. It is distrustful of both those it hopes to liberate as well as those whom it perceives as its most ruthless opposition. The Blanquist anarchists operate in small bands and hope to bring down the state by means of well-coordinated strikes against key officials, organizations, and installations.

Other anarchists champion the writings and philosophy of the Russian anarchist Mikhail Aleksandrovich Bakhunin. The Bakhuninists argue that any serious blow to the state must include elements from at least four sectors of society: (a) *the criminal underworld* (the most alienated and independent of all citizens); (b) *the workers* (the urban proletariat) who are exploited by mechanization and urbanization regardless of the label its organizers and overlords may bear (capitalist, fascist, socialist, or communist); (c) *the students and intelligentsia*, who fit into no world quietly or easily; (d) *the peasant class* (the agarian workers) exploited by agrarian capitalism as well as socialist and communist collectivism.

Still other anarchists embrace such revolutionary catechisms as nihilism — the belief that the proper role for the anarchist revolutionary (the nihilist) is that of active destruction of that which is present, thus making way for a more perfect existence yet to come. This new world is brought into effect by means of the cathartic effect of struggle which destroys all that was not worthy of existence.

Table 12.2 presents a brief summary of the most basic anarchist tenets, tenets which I believe are (or were) shared by most major anarchist groups — nihilistic, Blanquist, and Bakhuninist.

TABLE 12.2 Basic Tenets of Anarchist Doctrine

1. Man is essentially a benign creature.
2. Man is a social animal, and men reach their fulfillment when voluntarily and spontaneously cooperating with one another.
3. Prevailing institutions of society — particularly private property and the state — are artificial agencies through which men exploit and corrupt each other.
4. Social change must be spontaneous, direct, and mass-based.
5. Industrial civilizations, no matter what form of ownership of the means of production, warps the human spirit.

(2) Moscow-oriented communists such as recent Guatemalan Communists look to the 1917 Russian Revolution and Mother Russia for inspiration and guidance in their own struggles for a different, if not better world. These terrorists embrace the ideology of Stalinized Marxist-Leninism; that is, bureaucratic centralism, the combat party, and, to a lesser extent, a variation of the "Socialism in One Country Theme" — the belief that the U.S.S.R., the largest, most powerful, and progressive nation-state in the contemporary world, may be looked to for guidance and assistance in their own indigenous struggle. They

believe that certain objective "revolutionary conditions" are necessary for a successful socialist revolution; (1) a self-conscious, segregated ethnic, cultural, or religious minority which feels itself to be economically deprived or politically oppressed (a feeling exacerbated by the effect of modern communications) with poor job opportunities and lack of voting rights, but which has been encouraged to believe that change is coming ("rising expectations") and is then disappointed; (2) in a situation of unemployment/inflation; (3) externally encouraged; (4) with a historical "THEM" to blame; (5) and with frustrated elites to provide leadership and to overcome the natural distaste (of all save the psychopathic fringe) to initiate violence by giving it an ideological justification (Burton, 1975); and (6) nation-state inability to make reforms or suppress opposition.

(3) The nationalist groups (sectional chauvinists) have been among the most successful *and* the least successful terrorists — for example, note the successes of the FLN in Algeria, the MPLA in Angola, and FRELIMO in Mozambique. Yet, we should also note the failure or limited success of the FALN in the United States and Puerto Rico, ETA in Spain, and the FLQ in Canada. In brief, the nationalist groups are first and foremost engaged in a struggle for what they perceive as "national liberation"; their concern is the birth of a "nation-state." They may be fascistic, communistic, or socialistic (or they may consist of an odd amalgam of groups which cross the political spectrum, such as the PLO and the IRA-PROVOS and IRA officials).

(4) Composite and eclectic groups have been among the least successful of the contemporary terrorists if we take their espoused goals at "face value." That is, their pro-socialist ideologies and strategies have often led to brutal repression as a result of their limited successes against weak authoritarian states or moderate or liberal democracies (note the MLN and the ALN in Urguay and Brazil, respectively). It should be noted that many of these terrorists see themselves as the "true communists," forcing the existing left-wing and communist groups to embrace a purer form of Bolshevism (Marxist-Leninism). In part, their

theory and approach have argued that only by forcing the morally and politically bankrupt parties into a life-and-death struggle with a progressively repressive and ineffective state can one hope for the birth of a "Communist state" (note the philosophy and activity of Italy's Red Brigades).

(5) The Maoist, Peking-oriented splinter groups — have tended to look toward Communist China for inspiration, material support, and guidance. In theory, if not always in practice, they have advocated the formation of "urban brigades" to support the mainline activity of peasant guerilla war. It is interesting to note that America's most successful Maoist group — the New World Liberation Front — has not really evolved into a rural-oriented struggle group (Byrne, 1976), but has become a Maoist-oriented terrorist organization with an urban focus.

(6) Black racist terrorists have embraced Franz Fanon's theory of an oppressed, nonwhite Third World and the liberating (cathartic) effect of struggle; an effect that can lead to black unity, if not the immediate birth of a Pan-African nation-state as seen by Marcus Garvey (one of North and South America's most charismatic leaders). The Black Liberation Army, the Black Panthers before the "constitutional" phase, and the Afro-American Liberation Army have been disciples of Garvey's dream of "One God, One nation, One People." Black Racist terrorists have been members of "revolutionary nationalist"[3] as well as "cultural nationalist" organizations.

(7) "New left" student-based middle-class terrorists have been quite eclectic in regard to political, economic, and philosophical borrowings. In the United States this group has tended to be white and middle-class with a substantial female input (as leaders and ideologues, if not as considerable numbers of female cadre; see Georges and Rockell forthcoming). Groups such as the Weather Underground and the SLA (a nonstudent group) have been quick to seize upon and exploit current societal traumas and issues such as the "prisoner rights movements"; feminism; the war in Vietnam, Laos, and Cambodia; rent strikes; activities against slum (what they have called "scum") lords; as well as a thousand other very real concerns of America's urban poor.

(8) Castroite groups have taken their inspiration and guidance from Fidel Castro's successful revolution against Batista, the pre-Castro liberal-moderate dictator who, as inconceivable as it may sound, had tacit Cuban Communist support prior to Castro's late 1950s revolution. The Debrayian-Guevaraian terrorists with a rural focus have tended to be markedly unsuccessful in Latin America, in part because they have misread the actual, as opposed to the Castro-professed, history of the Cuban Revolution (see Laquer, 1976; Moss, 1972). A following section will discuss the Debrayian-Guevaraian model of guerilla warfare.

(9) Trotskyist terrorists, like their Moscow-oriented communist counterparts, believe that objective socioecopolitical conditions must exist if a successful socialist revolution is to occur. These objective "revolutionary conditions" will be discussed in the concluding segment of this chapter. One should note that Trotskyist terrorists believe that the 1917 Russian Revolution has been betrayed, that "Mother Russia" cannot and should not be looked to for material or moral support. The Trotskyists embrace Leon Trotsky's "Theory of the Permanent Revolution," a belief that indigenous people must struggle for their independence and cannot look for substantial assistance from outside forces. This theory also posits the belief that the revolutionary process is an ongoing one which will and must continue until the entire world is ruled by communist regimes. Trotskyists believe that the present so-called communist states are really "worker's states" where private monopoly capitalism has been replaced by something approaching state capitalism ruled by a stagnant political bureaucratic elite. Trotskyist groups in theory, if not in practice, are formed in combat parties which follow (1) a "mass action approach" (a belief that a successful socialist revolution must involve mass action by society's oppressed); (2) belief in "The Law of Uneven and Combined Development" (the belief that different sectors, ethnic and racial groups, and others manifest different levels of awareness in regard to their oppression and alienation, and will struggle against what they perceive as their oppression — even if that perception does not take immediate cognizance of the core

element in that oppression — the capitalist system); (3) a democratic centralist party organization; and (4) an active distrust of present-day communist systems.

(10) The right wing reaction — are groups, often government inspired, supported, and formed, which supplement government activities and support the present status quo in regard to civil, economic, political, and social rights. These groups may support the return to a centralist or right-of-center sociopolitical order in states currently ruled by socialist or communist regimes. These groups have tended to be well armed, protected, and highly trained by so-called moderate and conservative governments; for example, the U.S. support of Anti-Castro terrorist groups that were trained and based in Florida, Louisiana, and Mexico. Another example would be the KKK; the Ku Klux Klan is (and has been) perhaps American's foremost right-wing terrorist organization. Other infamous American examples include the amalgam of Anti-Oriental terrorist groups of the John Kearneyist ideology (for example, the White Working Man's Socialist Party of California).

(11) Religious fanatics of the right and left. Some of these have been (a) Jewish and Zionist (the Irgun, the Stern Gang), (b) Christian nationalist groups both Catholic and Protestant (the IRA and the Ulster Defense Leagues), while others have been (c) Moslem (Peoples Feedeyeen in Iran). These groups avoid easy generalization and can readily be placed within any of a number of the previously cited categories — some are Marxist, some are Trotskyist, others are right wing or eclectic. Suffice it to say that men and women of fanatical religious persuasion have made their bloody mark upon the world politic in the name of "god" and "god promised lands" and no doubt will continue to do so if Palestine and Iran are not contemporary aberrations. It should also be noted that religious fanaticism often is tied to a specific political ideology, an ideology that can range anywhere along the political continuum of left-wing extremism to right-wing fanaticism.

In summary, the spectrum of often-cited terrorist groups is considerable and impressive. Terrorists have been known to embrace left-wing and right-wing political dogmas as well as religious fanaticism.

PREVALENT FORMS OF
TERRORIST STRUGGLE

The most common forms of recent political terrorism have been variations of the Marighela Model of urban terrorism or the Guevara-Debray Model of rural struggle. The Marighela Model is a four-stage model which calls for (1) the immediate inception of guerilla activity (based on the belief that organizations grow through unleasing revolutionary action and the call for extreme violence); (2) provoking the government into repression, thus transforming the political situation into a military one, while also polarizing social groups; (3) the creation of a People's Army as an outgrowth of mobile rural guerilla group attacks on minor government installations and large estates; and (4) the Seizure of State Power brought about by the People's Army inflicting defeats on government forces and the success of the initiation of General Strikes. The *Guevara-Debray Model* is a three-phrase offensive which includes (1) the Guerilla Focus (aided by foreign career revolutionaries and indigenous participants and the formation of a secure base of operations (such as jungle/mountain reconnaissance, adoption of the guerillas to the environment, and the initiation of small training operations against the regime); (2) the Formation of Operational Columns and a People's Army (that is, establishment of a guerilla base, regional guerillas, urban squads, and the increase in numbers and evolution into a People's Army); and (3) conventional offensive on the capital which is marked by regional/urban groups keeping the government forces tied down, a mobile force attacking selected targets, and a general strike (Burton, 1975).

Contemporary urban terrorists such as Italy's Red Brigades and West Germany's Baader-Meinhoff Gang should be viewed as variations on the Marighela Model, a model that loosely champions "The Worst The Better Thesis." "The Worst The Better Thesis" may be interpreted as the belief that terrorist violence will force the national government to overreact, thereby alienating liberals and radicals alike, while forcing left-wing political parties and labor organizations to further radicalize and join the struggle against a fascistic government which functions outside of the law (see Table 12.3). The "key" to the Guevara-Debray Model is the "rural focus"; that is, the belief that much of the struggle takes place in the rural setting and that a small, well-armed, dedicated, and disciplined cadre can set in motion those factors necessary for a successful social revolution. This position champions the belief that the small-struggle organization is the party in embryo and that the mass movement (and the subsequent mass struggle) follows the initiation of violence by the small-struggle organization that carries out a series of well-planned and coordinated *golpas* (note the Blanquist and Maoist influences shared by this orientation).

TABLE 12.3   An Urban Strategy for Guerillas and Government

1. Stage One: The world is watching (violent propaganda).
2. Organizational growth.
3. A "Fort Apache" mentality: instill fear in the social control forces.
4. Repression is rapture: overreaction.
5. The tactics of a few must be coordinated with a mass: social revolution.

SOURCE: This chart is based on Jenkins (1972).

THE GOVERNMENT RESPONSE
TO THE TERRORIST THREAT

In a word, "repression" has been the usual (but not only) response of nation-states to terrorist violence. Other responses have included (a) infiltration of terrorist groups; (b) the issuance of financial rewards or bounties for information leading to the arrest and/or elimination of terrorists or terrorist groups; (c) the call for "democratic" elections with the hope of discrediting the terrorist demands for freely held and open elections;[4] and (d) the passage of tough counterterrorism laws which allow for increased penalties and decreased civil and political rights of the civilian population in a country under seige. For example, note West Germany's "Contract Ban Law" (Frankfurther Allgemein Zeitung, 1977) which was enacted on October 1, 1977. This law dealt with imprisoned terrorists in the following manner:

(1) Permits complete isolation of a terrorist inmate who is suspected of involvment in outside terrorist activities — applying especially to his attorney;
(2) provides for acceleration of court proceedings;
(3) tightens up the law on illegal possession of weapons; and
(4) introduces regulations for "theft-proof" license plates and plate numbers and automobile papers.

West Germany is not the only country to legislate and enforce what might be viewed as oppressive counterterrorism laws. I have already cited South Africa's tough counterterrorism law. To the South African and West German examples one can add Israel's Adminsitrative Detention Law, which allows (without a search warrant) for (a) the search, seizure, and arrest of Palestinians within the Israeli-occupied West Bank of Jordan as well as Israel itself, and (b) the imprisonment for up to one year without trial of Palestinians in the Israeli-occupied territories as well as Israel itself. Northern Ireland has the Emergency Provisions Act of 1973 which allows the army (British) to arrest and question any suspected terrorist for periods of four hours, after which he must either be released or handed over to the police for formal charging or for a further period of questioning, up to the limit of 72 hours (Boyle et al., 1978:103).[5]

The Amnesty International Report 1978 notes that it took action on violations of human rights in 110 countries during the period July 1, 1977 to June 30, 1978, many of which included active terrorist threats. *Freedom House's 1978 Annual Report* also acknowledges the lack of full freedom in 23 countries or territories with terrorist organizations.

GENERAL CONCLUSION

In conclusion, one can state that political crime and terrorism is a very real problem in at least five continents — North America, South America, Africa, Asia, and Europe. It can also be concluded that there is no single terrorist motivation or government response. Terrorists (that is, political terrorists) have been motivated by political and religious dogmas as diverse as fascism and communism, Judaism, Christianity, and Islam, while government response has been as diverse as outright illegal suppression of civil and political rights, as in the Urugayian Military's response to the MLN threat, Brazil's to the ALN, or Argentina's to the ERP and the Monteneros. At other times, in other countries, the response has been brutal but legal: for example, the passage of administrative detention laws by the Israeli government, the "Contract Ban Law" in West Germany, and the Emergency Provisions Act of 1973 (Internment Act) for Northern Ireland. Frederick Hacker's *Crusaders, Criminals, Crazies* (1976) offers a comprehensive review of official as well as unofficial "terror" from above in an attempt to suppress "terrorism" from below, which is a reminder of the very real fact that nation-states have been more than willing to meet violence with even greater and better-organized violence.

NOTES

1. Collective violence occurs when property and/or symbols of authority, such as policemen, social workers, firemen, or entrepreneurs, are the objects of attack rather than the members of a different ethnic or racial group (this violence must involve three or more persons acting in concert).

2. August Blanqui was a French anarchist who lived from 1805-1881 (see Laqueur's *Guerilla*, 1976).

3. A "revolutionary nationalist" advocates the immediate creation of a black-owned and black-ruled nation-state for black people, while "cultural nationalists" often argue that a black state of identity (an African or distinctly Afro-American culture) is necessary before the birth of a nation-state. Some "cultural nationalists" would even posit the belief that the "nation" is a state of mind rather than a sociopolitical spatial entity.

4. The terrorists are, of course, placed in a position of extreme disadvantage by the call for a so-called democratic election by the nation-state since the terrorists (1) must oppose an incumbent (always a difficult task in the best of all political circumstances); (2) must overcome the "outlaw" stigma which is usually tied to the terrorist label; (3) have not had an equal opportunity (much less experience) to establish a political campaign organization; (4) will probably not have equal positive access to the mass media (which might be government-run, or controlled by an economic/social/or religious elite in favor of the status quo).

5. A comprehensive review of the official and unofficial government response to the terrorist threat is provided in *Disorders and Terorrism* (1976) as well as in the work of the following editors and authors (Alexander and Finger, 1978; Evans and Murphy, 1978; Crelinsten et al., 1978; Bassiouni, 1975; Alexander, 1976; Moss, 1972; and Livingston et al., 1978).

REFERENCES

ALEXANDER, Y. and S. M. FINGER [eds.] (1978). Terrorism: Interdisciplinary Perspectives. New York: John Jay Press.

Amnesty International Report, 1978 (1978) London: Amnesty International Publications.

BASSIOUNI, M. C. [ed.] (1975) International Terrorism and Political Crimes. Springfield, IL: Charles C. Thomas.

BURTON, A. (1975) Urban Terrorism: Theory, Practice, and Response. New York: Free Press.

BYRNE, B. T. (1976) Report of the Task Force on Disorders and Terrorism, National Advisory Committee on Criminal Justice Standards and Goals. Washington, DC: U.S. Government Printing Office.

CRELINSTEN, R. D. et al. [ed.] (1978) Terrorism and Criminal Justice. Lexington, MA: D. C. Heath.

ELWIN, G. (1977) "Swedish anti-terrorist legislation." Contemporary Crises 1: 289-301.

EVANS, A. E. and J. F. MURPHY (1978) Legal Aspects of International Terrorism. Lexington, MA: D. C. Heath.

GEORGES, D. E. and B. ROCKELL (forthcoming) "Toward a theory of women as terrorists: an etiology of female terrorism."

GASTIL, R. D. (1976-1979) Freedom at Issue. New York: Freedom House.

HAAS, L. H. and D. E. GEORGES (1979) "Towards a strategy of psychological warfare — A brief overview." (forthcoming)

HACKER, F. (1976) Crusaders, Criminals, Crazies. New York: W. W. Norton.

HALPERIN, E. (1976) Terrorism in Latin America. Beverly Hills, CA: Sage.

HEREN, L. (1978) "Curbing terrorism." Atlas World Press Review 25:31-37.

JENKINS, B. (1972) An Urban Strategy for Guerillas and Government. Santa Monica, CA. Rand.

——— (1975) International Terrorism: A Chronology 1968-1974. Santa Monica. CA: Rand.LAQUEUR, W. (1976) Guerrilla. Boston: Little, Brown.

——— (1978) Terrorism. Boston: Little, Brown.

LIVINGSTON, M. H. et al. [ed.] (1978) International Terrorism in the Contemporary World. Westport, CT: Greenwood Press.

MOSS, R. (1972) The War for the Cities. New York: Coward, McCann and Geoghegan.

PAUST, J. (1975) "A survey of possible legal responses to international terrorism: prevention, punishment and cooperative action." Georgia Journal of International Cooperative Law 5.

WILKINSON, P. (1977) Terrorism and the Liberal State. New York: John Wiley.

ABOUT THE CONTRIBUTORS

FAHAD AL-THAKEB received his Ph.D. in sociology from Ohio State University in 1974. He is Chairman of the Department of Sociology and Social Work at the University of Kuwait. His research interests have focused on the revitalization of Islamic law and its impact on the family and law in the Arab world.

GEORGE DeVOS is Professor of Anthropology, University of California at Berkeley. He received his M.A. in anthropology in 1948 and Ph.D. in psychology in 1951, both from the University of Chicago, and is a pioneer in the new field of psychological anthropology. Although his research interests have taken him to many parts of the world, his sustained research interest has centered on Japan. His major books include *Japan's Invisible Race: Caste in Culture and Personality,* and *Socialization for Achievement: Essays on the Cultural Psychology of the Japanese* (with Hiroshi Wagatsuma). Forthcoming is a trilogy with Hiroshi Wagatsuma reporting the results of ten years of joint research in an urban lower-class district of Tokyo.

FRANCO FERRACUTI is Professor of Criminological Medicine and Forensic Psychiatry at the University of Rome Medical School. He has advanced criminological research in many parts of the world, including Eastern and Western Europe, Latin America, and the Far and Middle East. He has been active as a consultant and adviser on crime and deviance to many international bodies, including the Council of Europe and the United Nations, UNESCO, and the World Health Organization. Among his many publications, his best-known are *The Subculture of Violence* (with Marvin Wolfgang) and *Delinquents and Nondelinquents in the Puerto Rican Slum Culture* (with Simon Dinitz and Esperanza Acosta de Buenes).

PAUL C. FRIDAY is Director of Criminal Justice and Associate Professor of Sociology at Western Michigan University, Kalamazoo, Michigan. He is the author of numerous articles on youth crime and delinquency and co-editor of *Youth and Juvenile Justice: International Perspectives.* He is past-vice-president and executive counselor of the American Society for Criminology, and is currently Chair of International Liaison. He is the author of *International Assessment of Adult Probation,* and is currently President of the International Sociological Association Section on Deviance and Social Control.

DANIEL E. GEORGES-ABEYIE is an Urban Social Ecologist/Criminologist currently employed at the State University of New York at Albany. Professor Georges-Abeyie received his Ph.D. degree in urban social geography from Syracuse University in 1974. His research interests have centered on terrorism and collective violence, criminal violence, and Black crime perpetration and criminal victimization. He is a member of the editorial board of *The Journal of Environmental Systems* and has held teaching and research positions a the University of Texas at Arlington, City University of New York, Johns Hopkins University, and Amherst College. Professor Georges-Abeyie has also served as a lecturer at the New York State Police Hostage Negotiator School's Counterterrorism/Hostage Negotiation Program.

CHERYL HAFT-PICKER is a doctoral candidate at the School of Criminal Justice, State University of New York at Albany, where she has been a research assistant and teaching fellow. She is presently Assistant Professor of Criminal Justice at Central Missouri State University. Prior to her interest in comparative criminology, she studied linguistics and modern foreign languages at the State University of New York and abroad at the Universite de Nice, France. Under a Title XX grant to Philadelphia's Joseph J. Peters Institute, she recently developed and implemented training courses for Philadelphia's mental health professionals on the sex offender, the adult rape victim, and the sexually victimized child. She is presently researching criminality among Jews during New York City's East European immigration period.

FRANCIS A.J. IANNI is Professor and Director of the Horace Mann-Lincoln Institute in Teachers College, Columbia University, and Consultant in Medical Psychology in the Psychiatric Center of St. Luke's Hospital, New York. He was formerly Associate Commissioner for Research in the United States Office of Education, and has been on the faculty at Yale University and University College, Addis Abbaba, Ethiopia. In addition to serving on the Mayor's Task Force on Organized Crime (New York City), he has served as consultant to the President's Commission on Criminal Justice Standards and Goals. Among his publications are *A Family Business; Kinship and Social Control in Organized Crime* (New York: Russell Sage-Basic Books, 1972), *Black Mafia: Ethnic Succession in Organized Crime* (New York: Simon and Schuster, 1974), and *The Crime Society: Organized Crime and Corruption in America* (New York: New American Library, 1977).

ELIZABETH REUSS-IANNI is Research Director of the Institute for Social Analysis where she has conducted studies of community attitudes toward organized crime, evaluations of employment and work programs, and, most recently, a two-year participant observation study of a New York City police precinct. She is co-author of *A Family Business: Kinship and Social Control in Organized Crime* and *The Crime Society: Organized Crime and Corruption in America,* and is currently completing a book on the social organization of police precincts.

JEROME KRASE received his Ph.D. in sociology from New York University, and is presently Associate Professor at Brooklyn College of the City University of New York. He has published articles on secret societies and community organization, and is currently engaged in research and writing on ethnicity and urban problems.

MARIA ŁOŚ received her Ph.D. in humanities at the University of Warsaw in 1971. She has taught at the University of Warsaw, and is currently SSRC Research Fellow in Sociolegal Studies, Faculty of Law, University of Sheffield. She has written two books in Polish, *Attitudes of Polish Society Towards Morality and Law* and *Aspirations and Milieu,* along with many articles in Polish, German, Italian, and Spanish. Among her many English publications is *Multidimensional Sociology,* co-authored with A. Podgorecki.

GRAEME R. NEWMAN received his Ph.D. in sociology from the University of Pennsylvania in 1972. He has been an elementary school teacher, a school psychologist, and a research expert for the United Nations. He joined the School of Criminal Justice of the State University of Albany in 1972, where he is currently Professor and Associate Dean. Among his publications are *Comparative Deviance, The Punishment Response,* and *Understanding Violence.*

EDWARD SAGARIN is Professor of Sociology at City College and City University of New York, is former president of the American Society of Criminology, and former co-editor of its journal *Criminology*. He has published widely in the fields of crime, deviance, and sexual behavior; with Charles Winick, he launched the Sage Annual Review of Studies in Deviance, and was editor of the first volume in the series, *Deviance and Social Change*.

LUIS P. SALAS received his J.D. degree from Wake Forest School of Law in 1971. He is currently Associate Professor in the School of Public Affairs and Services, Florida International University. Apart from his academic activities, he has been in private law practice and consulted for a number of research and action programs supported by state and federal authorities. He has published in a variety of law and social science journals. His most important work is his new book *Social Control and Deviance in Cuba*. His translation of the Cuban Criminal Codes will shortly be published by New York University Press.

JOSEPH E. SCOTT received his Ph.D. in sociology from Indiana University in 1972. He is Director of the Criminology and Criminal Justice Major at Ohio State University. His most recent research interests have focused on comparative criminology and the sociology of law.

S. GIORA SHOHAM is Professor of law at Tel Aviv University. In the late 1950s he was Assistant District Attorney of Jerusalem and assistant to the Attorney General of Israel. From his position he joined the Institute of Criminology at Bar Ilan University in 1961 as senior lecturer and director. Professor Shoham has also held academic posts in the United States at Ohio State University and in the Department of Sociology at the University of Pennsylvania. He took up his present position in 1973. Professor Shoham has published widely and is probably best known for the publications, *The Mark of Cain* (1970) and *Social Deviance* (1976). His most recent books are *The Myth of Tantalus* and *Salvation Through the Gutters*.

LESLIE T. WILKINS has been Professor at the State University of New York's School of Criminal Justice, Albany, since 1969. His first excursion into criminology was in 1952, when he collaborated with Dr. Hermann Mannheim in research published under the title, *Prediction Methods in Relation to Borstal Training*. In 1972 he was presented the Edwin H. Sutherland Award of the American Criminological Society. He has published widely, both books and journal articles, and served as editor of learned journals and consultant to several national and international bodies. His work on guidelines has had a major impact on parole and sentencing practices in the United States.